2019 SQA Past Papers with Answers

Higher
ENGLISH

2017, 2018 & 2019 Exams

HODDER
GIBSON
AN HACHETTE UK COMPANY

This book contains the official SQA 2017, 2018 and 2019 Exams for Higher English, with associated SQA-approved answers modified from the official marking instructions that accompany the paper.

In addition the book contains study skills advice. This advice has been specially commissioned by Hodder Gibson, and has been written by experienced senior teachers and examiners in line with the Higher syllabus and assessment outlines. This is not SQA material but has been devised to provide further guidance for Higher examinations.

Hodder Gibson is grateful to the copyright holders, as credited on the final page of the Answer section, for permission to use their material. Every effort has been made to trace the copyright holders and to obtain their permission for the use of copyright material. Hodder Gibson will be happy to receive information allowing us to rectify any error or omission in future editions.

Hachette UK's policy is to use papers that are natural, renewable and recyclable products and made from wood grown in well-managed forests and other controlled sources. The logging and manufacturing processes are expected to conform to the environmental regulations of the country of origin.

Orders: please contact Bookpoint Ltd, 130 Park Drive, Milton Park, Abingdon, Oxon OX14 4SE. Telephone: (44) 01235 827827. Fax: (44) 01235 400454. Email education@bookpoint.co.uk Lines are open 9.00–5.00, Monday to Friday, with a 24-hour message answering service. Visit our website at www.hoddereducation.co.uk. If you have queries or questions that aren't about an order, you can contact us at hoddergibson@hodder.co.uk

This collection first published in 2019 by
Hodder Gibson, an imprint of Hodder Education,
An Hachette UK Company
211 St Vincent Street
Glasgow G2 5QY

Typeset by Aptara, Inc.

Printed in the UK

A catalogue record for this title is available from the British Library

ISBN: 978 1 5104 7825 1

2 1

2020 2019

SCOTLAND EXCEL

We are an approved supplier on the Scotland Excel framework.

Schools can find us on their procurement system as:

Hodder & Stoughton Limited t/a Hodder Gibson.

Introduction

Higher English

The course

The Higher English course aims to enable you to develop the ability to:

- read, write, talk and listen in detailed and complex contexts, as appropriate to purpose and audience
- understand, analyse and evaluate detailed and complex texts, including Scottish texts, in the contexts of literature, language and the media
- create and produce written texts and spoken language, as appropriate to purpose, audience and context, through the application of knowledge and understanding of detailed and complex language

The basics

The grade you finally get for Higher English depends on three things:

- The "Performance–Spoken Language" component which is assessed in your school or college; this doesn't count towards your final grade, but you must have achieved the minimum requirements in it in order to get a final graded award.
- Your Portfolio of Writing – this is submitted in April for marking by SQA and counts for 30% of your final grade.
- The two exams you sit in May – that's what this book is all about.

The exams

Reading for Understanding, Analysis and Evaluation

- exam time: 1 hour 30 minutes
- total marks: 30
- weighting in final grade: 30%
- what you have to do: read two passages and answer questions about the ideas and use of language in one of them (25 marks), and then compare the ideas in both passages (5 marks)

Critical Reading

- exam time: 1 hour 30 minutes
- total marks: 40 (20 marks for each Section)
- weighting in final grade: 40%
- what you have to do: (Section 1) read an extract from one of the Scottish Texts which are set for Higher and answer questions about it; (Section 2) write an essay about a work of literature you have studied during your course.

1 Reading for Understanding, Analysis and Evaluation

Questions which ask for understanding (e.g. questions which say "Identify ... " or "Explain what ... " etc.)

- Keep your answers fairly short and pay attention to the number of marks available.
- Use your own words as far as possible. This means you mustn't just copy chunks from the passage – you have to show that you understand what it means by rephrasing it in your own words.

Questions about language features (e.g. questions which say "Analyse how ... ")

- This type of question will ask you to comment on features such as Word Choice, Imagery, Sentence Structure and Tone.
- You should pick out a relevant language feature and make a valid comment about its impact. Try to make your comments as specific as possible and avoid vague comments (such as "It is a good word to use because it gives me a clear picture of what the writer is saying"). Remember that you will get no marks just for picking out a word, image or feature of a sentence structure – it's the comment that counts.
- Some hints:
  - **Word choice:** Always try to pick a single word and then give its connotations, i.e. what it suggests.
  - **Sentence structure:** Don't just name the feature – try to explain what effect it achieves in that particular sentence.
  - **Imagery:** Try to explain what the image means literally and then go on to explain what the writer is trying to say by using that image.
  - **Tone:** This is always difficult – a good tip is to imagine the sentence or paragraph being read out loud and try to spot how the words or the structure give it a particular tone.

The last question

- Make sure you follow the instruction about whether you're looking for agreement or disagreement (or possibly both).
- When you start on Passage 2, you will have already answered several questions on Passage 1, so you should know its key ideas quite well. As you read Passage 2, try to spot important ideas in it which are similar or different (depending on the question).
- Stick to **key ideas** and don't include trivial ones; **three** relevant key ideas will usually be enough – your task is to decide what the most significant ones are.

2 Critical Reading

Section 1 – Scottish Text

The most important thing to remember here is that there are two very different types of question to be answered:

- Three or four questions (for a total of 10 marks) which focus entirely on the extract.
- One question (for 10 marks) which requires knowledge of the whole text (or of another poem or short story by the same writer).

The first type of question will typically ask you to use the same types of skills as you use in the RUAE paper, e.g. word choice, sentence structure, etc. As always, the golden rule is to do exactly as the question directs you, and to remember that (as in the RUAE paper) there are no marks just for picking out a word or a feature of sentence structure, so all the marks have to be earned by your comments.

The second type of question requires you to discuss common features (of theme and/or technique) in the extract and elsewhere in the writer's work. You can answer this question with a series of bullet points or by writing a mini-essay, so choose the approach you feel most comfortable with.

Finally, a bit of advice for the Scottish Text question: when you see the extract in the exam paper, don't get too confident just because you recognise it (you certainly should recognise it if you've studied properly!). And even if you've answered questions on it before, remember that the questions in the exam are likely to be different, so stay alert.

Section 2 – Critical Essay

A common mistake is to rely too heavily on ideas and whole paragraphs you have used in practice essays and try to use them for the question you have chosen in the exam. The trick is to come to the exam with lots of ideas and thoughts about at least one of the texts you have studied and use these to tackle the question you choose from the exam paper. You mustn't use the exam question as an excuse to trot out an answer you've prepared in advance.

Structure

Every good essay has a structure, but there is no "correct" structure, no magic formula that the examiners are looking for. It's **your** essay, so structure it the way **you** want. As long as you're answering the question all the way through, then you'll be fine.

Relevance

Be relevant to the question **all of the time** – not just in the first and last paragraphs.

Central concerns

Try to make sure your essay shows that you have thought about and understood the central concerns of the text, i.e. what it's "about" – the ideas and themes the writer is exploring in the text.

Quotation

In poetry and drama essays, you're expected to quote from the text, but never fall into the trap of learning a handful of quotations and forcing them all into the essay regardless of the question you're answering. In prose essays, quotation is much less important, and you can show your knowledge more effectively by referring in detail to what happens in key sections of the novel or the short story.

Techniques

You are expected to show understanding of how various literary techniques work within a text, but simply naming them will not get you marks, and structuring your essay around techniques rather than around relevant ideas in the text is not a good idea.

Good luck!

Remember that the rewards for passing Higher English are well worth it! Your pass will help you get the future you want for yourself. In the exam, be confident in your own ability. If you're not sure how to answer a question, trust your instincts and just give it a go anyway – keep calm and don't panic! GOOD LUCK!

Study Skills – what you need to know to pass exams!

General exam revision: 20 top tips

When preparing for exams, it is easy to feel unsure of where to start or how to revise. This guide to general exam revision provides a good starting place, and, as these are very general tips, they can be applied to all your exams.

1. Start revising in good time.

Don't leave revision until the last minute – this will make you panic and it will be difficult to learn. Make a revision timetable that counts down the weeks to go.

2. Work to a study plan.

Set up sessions of work spread through the weeks ahead. Make sure each session has a focus and a clear purpose. What will you study, when and why? Be realistic about what you can achieve in each session, and don't be afraid to adjust your plans as needed.

3. Make sure you know exactly when your exams are.

Get your exam dates from the SQA website and use the timetable builder tool to create your own exam schedule. You will also get a personalised timetable from your school, but this might not be until close to the exam period.

4. Make sure that you know the topics that make up each course.

Studying is easier if material is in manageable chunks – why not use the SQA topic headings or create your own from your class notes? Ask your teacher for help on this if you are not sure.

5. Break the chunks up into even smaller bits.

The small chunks should be easier to cope with. Remember that they fit together to make larger ideas. Even the process of chunking down will help!

6. Ask yourself these key questions for each course:

- Are all topics compulsory or are there choices?
- Which topics seem to come up time and time again?
- Which topics are your strongest and which are your weakest?

Use your answers to these questions to work out how much time you will need to spend revising each topic.

7. Make sure you know what to expect in the exam.

The subject-specific introduction to this book will help with this. Make sure you can answer these questions:

- How is the paper structured?
- How much time is there for each part of the exam?
- What types of question are involved? These will vary depending on the subject so read the subject-specific section carefully.

8. Past papers are a vital *revision tool!*

Use past papers to support your revision wherever possible. This book contains the answers and mark schemes too – refer to these carefully when checking your work. Using the mark scheme is useful; even if you don't manage to get all the marks available first time when you first practise, it helps you identify how to extend and develop your answers to get more marks next time – and of course, in the real exam.

9. Use study methods that work well for you.

People study and learn in different ways. Reading and looking at diagrams suits some students. Others prefer to listen and hear material – what about reading out loud or getting a friend or family member to do this for you? You could also record and play back material.

10. There are three tried and tested ways to make material stick in your long-term memory:

- Practising – e.g. rehearsal, repeating
- Organising – e.g. making drawings, lists, diagrams, tables, memory aids
- Elaborating – e.g. incorporating the material into a story or an imagined journey

11. Learn actively.

Most people prefer to learn actively – for example, making notes, highlighting, redrawing and redrafting, making up memory aids, or writing past paper answers. A good way to stay engaged and inspired is to mix and match these methods – find the combination that best suits you. This is likely to vary depending on the topic or subject.

12. Be an expert.

Be sure to have a few areas in which you feel you are an expert. This often works because at least some of them will come up, which can boost confidence.

13. Try some visual methods.

Use symbols, diagrams, charts, flashcards, post-it notes etc. Don't forget – the brain takes in chunked images more easily than loads of text.

14. Remember – practice makes perfect.

Work on difficult areas again and again. Look and read – then test yourself. You cannot do this too much.

15. Try past papers against the clock.

Practise writing answers in a set time. This is a good habit from the start but is especially important when you get closer to exam time.

16. Collaborate with friends.

Test each other and talk about the material – this can really help. Two brains are better than one! It is amazing how talking about a problem can help you solve it.

17. Know your weaknesses.

Ask your teacher for help to identify what you don't know. Try to do this as early as possible. If you are having trouble, it is probably with a difficult topic, so your teacher will already be aware of this – most students will find it tough.

18. Have your materials organised and ready.

Know what is needed for each exam:

- Do you need a calculator or a ruler?
- Should you have pencils as well as pens?
- Will you need water or paper tissues?

19. Make full use of school resources.

Find out what support is on offer:

- Are there study classes available?
- When is the library open?
- When is the best time to ask for extra help?
- Can you borrow textbooks, study guides, past papers, etc.?
- Is school open for Easter revision?

20. Keep fit and healthy!

Try to stick to a routine as much as possible, including with sleep. If you are tired, sluggish or dehydrated, it is difficult to see how concentration is even possible. Combine study with relaxation, drink plenty of water, eat sensibly, and get fresh air and exercise – all these things will help more than you could imagine. Good luck!

HIGHER

2017

National Qualifications 2017

X724/76/11

English
Reading for Understanding, Analysis and Evaluation — Text

THURSDAY, 11 MAY
9:00 AM – 10:30 AM

Total marks — 30

Read the passages carefully and then attempt ALL questions, which are printed on a separate sheet.

This Question Paper replaces the original SQA 2017 Past Paper, which cannot be reproduced for copyright reasons. As such, it should be stressed that it is not an official SQA-verified section, although every care has been taken by the Publishers to ensure that it offers appropriate practice material for Higher English.

The following two passages focus on video games.

Passage 1

Read the passage below and then attempt questions 1 to 5.

In the first passage, Steven Johnson, writing in The Times newspaper, considers whether video games are as bad for young people as is often claimed.

Reading books enriches the mind; playing video games deadens it — you can't get much more conventional than the conventional wisdom that kids today would be better off spending more time reading books, and less time zoning out in front of their video games.

5 For the record, I think that the virtues of reading books are great. We should all encourage our kids to read more. But even the most avid reader is inevitably going to spend his or her time with other media — games, television, movies, the internet. Yet the question is whether these other forms of culture have intellectual virtues in their own right — different from, but comparable to, reading. Where most critics allege a dumbing down, I see a progressive story: popular culture steadily, but almost imperceptibly, making our brains sharper as we soak in

10 entertainment usually dismissed as so much lowbrow fluff. I hope to persuade you that increasingly the non-literary popular culture is honing different mental skills that are just as important as the ones exercised by reading books.

The most powerful example of this trend is found in the world of video games. And the first and last thing that should be said about the experience of playing today's video games, the thing

15 you almost never hear, is that games are fiendishly, sometimes maddeningly, hard. The dirty little secret of gaming is how much time you spend not having fun. You may be frustrated; you may be confused or disorientated; you may be stuck. But when you put the game down and move back into the real world, you may find yourself mentally working through the problem you have been wrestling with, as though you were worrying a loose tooth.

20 So why does anyone bother playing these things? And why does a seven-year-old soak up, for instance, the intricacies of industrial economics in the game form of SimCity 2000, when the same subject would send him screaming for the exits in a classroom? To date, there has been little direct research into the question of how games get children to learn without realising that they are learning. But I believe a strong case can be made that the power of games to captivate

25 largely involves their ability to tap into the brain's natural reward circuitry. If you create a system in which rewards are both clearly defined and achieved by exploring an environment, you will find human brains drawn to those systems, even if they are made up of virtual characters and simulated sidewalks. In the game world, reward is everywhere. The gaming universe is literally teeming with objects that deliver very clearly articulated rewards: more life, access to

30 new levels, new equipment, new spells. Most of the crucial work in game design focuses on keeping players notified of potential rewards available to them, and how much these rewards are currently needed. Most games offer a fictional world where rewards are larger, and more vivid, and more clearly defined than life.

35 You may just want to win the game, of course, or perhaps you want to see the game's narrative completed, or in the initial stages of play, you may just be dazzled by the game's graphics. But most of the time, when you're hooked on a game, what draws you in is an elemental form of desire: the desire to see the Next Thing. After all, with the occasional exception, the actual content of the game is often childish or gratuitously menacing. Much of the role play inside the gaming world alternates between drive-by shooting and princess-rescuing. It is not the
40 subject matter that attracts; it is the reward system that draws those players in, and keeps their famously short attention spans locked on the screen.

Playing down the content of video games shouldn't be seen as a cop-out. We ignore the content of many other activities that are widely considered to be good for the brain. No one complains about the simplistic, militaristic plot of chess games. We teach algebra to children
45 knowing full well that the day they leave the classroom 99 per cent of those kids will never again directly employ their algebraic skills. Learning algebra isn't about acquiring a specific tool; it's about building up a mental muscle that will come in handy elsewhere.

So it is with games. It's not what you're thinking about when you're playing a game, it's the way you're thinking that matters. Novels may activate our imagination and may conjure up powerful
50 emotions, but games force you to analyse, to choose, to prioritise, to decide. From the outside, the primary activity of a gamer looks like a fury of clicking and shooting. But if you peer inside the gamer's mind, the primary activity turns out to be another creature altogether: making decisions, some of them snap judgements, some of them long-term strategies.

Adapted from an article in The Times newspaper, May 2005

Passage 2

Read the passage below and attempt question 6. While reading, you may wish to make notes on the main ideas and/or highlight key points in the passage.

In the second passage, the politician and journalist Boris Johnson, writing on his own website, takes a different view about video games.

It's the snarl that gives the game away. It's the sobbing and the shrieking and the horrible pleading — that's how you know your children are undergoing a sudden narcotic withdrawal. As the strobing colours die away and the screen goes black, you listen to the wail of protest from the offspring and you know that you have just turned off their drug, and you know that they are,
5 to a greater or lesser extent, addicts.

Millions of seven-to-fifteen-year olds are hooked, especially boys, and it is time someone had the guts to stand up, cross the room and just say no to Nintendo. It is time to garrotte the Game Boy and paralyse the PlayStation, and it is about time, as a society, that we admitted the catastrophic effect these blasted gizmos are having on the literacy and the prospects of young
10 males.

We demand that teachers provide our children with reading skills; we expect the schools to fill them with a love of books; and yet at home we let them slump in front of the consoles. We get on with our hedonistic 21st-century lives while in some other room the nippers are bleeping and zapping in speechless rapture, their passive faces washed in explosions and gore. They sit for so
15 long that their souls seem to have been sucked down the cathode ray tube.

They become like blinking lizards, motionless, absorbed, only the twitching of their hands showing that they are still conscious. These machines teach them nothing. They stimulate no ratiocination, discovery or feat of memory — though some of them may cunningly pretend to be educational. I have just watched an eleven-year-old play a game that looked fairly historical, on
20 the packet. Your average guilt-ridden parent might assume that it taught the child something about the Vikings and medieval siege warfare. Phooey! The red soldiers robotically slaughtered the white soldiers, and then they did it again, that was it. Everything was programmed, spoon-fed, immediate — and endlessly showering the player with undeserved praise, richly congratulating him for his bogus massacres.

25 The more addictive these games are to the male mind, the more difficult it is to persuade boys to read books. It's not that these young people lack the brains; the raw circuitry is better than ever. It's the software that's the problem. They have not been properly programmed, because they have not read enough. The only way to learn to write is to be forced time and again to articulate your own thoughts in your own words, and you haven't a hope of doing this if you haven't read enough
30 to absorb the basic elements of vocabulary, grammar, rhythm, style and structure; and young males in particular won't read enough if we continually capitulate and let them fritter their lives away in front of these drivelling machines.

So I say now: go to where your children are sitting in auto-lobotomy in front of the console. Summon up all your strength, all your courage. Steel yourself for the screams and yank out that
35 plug. And if they still kick up a fuss, then get out the sledgehammer and strike a blow for literacy.

Adapted from an article published on Boris Johnson's website in June 2006

[END OF QUESTION PAPER]

National
Qualifications
2017

X724/76/21

English
Reading for Understanding,
Analysis and Evaluation — Questions

THURSDAY, 11 MAY

9:00 AM – 10:30 AM

Total marks — 30

Attempt ALL questions.

Write your answers clearly in the answer booklet provided. In the answer booklet you must clearly identify the question number you are attempting.

Use **blue** or **black** ink.

Before leaving the examination room you must give your answer booklet to the Invigilator; if you do not, you may lose all the marks for this paper.

MARKS

Attempt ALL questions
Total marks — 30

1. Read lines 1–12.

   (a) Analyse how the writer's word choice in lines 1–3 emphasises the "conventional wisdom" that reading books is better than playing video games.   2

   (b) Explain in your own words "the question" the writer asks in line 6 about "other forms of culture".   2

   (c) **By referring to at least two features of language in lines 8–12** ("Where … books"), analyse how the writer emphasises the contrast between his positive view of "other forms of culture" and the negative view held by "most critics".   4

2. By referring to lines 13–19, analyse how the writer uses both sentence structure and imagery to convey the difficulty of playing video games   4

3. Read lines 20–33.

   Identify **three** reasons why "reward" is so important to the learning process involved in playing video games. Use your own words as far as possible.   3

4. Read lines 34–47.

   Identify **two** criticisms and **two** defences the writer makes of video games.   4

5. Read lines 48–54.

   (a) Explain in your own words the key distinction the writer makes between reading a novel and playing a video game.   2

   (b) Analyse how the writer's use of language in lines 50–54 ("From … strategies") conveys the contrast between what a gamer looks like from "the outside" and what is happening "inside the gamer's mind".   4

Question on both passages

6. Look at both passages.

   The writers disagree about video games.

   Identify three key areas on which they disagree.

   You should support the points by referring to important ideas in both passages.

   You may answer this question in continuous prose or in a series of developed bullet points.   5

[END OF QUESTION PAPER]

National
Qualifications
2017

X724/76/12

English
Critical Reading

THURSDAY, 11 MAY

10:50 AM – 12:20 PM

Total marks — 40

SECTION 1 — Scottish Text — 20 marks

Read an extract from a Scottish text you have previously studied and attempt the questions.

Choose ONE text from either

Part A — Drama   Pages 2–13

or

Part B — Prose   Pages 14–23

or

Part C — Poetry   Pages 24–35

Attempt ALL the questions for your chosen text.

SECTION 2 — Critical Essay — 20 marks

Attempt ONE question from the following genres — Drama, Prose Fiction, Prose Non-Fiction, Poetry, Film and Television Drama, or Language.

Your answer must be on a different genre from that chosen in Section 1.

You should spend approximately 45 minutes on each Section.

Write your answers clearly in the answer booklet provided. In the answer booklet, you must clearly identify the question number you are attempting.

Use **blue** or **black** ink.

Before leaving the examination room you must give your answer booklet to the Invigilator; if you do not, you may lose all the marks for this paper.

SECTION 1 — SCOTTISH TEXT — 20 marks

Choose ONE text from Drama, Prose or Poetry.

Read the text extract carefully and then attempt ALL the questions for your chosen text.

You should spend about 45 minutes on this Section.

PART A — SCOTTISH TEXT — DRAMA

Text 1 — Drama

If you choose this text you may not attempt a question on Drama in Section 2.

Read the extract below and then attempt the following questions.

The Slab Boys **by John Byrne**

In this extract, from Act 2 of the play, Spanky and Phil believe that Hector has just lost his job.

	SPANKY:	We'd like to present this little . . . er . . . this token of . . . er . . .
	HECTOR:	There was five of them . . . plus a squared-off fitch with my name on it . . .
	SPANKY:	Are you going to shut your face and listen, Shorty? Me and Phil's trying to make a presentation here.
5	PHIL:	It's a quid.
	SPANKY:	Shut up.
	HECTOR:	Sorry, what were you saying?
	SPANKY:	We know it's come as a bit of a surprise to you, Hector . . . you having to leave the Slab Room . . .
10	HECTOR:	It's a bombshell . . . no kidding . . .
	SPANKY:	(*to Phil*) Doesn't make it easy, does he? Er . . . so what me and Phil's done is . . . er . . . well, we put round the hat and . . . er . . .
	PHIL:	Carry on, you're doing fine.
	SPANKY:	It's not a lot, you understand . . .
15	PHIL:	It's a quid, son.
	SPANKY:	Shut up, will you!
	PHIL:	Give us it. (*Snatches 'presentation'.*) What Spanky was trying to say, Hector, is . . . er . . . och, here.
	SPANKY:	It's a quid.
20	*They clap.*	
	HECTOR:	What's this for?
	PHIL:	Not even a "Thank you, boys, I'm really touched." You are leaving the Slab Room, right?
	HECTOR:	Yeh, but . . .
25	SPANKY:	Then that'll tide you over . . . you and your maw . . .

PHIL:	Till you get another job.
HECTOR:	Eh?
SPANKY:	He said, till you get another job.
HECTOR:	Eh?

30 SPANKY *and* PHIL (*together*): Till you get another job!

HECTOR:	I've already got another job.
PHIL:	Christ, that was quick. Is there a mobile Broo outside?
HECTOR:	That's what I was along seeing Willie about . . . my new job . . . I start on a desk on Monday.

35 SPANKY *and* PHIL (*together*): What????

HECTOR:	I'm a Designer now. Seven quid a week back-dated a fortnight, rising in annual increments to twelve pounds fifteen and eleven after tax at the end of four years. God, I don't think I feel too well . . .
SPANKY:	Me too . . .

40 HECTOR: It's the excitement.

(*Enter* Alan.)

ALAN:	Hey . . . guess what? Since two of you guys are vacating the Slab, Curry thought I should step in and fill the breach . . . how about that? Where are the gum crystals kept again? (*Hunts around.*) Oh . . . there was a phone call came through to Willie's office . . . I said I'd pass the message on . . .
PHIL:	Eh? Is my maw safe??
ALAN:	You didn't get in.
PHIL:	What?
ALAN:	Exceptionally high number of applicants this year . . . something like that . . .

MARKS

Questions

1. Look at lines 1—20.

    By referring to **at least two** examples, analyse how dialogue is used to reveal the attitudes of the slab boys (Phil and Spanky) to Hector's situation at this point.

    3

2. Look at lines 21—40.

    By referring to **at least two** examples, analyse how humour is used in relation to Hector's announcement.

    4

3. Look at lines 42—49.

    By referring to **at least two** examples, analyse how language is used to convey Alan's character **and/or** attitudes.

    3

4. By referring to this extract and to elsewhere in the play, discuss how Byrne develops the theme of opportunity.

    10

[OPEN OUT FOR QUESTIONS]

DO NOT WRITE ON THIS PAGE

OR

Text 2 — Drama

If you choose this text you may not attempt a question on Drama in Section 2.

Read the extract below and then attempt the following questions.

***The Cheviot, the Stag and the Black, Black Oil* by John McGrath**

This extract focuses on a shooting party in the Highlands.

Enter shooting party with large armoury. GHILLIE, LORD CRASK, *and* LADY PHOSPHATE OF RUNCORN.

LADY PH:	Her Royal Majesty the Queen is so right about the charm of this divine part of the world, what? Your estates, Lord Crask, abound in brown trout and grouse — what? —
LORD CRASK:	Has your Ladyship sampled the salmon?
LADY PH:	The rugged beauty hereabouts puts one in mind of the poetic fancies of dear Lord Tennyson — what?
LORD CRASK:	Lady Phosphate of Runcorn you are too kind.
LADY PH:	Oh listen for the vale profound is overflowing with the sound.

5

10

Blast of gunfire.

GHILLIE (*tries to stop them*): No no no no — the beaters are just having their tea.

LADY PH:	As one does. What?
LORD CRASK:	What?

Goes to fire; GHILLIE *restrains him.*

15

GHILLIE (*to audience*): That's nothing, you should see him when he's fishing.

LADY PH:	How far do your domains extend over this beauteous countryside, Lord Crask?
LORD CRASK:	I have about 120,000 acres down that way, but most of it's over that way.
LADY PH:	Oh Archie . . . Capital, capital, capital . . .
LORD CRASK:	Oh yes I've got bags of that too — 200,000 shares in Argentine Beef, half a million tied up in shipping, and a mile or two of docks in Wapping.
LADY PH:	Topping —
LORD CRASK:	No Wapping —
LADY PH:	What?

20

25

LORD CRASK *goes to shoot* — GHILLIE *restrains him.*

GHILLIE:	No no no no no.
LADY PH:	Your highland air is very bracing — I quite fancy a small port . . .
LORD CRASK:	Oh — how would you like Lochinver?
LADY PH:	No no no, I mean I'd like to wet my whistle —
LORD CRASK (*waving hand*): We've left a bush over there for that sort of thing . . .

30

GHILLIE *whistles up the beaters.*

GHILLIE: Any moment now sir . . .

LORD CRASK: Here come the grouse, Lady Phosphate —

35   LADY PH: What?

LORD CRASK: The grouse —

LADY PH: Oh, how lovely. (*She gets out a sten gun.*) I find it so moving that all over the north of North Britain, healthy, vigorous people are deriving so much innocent pleasure at so little cost to their fellow human beings.

40   *Barrage.* GHILLIE *aims* LORD CRASK's *gun up higher, struggles with him.* LADY PHOSPHATE *fires her sten from the hip. Bombs, shells, etc. Barrage ends.*

GHILLIE: Oh no — Thon was a nice wee boy.

Music — guitar and mandolin begins. LORD CRASK *and* LADY PHOSPHATE *sing a duet.*

BOTH: Oh it's awfully, frightfully, ni-i-ice,
45   Shooting stags, my dear, and grice —
                      And there's nothing quite so righ-it-it
                      As a fortnight catching trite:

                      And if the locals should complain,
                      Well we can clear them off again.

50   LADY PH: We'll clear the straths

LORD CRASK: We'll clear the paths

LADY PH: We'll clear the bens

LORD CRASK: We'll clear the glens

BOTH: We'll show them we're the ruling class.

MARKS

Questions

5. Look at lines 1—19.

    By referring to **at least two** examples, analyse how language is used to convey the characters of **both** Lady Phosphate and Lord Crask.

    4

6. Look at lines 20—42.

    By referring to **at least two** examples, analyse how humour is used to reveal central concerns.

    4

7. Look at lines 44—54.

    Explain how the singers' attitudes to **both** the local people and environment are made clear.

    2

8. By referring to this extract and to elsewhere in the play, discuss how McGrath explores the effects of social class.

    10

Page nine

[OPEN OUT FOR QUESTIONS]

DO NOT WRITE ON THIS PAGE

OR

Text 3 — Drama

If you choose this text you may not attempt a question on Drama in Section 2.

Read the extract below and then attempt the following questions.

Men Should Weep by Ena Lamont Stewart

In this extract from Act 2, scene 1, Granny is waiting to be collected by her daughter-in-law, Lizzie.

Mrs Harris opens the door to Lizzie, a hard-faced harridan about fifty

	Lizzie:	*(ignoring the others)* Well? Ye ready?
	Mrs Bone:	Ready? She's been sittin here waitin on ye for the last hauf-oor.
	Lizzie:	Got a yer claes packed? An yer pension book?
5	Granny:	Aye, Lizzie; it's here.
	Lizzie:	See's a look at it. *(Granny starts to fumble with her bag. Mrs Bone goes to help her)* Hev they men no been for the bed yet?
	Mrs Harris:	If they'd hae been for the bed it wouldna be staunin up against yon wa, would it?
10	Lizzie:	*(taking the pension book from Mrs Bone)* Here! Ye've drawn this week's. Ye got the money?
	Granny:	Naw, Lizzie . . . I gied it tae Maggie.
	Lizzie:	Well, it's no Maggie's, it's mines. If ye're comin tae bide wi me, ye're no comin tae bide *aff* me.
15	Granny:	She got some things aff the grocer she'd tae pay for, an she wis needin a vest an socks for Bertie gaun up tae the hospital.
	Lizzie:	Oh? So Bertie gets new socks at ma expense, does he? And whit does she think you're gonna live on for the next week? Air?
20	Mrs Harris:	Ach, leave the puir aul wife alane. Shairly ye can scrape up a bit tae eat for her; it's no as if ye wis takin in a big hulkin brute o a man tae feed.
	Lizzie:	I'm no takin in naebody tae feed. Folks that canna pay for their meat'll find nae room in ma hoose.
	Mrs Bone:	Oo! An her yer puir dead husband's mither. Oo! I'm surprised at ye, Lizzie Morrison.
25	Mrs Harris:	I thought you said you wis never surprised — at anythin human.
	Mrs Bone:	That's jist whit I said: *anythin human.*

They both stare hard at Lizzie, then shake their heads at each other

	Lizzie:	I've tae earn every penny that comes intae ma hoose.
30	Mrs Harris:	Aye, we ken that. An you don't dae sae bad either, ye aul miser. Buyin up aul claes for a copper or twa and sellin them at sixpence a week . . .
	Mrs Bone:	Or she'll loan ye the dough tae buy them outright — at fifty percent.

Mrs Harris: Aye, she's got a right kind heart, she wouldae see ye stuck; no if she could mak a guid thing oot o it.

35 Lizzie: Ye're jealous! Ye hevna the brains tae mak a bit yersels. But ye're no above tradin wi me when it suits ye. Aye, an gettin a bargain.

Mrs Harris ⎫
Mrs Bone: ⎬ (together) A bargain? Frae *you*?

They look at each other and shake their heads

Mrs Harris: I canna mind ony bargain.

Lizzie: Whit aboot yon veloory hat ye bought aff me?

40 Mrs Harris: Veloory hat? Veloory hat . . . ? Oh, ye mean yon scabby aul felt bunnet wi the moultin bird on tap? Oh aye, I mind! If yon wis veloory, I'm a wally dug.

Lizzie: It wis veloory. It belanged tae a lady in Kelvinside whaur I did a bit on a Saturday.

Mrs Bone: A bit whit? Pinchin?

45 Lizzie: Here! I could pit ye tae the Polis for that.

Mrs Harris: No roon aboot here ye couldnae. They a ken ye.

Granny: Oh, I'm nae wantin tae leave here! I wisht I could bide wi Maggie till I dee!

Lizzie: Bide then!

Granny: Ye ken I cannae bide. Alec and Isa's needin the room.

50 Mrs Harris: Some folks is right selfish. You've naebody but yersel tae think aboot, an ye'll no tak the aul wife aff Maggie's hauns wi'oot kickin up a fuss.

Lizzie sits down and loosens her coat

Mrs Bone: I thought you wis in a hurry tae get aff?

Lizzie: I'm sittin right here till Maggie comes hame wi whit's left o Granny's pension.

55 Mrs Bone: Huh! Whit a hope you've got. Whit d'ye think'll be left?

Lizzie: Aye . . . mebbe y're right . . . In that case, I'll jist hae tae tak whit she bought.

She gets up and goes to open food cupboard. Mrs Harris grabs her

Mrs Harris: Here! Mrs Bone and me's in chairge o this hoose till Lily comes; you keep yer dirty aul neb oot of the cupboards or we'll shout for the Polis.

MARKS

Questions

9. Look at lines 1–27.

    By referring to **at least two** examples, analyse how **both** stage directions and dialogue are used to create a clear impression of Lizzie in these lines.   **4**

10. Look at lines 28–46.

    By referring to **at least two** examples, analyse how language is used to convey the feelings of the neighbours (Mrs Harris and Mrs Bone) towards Lizzie.   **4**

11. Although Granny says very little in these lines, she is important in highlighting central concerns. By considering the extract as a whole, explain why she is important.   **2**

12. By referring to this extract and to elsewhere in the play, discuss how Lamont Stewart develops the theme of community.   **10**

[OPEN OUT FOR QUESTIONS]

DO NOT WRITE ON THIS PAGE

SECTION 1 — SCOTTISH TEXT — 20 marks

Choose ONE text from Drama, Prose or Poetry.

Read the text extract carefully and then attempt ALL the questions for your chosen text.

You should spend about 45 minutes on this Section.

PART B — SCOTTISH TEXT — PROSE

Text 1 — Prose

If you choose this text you may not attempt a question on Prose (Fiction or Non-Fiction) in Section 2.

Read the extract below and then attempt the following questions.

The Red Door by Iain Crichton Smith

As he stared at the door he felt strange flutterings within him. First of all the door had been painted very lovingly so that it shone with a deep inward shine such as one might find in pictures. And indeed it looked like a picture against the rest of the house which wasn't at all modern but on the contrary was old and intertwined with all sorts of rusty
5   pipes like snakes.

He went back from the door and looked at it from a distance as people in art galleries have to do when studying an oil painting. The more he regarded it the more he liked it. It certainly stood out against the drab landscape as if it were a work of art. On the other hand the more he looked at it the more it seemed to express something in himself which
10   had been deeply buried for years. After a while there was something boring about green and as for blue it wouldn't have suited the door at all. Blue would have been too blatant in a cold way. And anyway the sky was already blue.

But mixed with his satisfaction he felt what could only be described as puzzlement, a slight deviation from the normal as if his head were spinning and he were going round in circles.
15   What would the neighbours say about it, he wondered. Never in the history of the village had there been a red door before. For that matter he couldn't remember seeing even a blue door himself, though he had heard of the existence of one.

The morning was breaking all over the village as he looked. Blue smoke was ascending from chimneys, a cock was crowing, belligerent and heraldic, its red claws sunk into the
20   earth, its metallic breast oriental and strange. There was a dew all about him and lying on the fences ahead of him. He recognised that the village would wake to a new morning, for the red door would gather attention to itself.

And he thought to himself, "I have always sought to hide among other people. I agree to whatever anybody tells me to do. If they think I should go to church, I go to church. If they
25   want me to cut peats for them, I do. I have never," he thought with wonder, "been myself." He looked down at his grey fisherman's jersey and his wellingtons and he thought, "I have always worn these things because everybody else does. I have never had the courage to wear what I wanted to wear, for example a coloured waistcoat and a coloured jacket."

The red door stood out against the whiteness of the frost and the glimmerings of snow. It
30   seemed to be saying something to him, to be asking him a question. Perhaps it was pleading with him not to destroy it. Perhaps it was saying, "I don't want to be green. There must be a place somewhere for me as myself. I wish to be red. What is wrong with red anyway?" The door seemed to him to have its own courage.

MARKS

35 Wine of course was red and so was blood. He drank none of the former and only saw the latter when he cut himself while repairing a fence or working with wood when a nail would prick his finger.

But really was he happy? That was the question. When he considered it carefully he knew that he wasn't. He didn't like eating alone, he didn't like sitting in the house alone, he didn't like having none who belonged to him, to whom he could tell his secret thoughts,
40 for example that such and such was a mean devil and that that other one was an ungrateful rat.

He had to keep a perpetually smiling face to the world, that was his trouble. But the red door didn't do that. It was foreign and confident. It seemed to be saying what it was, not what it thought others expected it to say. On the other hand, he didn't like wellingtons and
45 a fisherman's jersey. He hated them in fact: they had no elegance.

Now Mary had elegance. Though she was a bit odd, she had elegance. It was true that the villagers didn't understand her but that was because she read many books, her father having been a teacher. And on the other hand she made no concessions to anybody. She seemed to be saying, "You can take me or leave me." She never gossiped. She was proud
50 and distant. She had a world of her own.

Questions

13. Look at lines 1—12.

    By referring to **at least two** examples, analyse how the language emphasises the differences between the red door and the existing surroundings.   4

14. Look at lines 18—33.

    By referring to **at least two** examples, analyse how language is used to highlight the significance of the red door at this moment in Murdo's life.   4

15. Look at lines 37—45.

    Analyse how the language reveals Murdo's deep-rooted unhappiness.   2

16. By referring to this extract and to at least one other short story, discuss how Crichton Smith explores the conflict between individuality and conformity.   10

[Turn over

OR

Text 2 — Prose

If you choose this text you may not attempt a question on Prose (Fiction or Non-Fiction) in Section 2.

Read the extract below and then attempt the following questions.

Tartan by George Mackay Brown

They crossed a field to the third house, a hovel. From the door they heard muttering and sighing inside. "There's breath in this house," said Kol. He leapt into the middle of the floor with a loud beserk yell, but it might have been a fly buzzing in the window for all the attention the old woman paid to him. "Ah," she was singing over the sheeted dead child on
5   the bed, "I thought to see you a shepherd on Morven, or maybe a fisherman poaching salmon at the mouth of the Naver. Or maybe you would be a man with lucky acres and the people would come from far and near to buy your corn. Or you might have been a holy priest at the seven altars of the west."

There was a candle burning at the child's head and a cross lay on his breast, tangled in his
10 cold fingers.

Arnor, Havard, and Sven crossed themselves in the door. Kol slunk out like an old dog.

They took nothing from that house but trudged uphill to a neat grey house built into the sheer brae.

At the cairn across the valley, a mile away, a group of plaided men stood watching them.

15 At the fourth door a voice called to them to come in. A thin man was standing beside a loom with a half-made web in it. "Strangers from the sea," he said, "you are welcome. You have the salt in your throats and I ask you to accept ale from Malcolm the weaver."

They stood round the door and Malcolm the weaver poured horns of ale for each of them.

"This is passable ale," said Havard. "If it had been sour, Malcolm the weaver, we would
20 have stretched you alive on your loom. We would have woven the thread of eternity through you."

Malcolm the weaver laughed.

"What is the name of this place?" said Arnor.

"It is called Durness," said Malcolm the weaver. "They are good people here, except for the
25 man who lives in the tall house beyond the cairn. His name is Duncan, and he will not pay me for the cloth I wove for him last winter, so that he and his wife and his snovelly-nosed children could have coats when the snow came."

"On account of the average quality of your ale, we will settle matters with this Duncan," said Arnor. "Now we need our cups filled again."

30 They stayed at Malcolm the weaver's house for an hour and more, and when they got up to go Kol staggered against the door. "Doubtless somebody will pay for this," he said thickly.

They took with them a web of cloth without asking leave of Malcolm. It was a gray cloth of fine quality and it had a thick green stripe and a thin brown stripe running up and down and a very thick black stripe cutting across it horizontally. It was the kind of Celtic weave
35 they call tartan.

MARKS

"Take it, take it by all means," said Malcolm the weaver.

"We were going to take it in any case," said Sven.

"Tell us," said Havard from the door, "who is the girl in Durness with black hair and black eyes and a cleft chin?"

40 "Her name is Morag," said Malcolm the weaver, "and she is the wife of John the shepherd. John has been on the hill all week with the new lambs. I think she is lonely."

Questions

17. Look at lines 1—13.

   By referring to **at least two** examples, analyse how the writer uses language to convey the emotional impact of the child's death.   4

18. Look at lines 15—41.

   By referring to **at least two** examples, analyse how the writer uses language to reveal the character **and/or** attitudes of Malcolm the weaver.   4

19. Look at the whole extract.

   By referring closely to the extract, analyse how the characters of **two** of the Vikings are conveyed.   2

20. By referring to this extract and to at least one other short story, discuss how Mackay Brown explores the relationship between the individual and the community.   10

[Turn over

OR

Text 3 — Prose

If you choose this text you may not attempt a question on Prose (Fiction or Non-Fiction) in Section 2.

Read the extract below and then attempt the following questions.

The Trick Is To Keep Breathing by Janice Galloway

On the map, it's called Bourtreehill, after the elder tree, the bourtree, Judas tree; protection against witches. The people who live here call it Boot Hill. Boot Hill is a new estate well outside the town it claims to be part of. There was a rumour when they started building the place that it was meant for undesirables: difficult tenants from other places,
5   shunters, overspill from Glasgow. That's why it's so far away from everything. Like most rumours, it's partly true. Boot Hill is full of tiny, twisty roads, wild currant bushes to represent the great outdoors, pubs with plastic beer glasses and kids. The twisty roads are there to prevent the kids being run over. The roads are meant to make drivers slow down so they get the chance to see and stop in time. This is a dual misfunction. Hardly anyone
10 has a car. If one does appear on the horizon, the kids use the bends to play chicken, deliberately lying low and leaping out at the last minute for fun. The roads end up more conducive to child death than if they had been straight. What they do achieve is to make the buses go slow. Buses are infrequent so the shelters are covered in graffiti and kids hanging from the roofs. Nobody waits in these shelters even when it's raining. It rains a lot.
15 The buses take a long time.

When I was small I always wanted a red front door. This front door is bottle green. The key never surrenders first time. I have to rummage through my bag and every pocket while I stand at the door as though I'm begging to be mugged. The first time we came, there were two sets of numbers on the door; one large and black; the other brass and much smaller.
20 Like this:

13   13

We laughed and left them on, wondering if the previous tenants had been amnesiacs or phobics. When I came back alone, I took both sets off. There are four little holes on the door where they used to be

    •

    •   •
25   and a

different colour of paint underneath. I wondered what had moved away the previous tenants with their amnesia or their phobia. I wondered where they were now. Anyway, I didn't want those numbers on the door: it was a signal I could do without. I was angry I hadn't done it before. The nameplate was something he had bought, so I left it on. It says
30 his name. Not mine.

MARKS

Grit wells up when I open the door. There are always withered leaves in the porch. It seems to sit at the end of a natural tunnel of wind and makes itself difficult even on mild days. Litter accumulates on either side of the porch step: the porch is full of curled, brown leaves. Slaters run frantic in the sudden emptiness overhead while I fight my way inside.
35 This makes me shiver. Every time. I notice a little shell of something dead that's been there for weeks now because I can't pick it up, not even through paper. I hate the feel of them, gritty little packets. Insects make me sick. They have their skeletons outside, too many eyes, unpredictable legs and you can never tell where their mouths are. Spiders are worse. But today there are only the slaters. They disgust me but I'm not afraid of them. I push the
40 letters with my foot till they are well clear of the dead one and pick them up with the tips of my fingers.

A bill from the lawyer, a note from the Health Visitor and a postcard from Marianne.

I've been Whitewater Rafting

The postcard has a picture of a butterfly and a gushing torrent of water in the background.
45 The words on the back are smudged as though some of the water from the front of the card has splashed over and made the ink run. This makes it hard to read but I get the general drift.

Camping better than anticipated. Leaving for the
Canadian border tomorrow. Scenery wonderful.
50 You would hate it. Love   Mxx

I forget about the slaters and try to feel the other continent through the card. It doesn't work. I make tea and check out the livingroom. The spill on the rug is almost dry. I find the bottle open from last night but not the lid. I put an envelope over the neck, sitting the bottle aside so I don't kick it later, then reshape cushions trying to keep my feet on the rug
55 because my shoes make a terrible noise on the floorboards. But things have to be set in place. A lot depends on stillness later and I have to get a lot of moving around out of my system now. Stillness helps when I'm alone. It keeps me contained.

Questions

21. Look at lines 1—15.

   By referring to **at least two** examples, analyse how the writer uses language to convey a negative impression of Bourtreehill. 4

22. Look at lines 16—41.

   By referring to **at least two** examples, analyse how the writer's use of language reveals Joy's anxiety. 4

23. Look at lines 42—57.

   Analyse how the writer's use of language emphasises Joy's attempts to cope with her situation. 2

24. By referring to this extract and to elsewhere in the novel, discuss how Galloway explores the impact of loneliness. 10

OR

Text 4 — Prose

If you choose this text you may not attempt a question on Prose (Fiction or Non-Fiction) in Section 2.

Read the extract below and then attempt the following questions.

Sunset Song by Lewis Grassic Gibbon

In this extract, which is from Part II (Drilling), it is threshing time at Chae Strachan's farm.

Not that they'd much to shout for that winter themselves, the Strachans; folk said it was easy to see why Chae was so strong on Rich and Poor being Equal: he was sore in need of the sharing out to start ere he went clean broke himself. Maybe old Sinclair or the wife were tight with the silver that year, but early as December Chae had to sell his corn, he
5 brought the first threshing of the season down in Kinraddie. John Guthrie and Will were off at the keek of dawn when they saw the smoke rise from the engines, Chris followed an hour later to help Chae's wife with the dinner and things. And faith! broke he might be but he wasn't mean, Chae, when the folk came trampling in to eat there was broth and beef and chicken and oat-cakes, champion cakes they made at the Knapp; and loaf and jelly
10 and dumpling with sugar and milk; and if any soul were that gutsy he wanted more he could hold to the turnip-field, said Chae.

The first three men to come in Chris hardly saw, so busied she was pouring their broth for them. Syne, setting the plates, she saw Alec Mutch, his great lugs like red clouts hung out to dry: and he cried *Ay, Chris!* and began to sup as though he hadn't seen food for a
15 fortnight. Beside him was Munro of the Cuddiestoun, he was eating like a colie ta'en off its chain, Chae's thresh was a spree to the pair of them. Then more trampling and scraping came from the door, folk came drifting in two-three at a time, Chris over-busied to notice their faces, but some watched her and gave a bit smile and Cuddiestoun cried to father, *Losh, man, she's fair an expert getting, the daughter. The kitchen's more her style than the*
20 *College.*

Some folk at the tables laughed out at that, the ill-nature grinned from the faces of them, and suddenly Chris hated the lot, the English Chris came back in her skin a minute, she saw them the yokels and clowns everlasting, dull-brained and crude. Alec Mutch took up the card from Cuddiestoun then and began on education and the speak ran round the tables.
25 Most said it was a coarse thing, learning, just teaching your children a lot of damned nonsense that put them above themselves, they'd turn round and give you their lip as soon as look at you. But Chae was sitting down himself by then and he wouldn't have that. *Damn't man, you're clean wrong to think that. Education's the thing the working man wants to put him up level with the Rich.* And Long Rob of the Mill said *I'd have thought a bit*
30 *balance in the bank would do that.* But for once he seemed right in agreement with Chae — *the more education the more of sense and the less of kirks and ministers.* Cuddiestoun and Mutch were fair shocked at that, Cuddiestoun cried out *Well, well, we'll hear nothing coarse of religion,* as though he didn't want to hear anything more about it and was giving out orders. But Long Rob wasn't a bit took aback, the long rangy childe, he just cocked an
35 eye at Cuddiestoun and cried *Well, well, Munro, we'll turn to the mentally afflicted in general, not just in particular. How's that foreman of yours getting on, Tony? Is he still keeping up with his shorthand?* There was a snicker at that, you may well be sure, and Cuddiestoun closed up quick enough, here and there folk had another bit laugh and said Long Rob was an ill hand to counter. And Chris thought of her clowns and yokels, and was
40 shamed as she thought — Chae and Long Rob they were, the poorest folk in Kinraddie!

MARKS

Questions

25. Look at lines 1—11.

    By referring to **at least two** examples, explain how important aspects of Chae's character are revealed.   3

26. Look at lines 12—20.

    By referring to **at least two** examples, analyse how humour is created.   3

27. Look at lines 21—40.

    By referring to **at least two** examples, analyse how the writer conveys the differing attitudes of those present.   4

28. By referring to this extract and to elsewhere in the novel, discuss how Grassic Gibbon conveys Chris's conflicting emotions towards the community of Kinraddie.   10

[Turn over

OR

Text 5 — Prose

If you choose this text you may not attempt a question on Prose (Fiction or Non-Fiction) in Section 2.

Read the extract below and then attempt the following questions.

The Cone-Gatherers by Robin Jenkins

In this extract, a storm is brewing.

In the tip of the tall larch they were in a good position to watch the approach of the storm. At the sea end of the loch for the past half hour indigo clouds had been mustering, with rumbles of thunder still distant and half-hearted. More ominous was the river of radiance pouring straight down into the orange mass of the tree. After long excited consultations,
5 the finches had whisked away. The two men were the only living creatures left in the tree tops.

At the very crest, Calum was frightened and exhilarated. He chattered involuntarily, making no sense. Instead of dropping the golden cones safely into his bag he let them dribble out of his hands so that, in the expectancy before the violence of the storm, the
10 tiny stots from one transfigured branch to another could be clearly heard. Several times he reached up and raised his hand, so that it was higher than the tree.

Neil, a little lower down, was fastened by a safety belt. His rheumatism had heralded the rain, so that the climb to the top had been for him a long slow agony which he did not wish to repeat. That was why he did not give the order to go down; he hoped the storm
15 would pass over without striking them. He too was agitated, finding the cones exasperatingly small and his bag insatiable. The belt chafed his waist, and his arms and legs ached. Above all, Calum's meaningless chatters distressed him. He shouted to him several times to stop. Calum only screamed back, not in defiance, but in uncontrollable excitement.

20 Then that cascade of light streaming into the larch ceased, leaving it dark and cold. Black clouds were now overhead. Thunder snarled. Colour faded from the wood. A sough of wind shook the gloomy host of trees. Over the sea flashed lightning. Yet, far to the east, islands of peace and brightness persisted in the sky.

The first few drops of rain fell, as large as cones.

25 "We'd better get down," shouted Neil, and he tugged frantically at the buckle of his belt with his stiff sticky blackened fingers.

Calum slithered down and helped to loose him. He was giggling.

"Whether we go down or not," said Neil, "we'll get soaked to the skin. But up here the lightning might be dangerous."

30 "I don't like the lightning, Neil."

"Nobody does. What's been the matter with you? You're not a child. You've been in a storm before."

MARKS

"Did you see the light, Neil?"

"How could I miss seeing it? It was in my eyes, blinding me."

35 "Was it from heaven, Neil?"

"Heaven?" Neil's shout was astonished and angry. "What are you talking about?"

Calum pressed close to him eagerly.

"Do you mind what you said yon time, Neil? We were in the shed together, with the horse. You said it was always as bright as that in heaven."

40 "In the shed, with the horse? What shed and what horse?"

"It was called Peggy, Neil."

Neil remembered. "But that was more than twenty years ago," he cried.

"Aye, but you said it, Neil. You said heaven was always as bright as that."

His face wet with rain and tears, Neil clung to the tree and shut his eyes.

45 "Maybe I did, Calum," he said.

"And mind what else you said, Neil? You said that was where our mither was. You said that, Neil, in the shed."

"Maybe I did."

Questions

29. Look at lines 1—6.

    Analyse how the writer effectively describes the impending storm.   2

30. Look at lines 7—19.

    By referring to **at least two** examples, analyse how the writer's use of language conveys Calum's reaction to the storm.   4

31. Look at lines 25—48.

    By referring to **at least two** examples, analyse how dialogue is used to convey aspects of the relationship between Calum and Neil.   4

32. By referring to this extract and to elsewhere in the novel, discuss how Jenkins uses symbolism to develop the central concerns of the text.   10

[Turn over

SECTION 1 — SCOTTISH TEXT — 20 marks

Choose ONE text from Drama, Prose or Poetry.

Read the text extract carefully and then attempt ALL the questions for your chosen text.

You should spend about 45 minutes on this Section.

PART C — SCOTTISH TEXT — POETRY

Text 1 — Poetry

If you choose this text you may not attempt a question on Poetry in Section 2.

Read the extract below and then attempt the following questions.

Address To The Deil by Robert Burns

'O Prince! O chief of many thronéd Pow'rs
That led th' embattl'd Seraphim to war—'— Milton.

O Thou! whatever title suit thee—
Auld Hornie, Satan, Nick, or Clootie,
Wha in yon cavern grim an' sootie,
        Clos'd under hatches,
5 Spairges about the brunstane cootie,
        To scaud poor wretches!

Hear me, auld Hangie, for a wee,
An' let poor damnéd bodies be;
I'm sure sma' pleasure it can gie,
10   Ev'n to a deil,
To skelp an' scaud poor dogs like me,
        An' hear us squeel!

Great is thy pow'r, an' great thy fame;
Far kenm'd an' noted is thy name;
15 An' tho' yon lowin' heuch's thy hame,
        Thou travels far;
An' faith! thou's neither lag nor lame,
        Nor blate, nor scaur.

Whyles, ranging like a roarin' lion,
20 For prey, a' holes and corners tryin';
Whyles, on the strong-wind'd tempest flyin',
        Tirlin' the kirks;
Whyles, in the human bosom pryin',
        Unseen thou lurks.

25 I've heard my rev'rend graunie say,
In lanely glens ye like to stray;
Or where auld ruin'd castles grey
        Nod to the moon,
Ye fright the nightly wand'rer's way,
30   Wi' eldritch croon.

When twilight did my graunie summon,
To say her pray'rs, douse, honest woman!
Aft 'yont the dyke she's heard you bummin',
        Wi' eerie drone;
35 Or, rustlin', thro' the boortrees comin',
        Wi' heavy groan.

Ae dreary, windy, winter night,
The stars shot down wi' sklentin light,
Wi' you, mysel, I gat a fright,
40   Ayont the lough;
Ye, like a rash-buss, stood in sight,
        Wi' wavin' sough.

The cudgel in my nieve did shake,
Each brist'ld hair stood like a stake,
45 When wi' an eldritch, stoor 'quaick, quaick',
        Amang the springs,
Awa ye squatter'd like a drake,
        On whistlin' wings.

Questions

33. Look at lines 1—12.

    By referring to **at least two** examples, analyse how the poet's use of language presents a light-hearted depiction of the Deil.   **4**

34. Look at lines 13—24.

    Analyse how the poet's use of language portrays the Deil as a powerful being.   **2**

35. Look at lines 25—48

    By referring to **at least two** examples, analyse how Burns mocks superstitious beliefs.   **4**

36. By referring to this extract and to at least one other poem by Burns, discuss the poet's use of humour in his exploration of serious issues.   **10**

[Turn over

OR

Text 2 — Poetry

If you choose this text you may not attempt a question on Poetry in Section 2.

Read the poem below and then attempt the following questions.

Valentine **by Carol Ann Duffy**

Not a red rose or a satin heart.

I give you an onion.
It is a moon wrapped in brown paper.
It promises light
5 like the careful undressing of love.

Here.
It will blind you with tears
like a lover.
It will make your reflection
10 a wobbling photo of grief.

I am trying to be truthful.

Not a cute card or a kissogram.

I give you an onion.
Its fierce kiss will stay on your lips,
15 possessive and faithful
as we are,
for as long as we are.

Take it.
Its platinum loops shrink to a wedding ring,
20 if you like.
Lethal.
Its scent will cling to your fingers,
cling to your knife.

MARKS

Questions

37. Look at lines 1—5.

By referring to **at least two** examples, analyse how the poet uses language to challenge **and/or** reinforce traditional stereotypes associated with romantic love.

4

38. Look at lines 6—17.

By referring to **at least two** examples, analyse how the poet uses language to suggest a "truthful" view of love.

4

39. Look at lines 18—23.

By referring to the poet's use of language, evaluate the effectiveness of these lines as a conclusion to the poem.

2

40. By referring to this poem and to at least one other poem by Duffy, discuss how the poet explores emotional conflict within an individual.

10

[Turn over

OR

Text 3 — Poetry

If you choose this text you may not attempt a question on Poetry in Section 2.

Read the poem below and then attempt the following questions.

For my Grandmother Knitting **by Liz Lochhead**

There is no need they say
but the needles still move
their rhythms in the working of your hands
as easily
5 as if your hands
were once again those sure and skilful hands
of the fisher-girl.

You are old now
and your grasp of things is not so good
10 but master of your moments then
deft and swift
you slit the still-ticking quick silver fish.
Hard work it was too
of necessity.

15 But now they say there is no need
as the needles move
in the working of your hands
once the hands of the bride
with the hand-span waist
20 once the hands of the miner's wife
who scrubbed his back
in a tin bath by the coal fire
once the hands of the mother
of six who made do and mended
25 scraped and slaved slapped sometimes
when necessary.

But now they say there is no need
the kids they say grandma
have too much already
30 more than they can wear
too many scarves and cardigans —
gran you do too much
there's no necessity . . .

MARKS

At your window you wave
35 them goodbye Sunday.
With your painful hands
big on shrunken wrists.
Swollen-jointed. Red. Arthritic. Old.
But the needles still move
40 their rhythms in the working of your hands
easily
as if your hands remembered
of their own accord the pattern
as if your hands had forgotten
45 how to stop.

Questions

41. Look at lines 1—14.

    By referring to **at least two** examples, analyse how the poet's use of language conveys a sense of **both** the past and the present.   4

42. Look at lines 15—26.

    Analyse how the poet uses the idea of "hands" to convey **two** different stages in the grandmother's past life.   2

43. Look at lines 27—45.

    By referring to **at least two** examples, analyse how the poet's use of language creates a bleak mood or atmosphere.   4

44. By referring to this poem and to at least one other poem by Lochhead, discuss how she explores the theme of personal **and/or** social change.   10

[Turn over

OR

Text 4 — Poetry

If you choose this text you may not attempt a question on Poetry in Section 2.

Read the poem below and then attempt the following questions.

Basking Shark by Norman MacCaig

To stub an oar on a rock where none should be,
To have it rise with a slounge out of the sea
Is a thing that happened once (too often) to me.

But not too often — though enough. I count as gain
5   That once I met, on a sea tin-tacked with rain,
That roomsized monster with a matchbox brain.

He displaced more than water. He shoggled me
Centuries back — this decadent townee
Shook on a wrong branch of his family tree.

10   Swish up the dirt and, when it settles, a spring
Is all the clearer. I saw me, in one fling,
Emerging from the slime of everything.

So who's the monster? The thought made me grow pale
For twenty seconds while, sail after sail,
15   The tall fin slid away and then the tail.

MARKS

Questions

45. Look at lines 1—3.

    Analyse how the poet's use of language conveys the nature of the encounter.　　2

46. Look at lines 4—9.

    By referring to **at least two** examples, analyse how language is used to suggest the impact of the experience on the speaker.　　4

47. Look at lines 10—15.

    By referring to **at least two** examples, analyse how the poet's language reveals a sense of new understanding.　　4

48. By referring to this poem and to at least one other poem by MacCaig, discuss how the poet uses symbolism to develop central ideas in his poetry.　　10

[Turn over

OR

Text 5 — Poetry

If you choose this text you may not attempt a question on Poetry in Section 2.

Read the poem below and then attempt the following questions.

Heroes by Sorley MacLean

I did not see Lannes at Ratisbon
nor MacLennan at Auldearn
nor Gillies MacBain at Culloden,
but I saw an Englishman in Egypt.

5   A poor little chap with chubby cheeks
    and knees grinding each other,
    pimply unattractive face —
    garment of the bravest spirit.

    He was not a hit "in the pub
10 in the time of the fists being closed,"
    but a lion against the breast of battle,
    in the morose wounding showers.

    His hour came with the shells,
    with the notched iron splinters,
15 in the smoke and flame,
    in the shaking and terror of the battlefield.

    Word came to him in the bullet shower
    that he should be a hero briskly,
    and he was that while he lasted,
20 but it wasn't much time he got.

    He kept his guns to the tanks,
    bucking with tearing crashing screech,
    until he himself got, about the stomach,
    that biff that put him to the ground,
25 mouth down in sand and gravel,
    without a chirp from his ugly high-pitched voice.

    No cross or medal was put to his
    chest or to his name or to his family;
    there were not many of his troop alive,
30 and if there were their word would not be strong.
    And at any rate, if a battle post stands,
    many are knocked down because of him,
    not expecting fame, not wanting a medal
    or any froth from the mouth of the field of slaughter.

35 I saw a great warrior of England,
    a poor manikin on whom no eye would rest;
    no Alasdair of Glen Garry;
    and he took a little weeping to my eyes.

MARKS

Questions

49. Look at lines 1—8.

Analyse how the poet's use of language makes it clear that the soldier was not a conventional hero.

2

50. Look at lines 13—26.

By referring to **at least two** examples, analyse how the poet's use of language conveys the hardships suffered by the soldier in battle.

4

51. Look at lines 27—38.

By referring to **at least two** examples, analyse how the poet uses language to create a sense of pity.

4

52. By referring to this poem and to at least one other poem by MacLean, discuss how the poet explores the theme of destruction.

10

[Turn over

OR

Text 6 — Poetry

If you choose this text you may not attempt a question on Poetry in Section 2.

Read the extract below and then attempt the following questions.

Nil Nil by Don Paterson

From the top, then, the zenith, the silent footage:
McGrandle, majestic in ankle-length shorts,
his golden hair shorn to an open book, sprinting
the length of the park for the long hoick forward,
5   his balletic toe-poke nearly bursting the roof
of the net; a shaky pan to the Erskine St End
where a plague of grey bonnets falls out of the clouds.
But ours is a game of two halves, and this game
the semi they went on to lose; from here
10   it's all down, from the First to the foot of the Second,
McGrandle, Visocchi and Spankie detaching
like bubbles to speed the descent into pitch-sharing,
pay-cuts, pawned silver, the Highland Division,
the absolute sitters ballooned over open goals,
15   the dismal nutmegs, the scores so obscene
no respectable journal will print them; though one day
Farquhar's spectacular bicycle-kick
will earn him a name-check in Monday's obituaries.
Besides the one setback — the spell of giant-killing
20   in the Cup (Lochee Violet, then Aberdeen Bon Accord,
the deadlock with Lochee Harp finally broken
by Farquhar's own-goal in the replay)
nothing inhibits the fifty-year slide
into Sunday League, big tartan flasks,
25   open hatchbacks parked squint behind goal-nets,
the half-time satsuma, the dog on the pitch,
then the Boys' Club, sponsored by Skelly Assurance,
then Skelly Dry Cleaners, then nobody;
stud-harrowed pitches with one-in-five inclines,
30   grim fathers and perverts with Old English Sheepdogs
lining the touch, moaning softly.
Now the unrefereed thirty-a-sides,
terrified fat boys with callipers minding
four jackets on infinite, notional fields;
35   ten years of dwindling, half-hearted kickabouts
leaves two little boys — Alastair Watt,
who answers to "Forty", and wee Horace Madden,
so smelly the air seems to quiver above him —
playing desperate two-touch with a bald tennis ball

MARKS

40 in the hour before lighting-up time.
    Alastair cheats, and goes off with the ball
    leaving wee Horace to hack up a stone
    and dribble it home in the rain;
    past the stopped swings, the dead shanty-town
45 of allotments, the black shell of Skelly Dry Cleaners
    and into his cul-de-sac, where, accidentally,
    he neatly back-heels it straight into the gutter
    then tries to swank off like he meant it.

    Unknown to him, it is all that remains
50 of a lone fighter-pilot, who, returning at dawn
    to find Leuchars was not where he'd left it,
    took time out to watch the Sidlaws unsheathed
    from their great black tarpaulin, the haar burn off Tayport
    and Venus melt into Carnoustie, igniting
55 the shoreline; no wind, not a cloud in the sky
    and no one around to admire the discretion
    of his unscheduled exit

Questions

53. Look at lines 1—6 ("From . . . the net;).

     Analyse how the poet's language creates a celebratory mood.   2

54. Look at lines 9—29 ("from here . . . inclines").

     By referring to **at least two** examples, analyse how the poet's use of language creates
     an atmosphere of decline.   4

55. Look at lines 41—57.

     By referring to **at least two** examples, analyse how the poet's use of language
     conveys the tragic situation of **both** the community and the pilot.   4

56. By referring to this extract and to at least one other poem by Paterson, discuss how
     the poet explores the impact of loss.   10

[END OF SECTION 1]

[Turn over

SECTION 2 — CRITICAL ESSAY — 20 marks

Attempt ONE question from the following genres — Drama, Prose Fiction, Prose Non-Fiction, Poetry, Film and Television Drama, or Language.

Your answer must be on a different genre from that chosen in Section 1.

You should spend approximately 45 minutes on this Section.

PART A — DRAMA

Answers to questions on Drama should refer to the text and to such relevant features as characterisation, key scene(s), structure, climax, theme, plot, conflict, setting . . .

1. Choose a play in which a major character behaves in an impulsive **or** calculating **or** emotional manner.

   With reference to appropriate techniques, briefly explain the circumstances surrounding this behaviour and discuss how this behaviour adds to your understanding of the play as a whole.

2. Choose a play in which there is a scene which influences the course of future events.

   With reference to appropriate techniques, explain how the scene influences the course of events and discuss how it contributes to your appreciation of the text as a whole.

3. Choose a play which deals with the theme of honour **or** shame **or** betrayal.

   With reference to appropriate techniques, explain how the dramatist presents the theme and discuss why it is important to your understanding of the play as a whole.

PART B — PROSE FICTION

> *Answers to questions on Prose Fiction should refer to the text and to such relevant features as characterisation, setting, language, key incident(s), climax, turning point, plot, structure, narrative technique, theme, ideas, description . . .*

4. Choose a novel **or** short story in which there is a character who experiences rejection **or** isolation.

   With reference to appropriate techniques, explain the rejection **or** isolation, and discuss how this aspect adds to your appreciation of the text as a whole.

5. Choose a novel **or** short story which has an effective opening **or** conclusion.

   With reference to appropriate techniques, explain why the opening **or** conclusion is effective and discuss how it adds to your appreciation of the text as a whole.

6. Choose a novel **or** short story which deals with the theme of love **or** loss **or** redemption.

   With reference to appropriate techniques, explain how the writer develops this theme, and discuss how it adds to your understanding of the text as a whole.

PART C — PROSE NON-FICTION

> *Answers to questions on Prose Non-Fiction should refer to the text and to such relevant features as ideas, use of evidence, stance, style, selection of material, narrative voice . . .*
>
> *Non-fiction texts can include travel writing, journalism, autobiography, biography, essays . . .*

7. Choose a non-fiction text in which the writer reports on aspects of war **or** injustice **or** human suffering.

   With reference to appropriate techniques, discuss how the writer engages your interest in these aspects of war **or** injustice **or** human suffering.

8. Choose a non-fiction text which gives you a detailed insight into a place **or** a person's life.

   With reference to appropriate techniques, discuss how the writer successfully engages your interest in the place **or** the person's life.

9. Choose a non-fiction text which makes effective use of humour to make a significant point.

   With reference to appropriate techniques, discuss how the writer uses humour to make the significant point.

PART D — POETRY

Answers to questions on Poetry should refer to the text and to such relevant features as word choice, tone, imagery, structure, content, rhythm, rhyme, theme, sounds, ideas . . .

10. Choose a poem in which the poet challenges accepted beliefs **or** attitudes **or** conventions.

    With reference to appropriate techniques, discuss how the poet's challenge of these accepted beliefs **or** attitudes **or** conventions enhances your appreciation of the poem as a whole.

11. Choose a poem which deals with a powerful emotion.

    With reference to appropriate techniques, discuss how the poet's presentation of this powerful emotion enhances your appreciation of the poem as a whole.

12. Choose a poem which makes effective use of imagery **and/or** sound to convey central concern(s).

    With reference to appropriate techniques, discuss how the poet's use of imagery **and/or** sound contributes to the presentation of the poem's central concern(s).

PART E — FILM AND TELEVISION DRAMA

Answers to questions on Film and Television Drama* should refer to the text and to such relevant features as use of camera, key sequence, characterisation, mise-en-scène, editing, music/sound, special effects, plot, dialogue . . .

13. Choose a film **or** television drama in which the opening sequence is particularly effective in engaging the audience's interest.

    With reference to appropriate techniques, discuss how the film or programme makers succeed in engaging the audience's interest.

14. Choose a film **or** television drama in which the main character faces a significant moment of change.

    With reference to appropriate techniques, discuss how the film or programme makers convey the significance of this change.

15. Choose a film **or** television drama in which special effects make an important contribution to the impact of the film **or** television drama as a whole.

    With reference to appropriate techniques, discuss how the special effects are used to enhance your appreciation of the film **or** television drama as a whole.

* "television drama" includes a single play, a series or a serial.

PART F — LANGUAGE

> *Answers to questions on Language should refer to the text(s) and to such relevant features as register, accent, dialect, slang, jargon, vocabulary, tone, abbreviation . . .*

16. Choose the language of newspaper reporting associated with sport **or** celebrity **or** crime **or** war **or** the environment.

    Identify the key language features and discuss the effectiveness of these features in communicating with the readership.

17. Choose the language of persuasion as used in the world of advertising **or** politics.

    Identify specific examples and discuss to what extent the language is effective.

18. Choose the language associated with a particular group in society which shares a common interest **or** work environment.

    Identify specific examples and discuss the advantages of these language features in aiding communication.

[END OF SECTION 2]

[END OF QUESTION PAPER]

[BLANK PAGE]

DO NOT WRITE ON THIS PAGE

HIGHER

2018

National
Qualifications
SPECIMEN ONLY

S824/76/11

**English
Reading for Understanding,
Analysis and Evaluation — Text**

Date — Not applicable

Duration — 1 hour 30 minutes

Total marks — 30

Read the passages carefully and then attempt ALL questions, which are printed on a separate sheet.

The following two passages focus on the importance of trees.

This Specimen Question Paper replaces the original RUAE section of the official SQA Past Paper 2018, which cannot be reproduced for copyright reasons. The Specimen Question Paper is set and verified by SQA and offers appropriate practice material for Higher English.

Passage 1

Read the passage below and then attempt questions 1 to 6.

In the first passage Janice Turner, writing in The Times newspaper, considers the value of trees.

Watching the tree surgeon from the window, I felt I was witnessing a crime. One I'd authorised, like a Mafia hit. The holm oak — a dense, virulent, evergreen ball — loomed over the garden like a storm cloud. It had to be cut back. But as the chainsaw whined and branches tumbled, I wondered if I really had the right.

5 I'm a resolute city-dweller, but trees seem ever more precious these days, a rebuke to built-in obsolescence, a steady point in a churning world. My pear and apple trees are remnants from when South London orchards ran all the way down to meet the sea. The walnut reaches out a mammoth limb from my neighbour's garden to mine like God's arm on the ceiling of the Sistine Chapel in Rome.

10 They are our living past, clocking up the years, ring by ring. Trees are calming like cathedrals, reassuring us that they will endure even though we will not. No wonder the ancients believed they were gods; there are worse things to worship than a tree.

And this week, reading how some protesters had been arrested trying to prevent ancient woodland being destroyed to make way for a three-mile link road to Hastings, I thought: yes, I'd
15 go to prison for a tree. Indeed, the protesters who are digging tunnels in the mud and standing before the diggers are not 'eco-warriors' or 'hippies'. Among them are young families, retired folk and ordinary dog-walkers. 'Local grandmothers', it was reported, came to swing in giant hammocks strung between the 400-year-old oaks.

But this is their last stand. They can only slow the developers. By March the trees will be felled.
20 Local people have fought for 20 years to save them, but they are on the wrong side of what the government is determined to market as progress, however short-term and dubious the economic benefits. The Chancellor of the Exchequer gave £56·8 million of government money for this very road, which will fill up with extra traffic, as new roads do, and lead in time to a spanking new industrial estate, although Hastings town already has plenty of boarded-up premises from which
25 to trade.

Development versus the trees. The government tells us that those who want to protect open countryside and woodland from being turned into endless Lego-brick estates are not conservationists, they are selfish, privileged people who, sitting comfortably in their own cheaply bought piles, have no care for struggling young couples who can't afford a family home. Anyway,
30 what's a bunch of trees?

But people with no respect for trees show a special kind of arrogance: they think they're bigger than history. I'd argue that cutting down an ancient oak is worse than killing most types of animal. Certainly the more numerous species such as dogs, cows, monkeys or cats. A chainsaw slicing into a 300-year-old trunk is more brutal and grotesque than hunting 100 foxes. Chopping down a fine
35 old tree is more like shooting an elephant or harpooning a whale: the aching poignancy of an enormous creature whose size and strength nonetheless cannot save it. Except even the mightiest mammal can be bred to maturity in a few years. Not so a tree.

Yet it is astonishing, given how much people love them — planting them to mark special moments or honour dead loved ones, measuring their lives by their seasonal changes — that officialdom
40 loathes trees. Insurance companies fretting about subsidence would rather you took them all down just in case. Councils detest them, employing municipal butchers to hack away at whole groves. Embarrassed stumps with a couple of twigs are all that remain.

It's a wonder any tree survives a health and safety audit. One city council tried to remove a whole row of horsechestnuts because conkers fell on cars and children might slip on leaves. Our local
45 primary school cut down a fine tree beneath which generations of children had played, because the new head deemed its twigs and leaves too messy. A posh gardener once suggested we cut down most of our trees and start again with fresh, more groovy varieties. This misunderstood the very point: trees are the antithesis of fickle fashion. But some crass homeowners can't bear the fluff-balls from plane trees messing up their hall carpet or the lime sap puking down on their
50 shiny car bonnets. Neater to reach for the axe. Maybe garden centres should start selling plastic ones: say goodbye to autumnal hell.

Visiting Burma, I learnt that its teak forests were flogged off to China by the generals, who were desperate for quick cash, like a beautiful girl being forced to sell her hair. Iceland is barren because Vikings cut them all down in a year and Peru is logging away its resources.

55 Our country's trees will tumble to make way for the machines of progress. But for how much economic growth is it worth mowing down a wood? Trees are beyond priceless: they are our history inscribed in the natural world. Which rich men, planting beautiful orchards to their own glorious memory, have always known.

Adapted from an article in The Times newspaper, January 2013.

Passage 2

Read the passage below and attempt question 7. While reading, you may wish to make notes on the main ideas and/or highlight key points in the passage.

In the second passage, the science writer Colin Tudge gives his own views on trees.

In New Zealand a few years ago I experienced more powerfully than ever the sheer gravitas of trees: in the presence of the world's largest kauri. Kauris are conifers, the biggest of their family. The great trunk of the kauri rises like a lighthouse out of the gloom: fifteen metres in circumference — it would touch all four walls in an average living room — and straight up,
5 leafless, for twenty metres or so. And then on its great horizontal boughs rests a virtual park, a floating island with an entire ecosystem of ferns and flowers. Some kauris are 2000 years old. For the first 1400 years of the kauri's life, moas strutted their stuff around its base. Moas included the world's tallest-ever birds, like giant emus, which were preyed upon by commensurately huge but
10 short-winged eagles. The moas and their attendant eagles are now long gone. The kauri lives on.

The remaining kauri forest has been horribly reduced these past two hundred years, but the way modern New Zealanders look after the trees that are left to them is a model for all the world. Rare trees are no longer felled but existing planks are prized and meticulously re-cycled. Meanwhile, you can follow slatted wooden paths among the vast conifers. That's conservation;
15 that's intelligent ecotourism.

Similarly, if new farming economies are to come about, then trees must be at the centre of them. Yet, tree-based farming systems have to fight for survival against the massed ranks of the powers-that-be. How ludicrous. The world's most powerful governments have made themselves answerable to the big companies — and they take pride in this. They call it 'realism'.

20 So although the things that need doing seem obvious, governments — and the big corporations whose interests they serve — have a quite different agenda. If we want life to be agreeable or indeed to continue at all we just have to ignore the pressures from our ostensible leaders, and do things the way they should be done: building new ways of life, whatever the pressures from on high. Again, trees show the way.

Outstanding among the world's many popular initiatives is the Greenbelt Movement, a campaign
25 among Kenyan women to re-plant trees in places they used to grow. Now they have planted
30 million. They have transformed landscapes and changed entire economies and the whole tenor
of life. This kind of thing, very simple, and achieved in the teeth of the modern economy (for who
makes money out of it?), contributes far more to human wellbeing than, say, cheap white goods
from China, on which the economy of the modern world, egged on by our world leaders, is being
30 built.

The broadest issue of all is the western conceit that we can 'conquer' nature, or indeed control it.
This idea truly took off in the 19th century, and yet is taken still as a mark of modernity. In 1879
the poet Gerard Manley Hopkins lamented the felling of poplars: 'O if we but knew what we do/
When we delve or hew — Hack and rack the growing green!' We still don't know what we are
35 doing but the hacking and racking continue more vigorously than ever. The only halfway sane
approach if we want this world to remain habitable, is to approach it humbly. Trees teach
humility. We need to take the world far more seriously. It would be a good idea to begin with
trees.

Adapted from an article published on Colin Tudge's website in 2005.

[END OF SPECIMEN TEXT]

National
Qualifications
SPECIMEN ONLY

S824/76/21

English
Reading for Understanding,
Analysis and Evaluation — Questions

Date — Not applicable

Duration — 1 hour 30 minutes

Total mark — 30

Attempt ALL questions.

Write your answers clearly in the answer booklet provided. In the answer booklet, you must clearly identify the question number you are attempting.

Use **blue** or **black** ink.

Before leaving the examination room you must give your answer booklet to the Invigilator; if you do not, you may lose all the marks for this paper.

MARKS

Attempt ALL questions

Total marks — 30

1. Read lines 1–12.

   (a) From the first paragraph, identify **two** feelings the writer had as she watched the tree in her garden being cut back.

   2

   (b) By referring to **at least two** examples, analyse how the writer uses language in lines 5–12 to emphasise the importance of trees.

   4

2. Read lines 13–18.

   According to the writer, in what ways are the protesters different from how we might expect them to be?

   2

3. Read lines 19–25.

   By referring to **at least two** features of language, analyse how the writer conveys her feelings of unhappiness about the Hastings development.

   3

4. Read lines 26–37.

   (a) From lines 26–30 identify **two** claims the government makes about the protesters.

   2

   (b) By referring to **at least two** features of language in lines 31–37, analyse how the writer conveys the strength of her belief in tree conservation.

   4

5. Read lines 38–54.

   (a) Identify any **four** reasons given in these lines for cutting down trees. Use your own words as far as possible.

   4

   (b) By referring to **at least one** example, analyse how the writer's use of imagery emphasises her opposition to cutting down trees.

   2

6. Evaluate the final paragraph's effectiveness as a conclusion to the passage as a whole.

   2

Question on both passages

7. Look at both passages.

   Both writers express their views about the importance of trees.

   Identify **three** key areas on which they agree. You should support the points by referring to important ideas in both passages.

   You may answer this question in continuous prose or in a series of developed bullet points.

   5

[END OF SPECIMEN QUESTION PAPER]

National Qualifications 2018

X724/76/12

English Critical Reading

FRIDAY, 11 MAY

10:50 AM – 12:20 PM

Total marks — 40

SECTION 1 — Scottish Text — 20 marks

Read an extract from a Scottish text you have previously studied and attempt the questions.

Choose ONE text from either

Part A — Drama	Pages 2–7
or	
Part B — Prose	Pages 8–17
or	
Part C — Poetry	Pages 18–29

Attempt ALL the questions for your chosen text.

SECTION 2 — Critical Essay — 20 marks

Attempt ONE question from the following genres — Drama, Prose Fiction, Prose Non-Fiction, Poetry, Film and Television Drama, or Language.

Your answer must be on a different genre from that chosen in Section 1.

You should spend approximately 45 minutes on each Section.

Write your answers clearly in the answer booklet provided. In the answer booklet, you must clearly identify the question number you are attempting.

Use **blue** or **black** ink.

Before leaving the examination room you must give your answer booklet to the Invigilator; if you do not, you may lose all the marks for this paper.

SECTION 1 — SCOTTISH TEXT — 20 marks

Choose ONE text from Drama, Prose or Poetry.

Read the text extract carefully and then attempt ALL the questions for your chosen text.

You should spend about 45 minutes on this Section.

PART A — SCOTTISH TEXT — DRAMA

Text 1 — Drama

If you choose this text you may not attempt a question on Drama in Section 2.

Read the extract below and then attempt the following questions.

The Slab Boys by John Byrne

In this extract, from Act 1 of the play, Jack Hogg is showing Alan around and introducing him to colleagues.

	JACK:	This is the Slab Room, Alan . . . where the colours are ground and dished for the Designers . . . you saw the patterns out there. What the lads do, basically, is dole out a quantity of dry colour from those drums over there . . . Persian red, rose pink . . .
5	PHIL:	. . . bile green . . .
	SPANKY:	. . . acne yellow . . .
	JACK:	. . . dump it onto one of these marble slabs, add some gum arabic to prevent it flaking off the paper . . . do we have some gum arabic? Then it's just a matter of grinding . . . (*Demonstrates.*) Bit of a diff from the studio, eh?
10	SPANKY:	Why don't you vamoose, Jacky Boy?
	PHIL:	Yeh, Plooky Chops . . . them boils of yours is highly smittal.
	JACK:	I'm warning you, McCann . . .
	PHIL:	Keep away from me! Hector, fling us over the Dettol!
	JACK:	Jealousy will get you nowhere, McCann . . . just because I'm on a desk.
15	SPANKY:	It's a bloody operating table you want to be on, Jack. That face . . . yeugh.
	PHIL:	You can put in for plastic surgery, you know . . . on the National Health.
	SPANKY:	Or a 'pimplectomy' . . .
	PHIL:	It would only take about six months . . .
	SPANKY:	. . . and a team of surgeons . . .
20	PHIL:	. . . with pliers.
	JACK:	(*to Alan*) I've just got to dodge down the factory . . . have a look at a couple of 'trials' . . . shouldn't be too long. (*to Spanky and Phil*) The boss would like you to show Alan what goes on in here . . . in the way of work. (*to Alan*) Don't worry, you haven't been condemned to spend the rest of the day here . . . I'll have a word with Bobby Sinclair the colour consultant. He could take you through the dyeing process . . .
25		

> *Spanky collapses into Phil's arms.*
>
> See you shortly . . . (*Exits.*)

	PHIL:	Get a brush and some red paint, Heck.
30	HECTOR:	What for?
	SPANKY:	To paint a cross on the door, stupid. To warn the villagers . . .
	HECTOR:	What villagers?
	PHIL:	(*to Alan*) Okay, son, what did you say your name was again?
	ALAN:	Alan . . . Alan Downie.
35	PHIL:	Right, Eamonn . . . let's show you some of the mysteries of the Slab Room. Mr Farrell . . .
	SPANKY:	Mr Mac?
	PHIL:	I'm just showing young Dowdalls here some of the intricacies of our work. If you and the boy would care to stand to the one side . . .
40	SPANKY:	Certainly. Hector . . .
	PHIL:	Many thanks. Right, Alec . . . this here is what we call a sink . . . s-i-n-k. Now I don't expect you to pick up all these terms immediately but you'll soon get the hang of it. And this — (*Grabs Hector.*) — is what we cry a Slab Boy . . .
	SPANKY:	You say it . . . Slab Boy . . .
45	PHIL:	Note the keen eye . . . the firm set of the jaw . . .
	SPANKY:	They're forced up under cucumber frames . . .

MARKS

Questions

1. Look at lines 1–9.

    Analyse how language is used to convey the attitudes of both Jack **and** the slab boys (Phil and Spanky) to the work of the slab room.

    2

2. Look at lines 10–26.

    By referring to **at least two** examples, analyse how language is used to convey the hostility felt by both Jack **and** the slab boys (Phil and Spanky) towards each other.

    4

3. Look at lines 27–46.

    By referring to **at least two** examples, analyse how humour is used by the slab boys (Phil and Spanky).

    4

4. By referring to this extract and to elsewhere in the play, discuss how Byrne explores attitudes to authority.

    10

[Turn over

OR

Text 2 — Drama

If you choose this text you may not attempt a question on Drama in Section 2.

Read the extract below and then attempt the following questions.

The Cheviot, the Stag and the Black, Black Oil by John McGrath

In this extract, Loch and Sellar discuss aspects of Highland life and land ownership.

LOCH: The Marquis is not unaware of the responsibility his wealth places upon him, Mr. Sellar. The future and lasting interest and honour of his family, as well as their immediate income, must be kept in view.

5   *They freeze. A phrase on the fiddle. Two* SPEAKERS *intervene between them, speak quickly to the audience.*

SPEAKER 1: Their immediate income was over £120,000 per annum. In those days that was quite a lot of money.

SPEAKER 2: George Granville, Second Marquis of Stafford, inherited a huge estate in Yorkshire; he inherited another at Trentham in the Potteries; and he
10   inherited a third at Lilleshall in Shropshire, that had coal-mines on it.

SPEAKER 1: He also inherited the Bridgewater Canal. And, on Loch's advice, he bought a large slice of the Liverpool-Manchester Railway.

SPEAKER 2: From his wife, Elizabeth Gordon, Countess of Sutherland, he acquired three-quarters of a million acres of Sutherland — in which he wanted to invest some
15   capital.

Another phrase on the fiddle: they slip away.

SELLAR *and* LOCH *re-animate.*

SELLAR: The common people of Sutherland are a parcel of beggars with no stock, but cunning and lazy.

20 LOCH: They are living in a form of slavery to their own indolence. Nothing could be more at variance with the general interests of society and the individual happiness of the people themselves, than the present state of Highland manners and customs. To be happy, the people must be productive.

SELLAR: They require to be thoroughly brought to the coast, where industry will pay,
25   and to be convinced that they must worship industry or starve. The present enchantment which keeps them down must be broken.

LOCH: The coast of Sutherland abounds with many different kinds of fish. (LOCH *takes off his hat, and speaks directly to the audience.*) Believe it or not, Loch and Sellar actually used these words. (*Puts hat on again.*) Not only white fish,
30   but herring too. With this in mind, His Lordship is considering several sites for new villages on the East Coast — Culgower, Helmsdale, Golspie, Brora, Skelbo and Knockglass — Helmsdale in particular is a perfect natural harbour for a fishing station. And there is said to be coal at Brora.

SELLAR: You will really not find this estate pleasant or profitable until by draining to
35   your coast-line or by emigration you have got your mildewed districts cleared.

They are just in that state of society for a savage country, such as the woods of Upper Canada — His Lordship should consider seriously the possibility of subsidising their departures. They might even be inclined to carry a swarm of dependants with them.

40   LOCH: I gather you yourself Mr. Sellar, have a scheme for a sheep-walk in this area.

   SELLAR: The highlands of Scotland may sell £200,000 worth of lean cattle this year. The same ground, under the Cheviot, may produce as much as £900,000 worth of fine wool. The effects of such arrangements in advancing this estate in wealth, civilisation, comfort, industry, virtue and happiness are palpable.

45   *Fiddle in — Tune, 'Bonnie Dundee', quietly behind.*

   LOCH: Your offer for this area, Mr. Sellar, falls a little short of what I had hoped.

   SELLAR: The present rents, when they can be collected, amount to no more than £142 per annum.

   LOCH: Nevertheless, Mr. Sellar, His Lordship will have to remove these people at
50   considerable expense.

   SELLAR: To restock the land with sheep will cost considerably more.

Questions

MARKS

5. Look at lines 1—15.

    By referring to **at least two** examples, analyse how language is used to convey both Loch's **and** the Speakers' views of the Marquis' situation.   4

6. Look at lines 18—26.

    Analyse how language is used to create a dismissive tone in these lines.   2

7. Look at lines 27—51.

    By referring to **at least two** examples, analyse how language is used to reveal the characters' apparently positive aims **and** their true attitudes.   4

8. By referring to this extract and to elsewhere in the play, discuss how McGrath uses unusual dramatic techniques to highlight central concerns.   10

[Turn over

OR

Text 3 — Drama

If you choose this text you may not attempt a question on Drama in Section 2.

Read the extract below and then attempt the following questions.

Men Should Weep by Ena Lamont Stewart

This extract is from Act 2, Scene 2.

Alec and Isa are quarrelling in the bedroom: their raised voices are heard off

Isa comes out in a soiled, tawdry negligé with her hair about her shoulders, a cigarette hanging from her lip

	ISA:	Aw shut up! I'm sick o yer jawin.
5		*Alec appears behind her, half dressed*
	ALEC:	I'm tellin ye, Isa, I'll no staun much mair! I'm jist warnin ye. That's a.
	ISA:	An I'm warnin you! If you think I'm gaun on like this a ma life, ye've anither think comin. You're no the only pebble on ma beach, no by a lang chalk. If you want tae keep me, it's time ye wis makin a bit o dough again. I canna live on air.
10		
	ALEC:	(*placating*) Come an we'll go tae the dugs the night, Isa; mebbe we'll hae a bit o luck.
	ISA:	Aye. *Mebbe.*
	ALEC:	Mind the last time I won — —
15	ISA:	Aye, an I mind the last hauf dizzen times ye lost . . . Whit did ye dae wi yon bag?
	ALEC:	I flung it ower a wa.
	ISA:	Ye stupid fool! I'm needin a bag.
	ALEC:	It's no safe, Isa — ye've got tae get rid o the evidence — the Polis . . .
20	ISA:	Three quid and a handfu o coppers! A fat lot o use that is tae me. Why the Hell did ye no pick on a toff! We wis in the right district.
	ALEC:	She looked like a toff; honest, Isa! She'd on a fur coat . . .
	ISA:	Whit kind o fur? Rabbit? You're that dumb ye wouldnae ken. Next time, I'm no jookin up a lane, I'm stayin wi ye.
25	ALEC:	No ye're no! It's no safe. Ye've got tae be able tae rin fast.
	ISA:	Rin! That's a you're guid for. Rinnin. It's aboot time I wis daein the rinnin. I'm sick fed up wi you. If I'd went wi Peter Robb I'd hae a fur coat an it wouldna be rabbit. An he's got a caur . . .
	ALEC:	You say Peter Robb tae me again an I'll kill ye! I wull! I'll kill ye!
30		*He gets hold of her by the throat: she makes strangling noises. He panics and drops her*
	ISA:	(*frightened first, then angry*) You . . . ! Ma Goad! (*Rubbing her throat*) You'll pey for that!

ALEC: Isa! Did I hurt ye? I didnae mean tae hurt ye — I lost ma heid.

ISA: Get oot! Clear aff oot o ma sight!

35 ALEC: Isa, I'm sorry. I jist see red when ye talk aboot Peter Robb. I canna see naethin but him an you taegether an the way ye wis last night, cairryin oan wi him.

ISA: Aye! Ye can use yer hauns a right on a wumman; but if ye wis hauf a man, ye'd have kicked his teeth in last night.

ALEC: He's bigger nor me — he'd have hauf-killed me!

40 ISA: Fancy me mairryin a rat like you. The joke wis on me a right.

ALEC: Isa, I'll hae plenty again, you'll see . . . I've a coupla pals that's got ideas . . . wait on, Isa! I'll get ye onythin ye want . . . a fur coat an crockydile shoes — ye said ye wanted crockydile shoes — I proamise, Isa! I proamise! If ye'll stay wi me . . . I love ye, Isa; honest, I dae. I love ye.

45 ISA: *Love!* Hee-haw! There's nae sich a thing. There's wantin tae get intae bed wi someone ye fancy . . . or wantin someone'll let ye lie in yer bed an no have tae work; but there's nae love. No roon aboot here, onyway. Don't kid yersel.

ALEC: (*trying to take her in his arms*) That's no true! I love ye. I'm no fit for onythin when ye're oot o ma sight. I'm . . . lost waitin on ye comin back. I get tae
50   thinkin . . . an wonderin whaur ye are . . . and if — —

ISA: If I'm behavin masel? Well, hauf the time, I'm no.

ALEC: Isa!

ISA: Aw shut up! (*She pushes him away*) Ye're aye wantin tae slobber ower me. If ye wis onythin decent tae look at it wouldna be sae bad, but ye're like somethin
55   that's been left oot a night in the rain. G'on blow! I canna staun yer fumblin aboot — unless I'm canned. Get oot ma way. I'm gonnae get dressed.

She slams the bedroom door in his face

He stands looking at it

Questions

MARKS

9. Look at lines 1—28.

    By referring to **at least two** examples, analyse how language is used to convey Isa's attitude(s) towards Alec.   4

10. Look at lines 29—44.

    By referring to **at least two** examples, analyse how both dialogue **and** stage directions reveal the extreme nature of Alec's treatment of Isa.   4

11. Look at lines 45—58.

    Analyse how language is used to create a cynical tone in these lines.   2

12. By referring to this extract and to elsewhere in the play, discuss how Lamont Stewart explores the theme of love.   10

SECTION 1 — SCOTTISH TEXT — 20 marks

Choose ONE text from Drama, Prose or Poetry.

Read the text extract carefully and then attempt ALL the questions for your chosen text.

You should spend about 45 minutes on this Section.

PART B — SCOTTISH TEXT — PROSE

Text 1 — Prose

If you choose this text you may not attempt a question on Prose (Fiction or Non-Fiction) in Section 2.

Read the extract below and then attempt the following questions.

The Painter by Iain Crichton Smith

We felt a certain responsibility towards him also since he was sickly, and many maintained that he wouldn't live very long, as he was so clever. So our houses were decorated with his colourful paintings and if any stranger came to the village we always pointed to the paintings with great pride and mentioned the painter as one of our greatest assets. No
5   other village that we knew of had a painter at all, not even an adult painter, and we had a wonderful artist who was also very young. It is true that once or twice he made us uncomfortable for he insisted on painting things as they were, and he made our village less glamorous on the whole than we would have liked it to appear. Our houses weren't as narrow and crooked as he made them seem in his paintings, nor did our villagers look so
10   spindly and thin. Nor was our cemetery, for instance, so confused and weird. And certainly it wasn't in the centre of the village as he had placed it.

He was a strange boy, seeming much older than his years. He hardly ever spoke and not because there was anything wrong with him but because it seemed as if there was nothing much that he wished to say. He dressed in a very slapdash manner and often had holes in
15   the knees of his trousers, and paint all over his blouse. He would spend days trying to paint a particular house or old wall or the head of an old woman or old man. But as we had a lot of old people in the village, some who could play musical instruments — especially the melodeon — extremely well, he didn't stand out as a queer person. There is, however, one incident that I shall always remember.

20   Our village of course was not a wholly harmonious place. It had its share of barbarism and violence. Sometimes people quarrelled about land and much less often about women. Once there was a prolonged controversy about a right of way. But the incident I was talking about happened like this. There was in the village a man called Red Roderick who had got his name because of his red hair. As is often the case with men with red hair he was also a
25   man of fiery temper, as they say. He drank a lot and would often go uptown on Saturday nights and come home roaring drunk, and march about the village singing.

He was in fact a very good strong singer but less so when he was drunk. He spent most of his time either working on his croft or weaving in his shed and had a poor thin wife given to bouts of asthma whom he regularly beat up when it suited him and when he was in a
30   bad temper. His wife was the daughter of Big Angus who had been a famous fisherman in his youth but who had settled down to become a crofter and who was famed for his great strength though at this time he was getting old. In fact I suppose he must have been about

seventy years old. His daughter's name was Anna and during the course of most days she seemed to be baking a lot without much result. You would also find her quite often with a
35 dripping plate and a soggy dishcloth in her hand. She had seven children all at various stages of random development and with running noses throughout both summer and winter.

It must be said that, when sober, Red Roderick was a very kind man, fond of his children and picking them up on his shoulders and showing them off to people and saying how
40 much they weighed and how clever and strong they were, though in fact none of them was any of these things, for they were in fact skinny and underweight and tending to have blotches and spots on their faces and necks. In those moments he would say that he was content with his life and that no one had better children or better land than he had. When he was sunny-tempered he was the life and soul of the village and up to all sorts of
45 mischief, singing songs happily in a very loud and melodious voice which revealed great depth of feeling. That was why it seemed so strange when he got drunk. His whole character would change and he would grow violent and morose and snarl at anyone near him, especially the weakest and most inoffensive people.

MARKS

Questions

13. Look at lines 1—19.

    By referring to **at least two** examples, analyse how language is used to convey the community's differing attitudes to the painter.   4

14. Look at lines 20—26.

    Analyse how language is used to create an impression of the community in these lines.   2

15. Look at lines 27—48.

    By referring to **at least two** examples, analyse how language is used to convey contrasting aspects of Red Roderick's character.   4

16. By referring to this extract and to at least one other short story, discuss how Crichton Smith explores the theme of isolation.   10

[Turn over

OR

Text 2 — Prose

If you choose this text you may not attempt a question on Prose (Fiction or Non-Fiction) in Section 2.

Read the extract below and then attempt the following questions.

The Bright Spade by George Mackay Brown

That winter the gravedigger was the busiest man in the island.

They got the thin harvest in and then the wind squatted in the east, a winter witch, and blew the island gray with her breath.

5 James of Moss died in the last week of October. Jacob dug his grave and got a bottle of whisky for it from the widow of Moss. This death was not unexpected. James of Moss had been ill with dropsy all summer; he had clung to life like the last tattered leaf on a branch.

The gravedigger had hardly sobered up when he was called to the house of Maria of Graystones. There Maria lay as stiff and pale as a candle. He dug her grave near the wall of the kirk. Maria's nephew gave him a goose.

10 There was not much food in the island even at the beginning of winter, and the ale was sour and thin.

In early November the laird's youngest son was thrown from his horse at the bridge and broke his neck. 'This will need a deep grave,' said Jacob. He threw up many fine white bones, the laird's ancestors, with his spade. The laird gave him half a guinea, and a dram
15 both before and after the funeral.

Late November and early December brought death to Samuel Ling the fisherman, Jean the wife of Ebenezer of Ness, and the boy with the hare lip from the Quarry. They were all poor people and Jacob got nothing at all for his work but a box of coarse tobacco snuff from Ebenezer of Ness. 'I suppose I'll be glad of somebody to bury me when my time
20 comes,' said Jacob, and sneezed heroically for a month till the snuff was finished.

It was a hard winter, and nobody expected most of the old people and the sickly people to see the spring.

At harvest Kirstie had given birth to a daughter, just three months after she had married Amos of the Glebe. Kirstie and Amos raged at each other so much, both before and after
25 the birth, that there wasn't a bowl or a dish unbroken in the cupboard. In the season of snow and small fires the infant breathed her last; she died the week before Christmas. Jacob dug a small grave in the east corner of the kirkyard. He got a shilling from Kirstie and a pocket-full of potatoes from Amos. The day after the funeral Kirstie left Amos and went back to her parents' house. She never lived with Amos again.

30 The day after New Year a Dutch ship went ashore at the Red Head. Unfortunately the ship had no cargo; she was in ballast, bound for Labrador. Seven bodies were found on the shore next morning. The minister asked Jacob to dig one large grave for the foreigners.

'Who will pay my fee?' said Jacob.

'I don't know that,' said the minister, 'for the next-of-kin are in the Low Countries.'

35 In the end Jacob agreed to dig their grave for three spars of timber from the wrecked ship and half a barrel of oil out of the hold.

MARKS

Questions

17. Look at lines 1—11.

    By referring to **at least two** examples, analyse how language is used to create a bleak atmosphere.

    4

18. Look at lines 12—36.

    By referring to **at least two** examples, analyse how language is used to explore the idea of death.

    4

19. Look at the whole extract.

    Analyse how language is used to convey **two** aspects of Jacob's character.

    2

20. By referring to this extract and to at least one other short story, discuss how Mackay Brown uses characters as metaphorical and/or symbolic figures.

    10

[Turn over

OR

Text 3 — Prose

If you choose this text you may not attempt a question on Prose (Fiction or Non-Fiction) in Section 2.

Read the extract below and then attempt the following questions.

The Trick Is To Keep Breathing **by Janice Galloway**

In this extract Joy receives a visit from the Health Visitor.

I rearrange things, placing chairs over the bald patches of the rug, sweeping the boards. It never looks as good as I'd like.

By twenty past I'm running along the twisty road between the houses to the shop for biscuits. She likes biscuits. I get different ones each time hoping they are something else
5 she will enjoy. I can't choose in a hurry. I can't be trusted with custard creams so deliberately don't get them. Chocolate digestives are too expensive. I wait for too long in the queue while a confused little kid tries to bargain for his father's cigarettes with the wrong money, so I have to run back clutching fig rolls and iced coffees and nearly drop the milk. I get flustered at these times, but I know I'll manage if I try harder. These visits are
10 good for me. Dr Stead sends this woman out of love. He insisted.

    I said, I'm no use with strangers.

    He said, But this is different. Health Visitors are trained to cope with that. He said she would know what to do; she would find me out and let me talk. *Make me* talk.

HAH

15 I'm putting on the kettle, still catching my breath when she comes in without knocking and frightens me. What if I had been saying things about her out loud? I tell her to sit in the livingroom so I can have time to think.

    Tray

          jug

20   sweeteners

                   plates

                        cups and saucers

                            another spoon

                                christ

25 the biscuits

    the biscuits

I burst the wrap soundlessly and make a tasteful arrangement. I polish her teaspoon on my cardigan band. No teapot. I make it in the cup, using the same bag twice, and take it through as though I've really made it in a pot and just poured it out. Some people are sniffy
30 about tea-bags. It sloshes when I reach to push my hair back from falling in my eyes and I suddenly notice I am still wearing my slippers dammit.

Never mind. She smiles and says

Well!

35 This is to make out the tea is a surprise though it isn't. She does it every time. We sit opposite each other because that's the way the chairs are. The chairs cough dust from under their sheets as she crosses her legs, thinking her way into the part. By the time she's ready to start I'm grinding my teeth back into the gum.

HEALTH VISITOR So, how are you/how's life/what's been happening/anything interesting to tell me/what's new?

40 PATIENT   Oh, fine/nothing to speak of.

I stir the tea repeatedly. She picks a piece of fluff off her skirt.

HEALTH VISITOR Work. How are things at work? Coping?

PATIENT   Fine. [Pause] I have trouble getting in on time, but getting better.

I throw her a little difficulty every so often so she feels I'm telling her the truth. I figure this
45 will get rid of her quicker.

HEALTH VISITOR [Intensifying] But what about the day-to-day? How are you coping?

PATIENT   OK. [Brave smile] I manage.

HEALTH VISITOR The house is looking fine.

PATIENT   Thank-you. I do my best.

50 This is overdone. She flicks her eyes up to see and I lower mine. She reaches for a biscuit.

HEALTH VISITOR These look nice. I like a biscuit with a cup of tea.

We improvise about the biscuits for a while, her hat sliding back as she chews. She doesn't like the tea. Maybe she eats so many biscuits just to get rid of the taste.

HEALTH VISITOR Aren't you having one? They're very good.

55 PATIENT   No, thanks. Maybe later. Having lunch soon.

She goes on munching, knowing I don't want her to be here/that I do want her to be here but I can't talk to her.

MARKS

Questions

21. Look at lines 1—10.

    By referring to **at least two** examples, analyse how the writer's use of language creates a sense of tension before the visit.

    3

22. Look at lines 11—33.

    By referring to **at least two** examples, analyse how the writer's use of language conveys Joy's anxiety about the visit.

    3

23. Look at lines 34—57.

    By referring to **at least two** examples, analyse how the writer's use of language conveys the artificiality of the situation.

    4

24. By referring to this extract and to elsewhere in the novel, discuss how Galloway explores Joy's difficulties with social interaction.

    10

OR

Text 4 — Prose

If you choose this text you may not attempt a question on Prose (Fiction or Non-Fiction) in Section 2.

Read the extract below and then attempt the following questions.

Sunset Song by Lewis Grassic Gibbon

This extract is from Part IV (Harvest).

Different from the old Rob he looked, she thought, but thought that carelessly, hurried to be in to young Ewan. But she stopped and watched him swing down the rigs to Ewan by the side of his horses, Ewan with his horses halted on the side of the brae and the breath of them rising up like a steam. And she heard Ewan call *Ay, man, Rob,* and Rob call *Ay, man,*
5   *Ewan,* and they called the truth, they seemed fine men both against the horizon of Spring, their feet deep laired in the wet clay ground, brown and great, with their feet on the earth and the sky that waited behind. And Chris looked at them over-long, they glimmered to her eyes as though they had ceased to be there, mirages of men dreamt by a land grown desolate against its changing sky. And the Chris that had ruled those other two selves of
10 herself, content, unquestioning these many months now, shook her head and called herself daft.

That year's harvest fell sharp away, but the price of corn made up for it, other prices might rise but farming folk did well. So it went in the winter and into the next year too, Ewan took in a drove of Irish steers to eat up the lush green grass of nineteen-sixteen. They grew
15 fat and round in the shortest while, Chris proud to see them, so many beasts had Blawearie. You'd hardly believe 'twas here father had chaved and fought for a living the way he did; but that was before the War.

For it still went on, rumbling its rumours like the thunder of summer beyond the hills. But nobody knew now when it would finish, not even Chae Strachan come home, a soldier all
20 the way from the front, as they called it; in the orra-looking khaki he came, with two stripes sewn on his arm, he said they had made him a corporal. He came up to Blawearie the night he got home and scraped his feet on the scraper outside and came dandering into the kitchen as aye he had done, not knocking but crying through the door *Ay, folk, are you in?*

25 So there was Chae, Chris gave a loud gasp to see him, Chae himself, so altered you'd hardly believe it, Chae himself, thin, his fine eyes queered and strained somehow. Even his laugh seemed different, hearty as it was, and he cried *God, Chris, I'm not a ghost yet!* and syne Chris and Ewan were shaking his hands and sitting him down and pouring him a dram and another after that. And young Ewan came running to see and cried *soldier!* and Chae
30 caught him and swung him up from the floor and cried *Chris's bairn — God, it can't be, I mind the day he was born, just yesterday it was!*

Young Ewan took little to strangers, most, not frightened but keep-your-distance he was, but he made no try to keep distant from Chae, he sat on his knee as Chris spread them supper and Chae spoke up about things in the War, it wasn't so bad if it wasn't the lice. He
35 said they were awful, but Chris needn't be feared, he'd been made to stand out in the close by Kirsty and strip off everything he had on, and fling the clothes in a tub and syne get into another himself. So he was fell clean, and God! he found it a change not trying to reach up his shoulders to get at some devil fair sucking and sucking the life from his skin.

And he gave a great laugh when he told them that, his old laugh queerly crippled it was.
40 And Ewan asked what he thought of the Germans, were they truly coarse? And Chae said he
was damned if he knew, he'd hardly seen one alive, though a body or so you saw now and
then, gey green and *feuch! there's a supper on the table!* Well, out there you hardly did
fighting at all, you just lay about in those damned bit trenches and had a keek at the soil
they were made of. And man, it was funny land, clay and a kind of black marl, but the
45 French were no good as farmers at all, they just pleitered and pottered in little bit parks
that you'd hardly use as a hanky to wipe your neb.

MARKS

Questions

25. Look at lines 1—11.

    By referring to **at least two** examples, analyse how the writer's use of language creates a dreamlike atmosphere.   3

26. Look at lines 12—17.

    By referring to **at least two** examples, analyse how the writer's use of language creates a sense of prosperity.   3

27. Look at lines 25—46.

    By referring to **at least two** examples, analyse how language is used to convey the impact of the War on Chae.   4

28. By referring to this extract and to elsewhere in the novel, discuss how Grassic Gibbon uses symbolism to explore the central concerns of the text.   10

[Turn over

OR

Text 5 — Prose

If you choose this text you may not attempt a question on Prose (Fiction or Non-Fiction) in Section 2.

Read the extract below and then attempt the following questions.

***The Cone-Gatherers* by Robin Jenkins**

In this extract from chapter five, Duror's presence threatens the cone-gatherers.

In the tree here was Calum's happiness. Here were his friends the finches, safe from the hawk scouting above. The ground of snares and stumbles was far below. In the loch the seals were playing, with audible splashes. In a nearby Douglas fir cushat doves were crooning. Above all, his brother beside him was singing. So much present joy was there for
5   him he did not have to look forward. He did not wonder, as Neil sometimes did, whether the cones he was gathering would be fertile; nor did he see the great trees born from this seed in his hands being toppled down in fifty years' time to make ammunition boxes for that generation's war. He was as improvident as the finches to whom he had fed more than half of his morning slice of bread.

10   Yet it was he who first saw the gamekeeper approaching through the sunshine and shadow of the wood, with his three glossy dogs running silently in front. In agitation he stretched over to touch Neil, and point.

Neil paused in his singing and picking to watch Duror. The latter, he thought, must be on a patrol of the wood, looking for deer or foxes or weasels to shoot. Even if he saw their
15   ladder against the tree, and from it learned where they were, he would still pass by. While they were gathering cones, they were none of his business: his own mistress had given them permission.

'It's all right,' he murmured to Calum. 'He's got nothing to do with us. He'll pass by.'

Indeed, as he watched the gamekeeper now in and now out of sight on the dappled ground
20   among the trees, he felt the sympathy he could never withhold when he saw any human being alone in a vast place, on a hillside say, or here in a wood. Unlike his brother, he saw nature as essentially hostile; and its resources to take away a man's confidence were immense. He felt sure, for instance, that the gamekeeper treading on the withered leaves must be thinking of his sick wife.

25   In a clearing Duror halted, laid down his gun, took his binoculars out of their case, and trained them on the top of the larch.

Neil knew that they must be clearly visible; it seemed to him typical of nature that the foliage was gone which would have hidden them. It took an effort to go on picking cones. He told Calum to keep on picking too. He objected to this spying on them, but would not
30   show it even by stopping work.

Calum could not concentrate on the cones. He became like an animal in danger with no way of escape. He began to whimper, and tilting over in a panicky attempt to hide from that distant scrutiny he let some cones dribble out of his bag.

'What's the matter with you?' asked Neil. 'Aye, I ken he's looking at us. But where's the
35   harm in that? He's just doing his work, like you and me. Maybe he's not looking at us at all. Maybe it's that hawk we saw that he's looking at. Didn't I tell you, that if we keep out of his way, he can't harm us? Well, we're out of his way up here.'

Calum was not reassured; he still whimpered and cowered, like a dog in the presence of someone who has been cruel to it.

40 Neil's own fear suddenly increased. He became angry.

'What are you moaning for?' he demanded. 'I ken he doesn't like us, but we don't like him either. This wood doesn't belong to him; it belongs to the lady and she's given us permission to climb the trees and pick the cones. You heard Mr Tulloch say it. As long as we don't saw branches off and injure the trees, nobody would interfere with us, he said.
45 Have we ever sawn any branches off?'

He repeated that last question in a passion of resentment, for on most trees the best harvest of cones was on the tips of branches too far out from the trunk to be reached. If sawing was permitted, then those branches, so small as hardly to be noticed, could be dropped to the ground where it would be easy and safe to strip them of every cone. The
50 trees' wounds would soon heal, the yield of cones would be doubled, and the strain on arms, legs, and back would be greatly relieved.

'The trees are more precious than we are,' he added bitterly.

MARKS

Questions

29. Look at lines 1—9.

Analyse how the writer's use of language conveys 'Calum's happiness'.   2

30. Look at lines 10—33.

By referring to **at least two** examples, analyse how the writer's use of language conveys the impact of Duror's presence on both Calum **and** Neil.   4

31. Look at lines 34—52.

By referring to **at least two** examples, analyse how the writer's use of language gives a clear impression of Neil's character.   4

32. By referring to this extract and to elsewhere in the novel, discuss how Jenkins explores the theme of power.   10

[Turn over

SECTION 1 — SCOTTISH TEXT — 20 marks

Choose ONE text from Drama, Prose or Poetry.

Read the text extract carefully and then attempt ALL the questions for your chosen text.

You should spend about 45 minutes on this Section.

PART C — SCOTTISH TEXT — POETRY

Text 1 — Poetry

If you choose this text you may not attempt a question on Poetry in Section 2.

Read the poem below and then attempt the following questions.

A Man's A Man For A' That by Robert Burns

```
     Is there, for honest poverty
        That hangs his head, and a' that;
     The coward slave, we pass him by,
        We dare be poor for a' that!
 5   For a' that, and a' that,
        Our toils obscure, and a' that,
     The rank is but the guinea's stamp,
        The Man's the gowd for a' that.


     What though on hamely fare we dine,
10      Wear hoddin grey, and a' that;
     Gie fools their silks, and knaves their wine,
        A man's a man for a' that!
     For a' that, and a' that,
        Their tinsel show, and a' that;
15   The honest man, though e'er sae poor,
        Is king o' men for a' that!


     Ye see yon birkie, ca'd a lord,
        Wha struts, and stares, and a' that;
     Though hundreds worship at his word,
20      He's but a coof for a' that.
     For a' that, and a' that,
        His riband, star, and a' that,
     The man of independent mind
        He looks and laughs at a' that.


25   A king can mak a belted knight,
        A marquis, duke, and a' that;
     But an honest man's aboon his might,
        Guid faith, he maunna fa' that!
     For a' that, and a' that,
30      Their dignities, and a' that,
     The pith o' sense, and pride o' worth,
        Are higher rank than a' that.
```

Then let us pray that come it may —
    As come it will for a' that —
35 That sense and worth, o'er a' the earth,
    May bear the gree, and a' that.
For a' that, and a' that,
    It's coming yet for a' that,
That man to man, the world o'er,
40   Shall brothers be for a' that!

MARKS

Questions

33. Look at lines 1—8.

    By referring to **at least two** examples, analyse how the poet's use of language conveys his views on poverty.   4

34. Look at lines 9—32.

    By referring to **at least two** examples, analyse how the poet's use of language conveys his contempt for wealth and/or status.   4

35. Look at lines 33—40.

    Analyse how the poet's use of language creates an inspirational tone.   2

36. By referring to this poem and to at least one other poem, discuss how Burns uses contrast to explore central concerns.   10

[Turn over

OR

Text 2 — Poetry

If you choose this text you may not attempt a question on Poetry in Section 2.

Read the poem below and then attempt the following questions.

Originally **by Carol Ann Duffy**

We came from our own country in a red room
which fell through the fields, our mother singing
our father's name to the turn of the wheels.
My brothers cried, one of them bawling, *Home,*
5 *Home,* as the miles rushed back to the city,
the street, the house, the vacant rooms
where we didn't live any more. I stared
at the eyes of a blind toy, holding its paw.

All childhood is an emigration. Some are slow,
10 leaving you standing, resigned, up an avenue
where no one you know stays. Others are sudden.
Your accent wrong. Corners, which seem familiar,
leading to unimagined pebble-dashed estates, big boys
eating worms and shouting words you don't understand.
15 My parents' anxiety stirred like a loose tooth
in my head. *I want our own country*, I said.

But then you forget, or don't recall, or change,
and, seeing your brother swallow a slug, feel only
a skelf of shame. I remember my tongue
20 shedding its skin like a snake, my voice
in the classroom sounding just like the rest. Do I only think
I lost a river, culture, speech, sense of first space
and the right place? Now, *Where do you come from?*
strangers ask. *Originally?* And I hesitate.

MARKS

Questions

37. Look at lines 1—8.

     Analyse how the poet uses language to convey the emotional impact of the journey on the speaker **and/or** her family.

     2

38. Look at lines 9—16.

     By referring to **at least two** examples, analyse how language is used to convey the speaker's alienation from her new surroundings.

     4

39. Look at lines 17—24.

     By referring to **at least two** examples, analyse how language is used to convey a sense of acceptance of the speaker's situation.

     4

40. By referring to this poem and at least one other by Duffy, discuss how the poet explores concerns about identity.

     10

[Turn over

OR

Text 3 — Poetry

If you choose this text you may not attempt a question on Poetry in Section 2.

Read the poem below and then attempt the following questions.

Some Old Photographs by Liz Lochhead

weather evocative as scent
the romance of dark stormclouds
in big skies over the low wide river
       of long shadows and longer shafts of light

5   of smoke
      fabulous film-noir stills of Central Station
of freezing fog silvering the chilled, stilled parks
      of the glamorous past
      where drops on a rainmate are sequins
10   in the lamplight, in the black-and-white

your young, still-lovely mother laughs, the
hem of her sundress whipped up
by a wind on a beach before you were even born

all the Dads in hats
15 are making for Central at five past five
in the snow, in the rain, in the sudden *what-a-scorcher*,
in the smog, their
belted dark overcoats white-spattered by the starlings

starlings swarming
20 in that perfect and permanent cloud
above what was
never really this photograph
but always all the passing now
and noise and stink and smoky breath of George Square

25 wee boays, a duchess, bunting, there's a
big launch on the Clyde
and that boat is yet to sail

MARKS

Questions

41. Look at lines 1—10.

By referring to **at least two** examples, analyse how the poet's language conveys the enjoyment gained from looking at the photographs.

4

42. Look at lines 11—18.

By referring to **at least two** examples, analyse how the poet's language creates a nostalgic mood.

4

43. Look at lines 19—27.

Analyse how the poet's language challenges what is presented in the photographs.

2

44. By referring to this poem and to at least one other poem, discuss how Lochhead explores important aspects of life through everyday objects **and/or** situations.

10

[Turn over

OR

Text 4 — Poetry

If you choose this text you may not attempt a question on Poetry in Section 2.

Read the poem below and then attempt the following questions.

Sounds of the Day by Norman MacCaig

When a clatter came,
it was horses crossing the ford.
When the air creaked, it was
a lapwing seeing us off the premises
5 of its private marsh. A snuffling puff
ten yards from the boat was the tide blocking and
unblocking a hole in a rock.
When the black drums rolled, it was water
falling sixty feet into itself.

10 When the door
scraped shut, it was the end
of all the sounds there are.

You left me
beside the quietest fire in the world.

15 I thought I was hurt in my pride only,
forgetting that,
when you plunge your hand in freezing water,
you feel
a bangle of ice round your wrist
20 before the whole hand goes numb.

MARKS

Questions

45. Look at lines 1—9.

    By referring to **at least two** examples, analyse how the poet uses language to build a sense of anticipation.

    4

46. Look at lines 10—12.

    Analyse how the poet's use of language creates a turning point.

    2

47. Look at lines 13—20.

    By referring to **at least two** examples, analyse how imagery **and/or** tone is used to convey the speaker's situation at this point.

    4

48. By referring to this poem and to at least one other poem by MacCaig, discuss how relationships are used to develop key themes.

    10

[Turn over

OR

Text 5 — Poetry

If you choose this text you may not attempt a question on Poetry in Section 2.

Read the extract below and then attempt the following questions.

Screapadal **by Sorley MacLean**

Screapadal in the morning
facing Applecross and the sun,
Screapadal that is so beautiful,
quite as beautiful as Hallaig.
5   No words can be put on beauty,
no picture, music or poem made for it.

Screapadal in May
when the young bracken is
but half a foot in height,
10 hardly above the grass.

Screapadal the sheep-pen and the cattle-fold
with walls to the south and west and north,
and to the east the sea-sound
over to the Sanctuary of Maol Rubha.

15 There is a half-dead memory of Maol Rubha
but only the dead written names
of the children, men and women
whom Rainy put off the land
between the north end of the Rock
20 and the Castle built for MacSwan
or for Mac Gille Chaluim
for violence and refuge.

Green, red-rocked and yellow
knolls to the horizon of the Carn Mor
25 in the west above the brae
coming down to green meadows,
and the pine wood dark and green
north right to the Castle
and the light-grey rocks beyond it.

30 And to the south the end of Creag Mheircil
hundreds of feet above the grass,
towers, columns and steeples
with speckled light-grey bands,
limestone whiteness in the sun.

35 A steep brae with scree-cairns
to the east down from the end of the Rock
under birch, rowan and alder,

and the Church of Falsehood in high water
when the spring tide is at its height.

40 It was not its lies that betrayed the people
in the time of the great pietist,
Rainy, who cleared
fourteen townships
in the Island of the Big Men,
45 Great Raasay of the MacLeods.

Rainy left Screapadal without people,
with no houses or cattle, only sheep,

MARKS

Questions

49. Look at lines 1—22.

By referring to **at least two** examples, analyse how the poet's language conveys a contrast in atmosphere within these lines.

4

50. Look at lines 23—34.

Analyse how the poet uses language to create a vivid sense of place.

2

51. Look at lines 35—47.

By referring to **at least two** examples, analyse how the poet's language makes clear his sympathy for the people of Screapadal.

4

52. By referring to this extract and to at least one other poem by MacLean, discuss how he explores change in relation to people **and/or** places.

10

[Turn over

OR

Text 6 — Poetry

If you choose this text you may not attempt a question on Poetry in Section 2.

Read the poem below and then attempt the following questions.

The Ferryman's Arms **by Don Paterson**

About to sit down with my half-pint of Guinness
I was magnetized by a remote phosphorescence
and drawn, like a moth, to the darkened back room
where a pool-table hummed to itself in the corner.
5 With ten minutes to kill and the whole place deserted
I took myself on for the hell of it. Slotting
a coin in the tongue, I looked round for a cue —
while I stood with my back turned, the balls were deposited
with an abrupt intestinal rumble; a striplight
10 batted awake in its dusty green cowl.
When I set down the cue-ball inside the parched D
it clacked on the slate; the nap was so threadbare
I could screw back the globe, given somewhere to stand.
As physics itself becomes something negotiable
15 a rash of small miracles covers the shortfall.
I went on to make an immaculate clearance.
A low punch with a wee dab of side, and the black
did the vanishing trick while the white stopped
before gently rolling back as if nothing had happened,
20 shouldering its way through the unpotted colours.

The boat chugged up to the little stone jetty
without breaking the skin of the water, stretching,
as black as my stout, from somewhere unspeakable
to here, where the foaming lip mussitates endlessly,
25 trying, with a nutter's persistence, to read
and re-read the shoreline. I got aboard early,
remembering the ferry would leave on the hour
even for only my losing opponent;
but I left him there, stuck in his tent of light, sullenly
30 knocking the balls in, for practice, for next time.

MARKS

Questions

53. Look at lines 1—10.

By referring to **at least two** examples, analyse how the poet's use of language conveys an unsettling atmosphere.   4

54. Look at lines 11—20.

Analyse how the poet's use of language conveys the speaker's attitude at this point.   2

55. Look at lines 21—30.

By referring to **at least two** examples, analyse how the poet uses imagery to convey the central concern(s).   4

56. By referring to this poem and to at least one other poem, discuss how Paterson explores the challenges of human experience.   10

[Turn over

[END OF SECTION 1]

SECTION 2 — CRITICAL ESSAY — 20 marks

Attempt ONE question from the following genres — Drama, Prose Fiction, Prose Non-Fiction, Poetry, Film and Television Drama, or Language.

Your answer must be on a different genre from that chosen in Section 1.

You should spend approximately 45 minutes on this Section.

PART A — DRAMA

*Answers to questions on **drama** should refer to the text and to such relevant features as characterisation, key scene(s), structure, climax, theme, plot, conflict, setting . . .*

1. Choose a play which focuses on a relationship which is destructive **or** is in crisis.

   By referring to appropriate techniques, explain the nature of the relationship and discuss how it contributes to your appreciation of the play as a whole.

2. Choose a play in which a character has a weakness **or** flaw.

   By referring to appropriate techniques, explain the importance of this weakness **or** flaw and discuss how it contributes to your appreciation of the play as a whole.

3. Choose a play which explores the theme of truth and lies, **or** good and evil, **or** appearance and reality.

   By referring to appropriate techniques, explain how the dramatist presents this theme and discuss how it contributes to your appreciation of the play as a whole.

PART B — PROSE FICTION

> *Answers to questions on **prose fiction** should refer to the text and to such relevant features as characterisation, setting, language, key incidents(s), climax, turning point, plot, structure, narrative technique, theme, ideas, description . . .*

4. Choose a novel **or** short story in which there is a complex character for whom the reader has some sympathy.

   With reference to appropriate techniques, explain the nature of the complexity and discuss how your response to this character adds to your appreciation of the text as a whole.

5. Choose a novel **or** short story in which important human values are explored.

   With reference to appropriate techniques, explain how these values are explored and discuss how this adds to your appreciation of the text as a whole.

6. Choose a novel **or** short story in which the setting in time **and/or** place is important to your understanding of the text.

   By referring to appropriate techniques, explain the nature of the setting and discuss how it is important to your understanding of the text as a whole.

PART C — PROSE NON-FICTION

> *Answers to questions on **prose non-fiction** should refer to the text and to such relevant features as ideas, use of evidence, stance, style, selection of material, narrative voice . . .*

7. Choose a non-fiction text which has an emotional **and/or** intellectual appeal for the reader.

   With reference to appropriate techniques, discuss how the writer has created this emotional **and/or** intellectual appeal.

8. Choose a non-fiction text which has made you think differently about an important moral **or** social issue.

   With reference to appropriate techniques, discuss how the writer has caused you to view the issue differently.

9. Choose a non-fiction text which provides fresh understanding of a group of people, **or** a way of life, **or** an important figure.

   With reference to appropriate techniques, discuss how the writer has provided this insight.

[Turn over

PART D — POETRY

*Answers to questions on **poetry** should refer to the text and to such relevant features as word choice, tone, imagery, structure, content, rhythm, rhyme, theme, sounds, ideas . . .*

10. Choose a poem which deals with an issue of importance to human experience.

    With reference to appropriate techniques, explain how the issue is presented and discuss how it enhances your appreciation of the poem.

11. Choose a poem which creates a mood of hope **or** despair **or** mystery.

    With reference to appropriate techniques, explain how the mood is created and discuss how it enhances your appreciation of the poem as a whole.

12. Choose a poem in which the ending is important in highlighting central concerns.

    With reference to appropriate techniques, explain how the ending highlights central concerns and discuss how it enhances your appreciation of the poem as a whole.

PART E — FILM AND TELEVISION DRAMA

*Answers to questions on **film and television drama*** *should refer to the text and to such relevant features as use of camera, key sequence, characterisation, mise-en-scène, editing, music/sound, special effects, plot, dialogue . . .*

13. Choose a film **or** television drama in which there is a sequence which is particularly moving **or** humorous **or** shocking.

    With reference to appropriate techniques, discuss how the film or programme makers succeed in engaging the viewer's emotions or reactions.

14. Choose a film **or** television drama in which setting in time **and/or** place is important to the development of the central concerns.

    With reference to appropriate techniques, discuss how the setting in time **and/or** place enhances your appreciation of the film or television drama as a whole.

15. Choose a film **or** television drama in which the viewer feels engaged with a character who is flawed **or** vulnerable.

    With reference to appropriate techniques, discuss how the film or programme makers succeed in creating engagement with the character, and how this adds to your appreciation of the film or television drama as a whole.

* 'television drama' includes a single play, a series or a serial.

PART F — LANGUAGE

> *Answers to questions on **language** should refer to the text and to such relevant features as register, accent, dialect, slang, jargon, vocabulary, tone, abbreviation . . .*

16. Choose language which is intended to persuade you to buy products, **or** to agree with a particular point of view.

    Identify specific examples of language use, and discuss to what extent they are effective.

17. Choose the language associated with digital communications.

    Identify specific language features, and discuss their effectiveness as a means of communication.

18. Choose the spoken **or** written language typically used by a particular vocational **or** leisure group.

    Identify specific language features, and discuss their contribution to efficient communication within the group.

[END OF SECTION 2]

[END OF QUESTION PAPER]

[BLANK PAGE]

DO NOT WRITE ON THIS PAGE

HIGHER

2019

National Qualifications 2019

X824/76/11

English
Reading for Understanding, Analysis and Evaluation — Text

WEDNESDAY, 8 MAY

9:00 AM – 10:30 AM

Total marks — 30

Read the passages carefully and then attempt ALL questions, which are printed on a separate sheet.

The following two passages discuss news in the modern world.

Passage 1

Read the passage below and attempt questions 1 to 8.

In the first passage, Katharine Viner considers the impact that the internet has on what we believe to be true.

Gutenberg invented the printing press in 1440. For the next 500 years the main form of information was the printed page. This meant that knowledge was primarily delivered in a fixed format, one that encouraged readers to believe in stable and settled truths.

5 Now, 25 years after the first website went online, it is clear that we are living through a period of dizzying transition. We are caught in a series of confusing battles between opposing forces: between truth and falsehood, fact and rumour, kindness and cruelty; between the connected and the alienated; between the original vision of the web as an open platform and the gated enclosures of social media; between an informed public and a misguided mob.

What is common to these struggles — and what makes their resolution an urgent matter — is
10 that they all involve the diminishing status of truth. This does not mean that there are no truths. It simply means that we cannot agree on what these truths are, and when there is no consensus about the truth and no way to achieve this consensus, chaos soon follows.

Increasingly, what counts as a fact is merely a view that someone feels to be true — and technology has made it very easy for these 'facts' to circulate with a speed and reach that was
15 unimaginable in the Gutenberg era (or even a decade ago). A dubious story appears in a tabloid one morning, and by noon it has flown around the world in social media. This may seem like a small matter, but its consequences are enormous. To pick one example among many, during the November 2015 Paris terror attacks, rumours quickly spread on social media that the Louvre and the Pompidou Centre had been hit, and that the French president had suffered a stroke. Trusted
20 news agencies found it difficult to correct such fake news.

Sometimes stories like these are spread out of panic, sometimes out of malice, and sometimes out of deliberate manipulation, in which a corporation or regime pays people to convey their message. Whatever the motive, falsehoods and facts now spread the same way in what is called an 'information cascade'. As one expert describes it, 'people forward on what others think, even
25 if the information is false, misleading or incomplete, because they think they have learned something valuable'. This cycle repeats itself, and before you know it, the cascade has unstoppable momentum. You share a friend's post on social media, perhaps to show support or agreement or that you're 'in the know', and thus you increase the visibility of their post to others.

Social media organisations design news feeds to give us more of what they think we want. This
30 means that the version of the world we encounter every day in our own personal stream has been invisibly crafted to reinforce our pre-existing beliefs. The term 'filter bubble', created by Eli Pariser in 2011, refers to personalised search functions which mean that we are less likely to be exposed to information that challenges us or broadens our worldview. We are also less likely to encounter facts that disprove false information that others have shared.

35 Eli Pariser believed that those running social media platforms should 'prioritise balanced views and news that's important, not just the stuff that's most popular or most self-validating'. But in less than five years, thanks to the incredible power of a few social media platforms, the filter bubble has become more extreme. Asking technology companies to do something about this issue presumes that it is a problem that can be easily fixed — rather than one hardwired into the very
40 idea of those social networks designed to give you what you and your friends want to see.

There's no denying that, in recent years, many news organisations have steered themselves away from public interest journalism and towards junk-food news, chasing page views in the hope of attracting clicks, advertising or profit. And, like junk food, you hate yourself when you've gorged on it. The most extreme version of this has been the creation of fake news farms, which attract
45 traffic with false reports that are designed to look like real news and are therefore widely shared on social networks.

Of course, news media have got things wrong in the past. But what is new and significant is that today, rumours and lies are read just as widely as facts — and often more widely — because they are stranger than reality and more exciting to share. This approach, instead of
50 strengthening social bonds or creating an informed population or reinforcing the idea of news as a democratic necessity, creates online 'gangs'. These gangs spread instant falsehoods fitting their views, reinforcing each other's beliefs, driving each other deeper into shared opinions rather than established facts.

It need not be like this. The truth is a struggle but the struggle is worth it. Media organisations
55 must put the search for truth at the heart of everything, building an informed, active public that scrutinises the powerful — not an ill-informed, reactionary gang that attacks the vulnerable. Traditional news values must be embraced and celebrated: reporting, verifying, gathering together eyewitness statements. All in the cause of making a serious attempt to discover what really happened, and taking responsibility for creating the kind of world we want to live in.

Passage 2

Read the passage below and attempt question 9. While reading, you may wish to make notes on the main ideas and/or highlight key points in the passage.

In the second passage, Matthew Parris reflects on the impact of new technology on communication.

Among the smiles with which future generations will reflect on early 21st-century thinking, the broadest may be reserved for our alarm over the arrival of the internet. We're probably right about only one thing: for good and ill, mass, cheap, instant global communication will have a tremendous and growing impact on humankind. But what that impact will be, how society will
5 respond to it, how it may change us and how it will finally bed down in our culture is impossible to predict. How we end up regulating the internet is at this stage equally impossible to anticipate.

By 'impossible' I don't mean problematical: I mean impossible. Pointless, hopeless, a waste of time. We're no more able to peer even a couple of decades into a future world's relationship with the internet than in 1440 Johannes Gutenberg could have guessed how fast and how completely
10 his printing press would shape the world to come. Did he know where his invention would lead? Of course not. Any contemporary speculation on the future impact of the printing press would have been futile. As futile as our guesses, now, about where the internet will take us.

In the end, all we're talking about is human communication. Based on the history of communications so far, there are two important points to remember.

15 First is the need to question the supposedly 'new situation' that social media and internet communication presents us with. Ask yourself what genuinely new ethical or legal dilemma we face and what genuinely new principle is involved. I've yet to see either. So criminals and terrorists can communicate with greater ease using the internet? But all communication opens up opportunities for criminality. The easier the communication, the easier the conspiracy. The
20 railways, the motor car, post and telegraphy, radio, the telephone, television, the mobile phone — each was greeted with the same anxieties, for each enlarged the scope not only for good but evil too.

Secondly, we should never forget that humans can evolve very fast to adapt to new circumstances. We are not looking at social media platforms in the way the next generation will. It's possible they
25 will learn to dismiss 'trolling' just as readers of the first newspapers learnt, after an initial shock, to dismiss the sensationalised reporting that soon appeared. I believe the immediate response of my generation — that such things must somehow be stopped by 'regulation' — is wrong: first because this is in practice impossible if we're to maintain platforms on which people can express opinions. And second because protecting people from nastiness makes them more vulnerable: it
30 impairs the production of the ultimate defence against abuse, which is learning to take no notice.

None of this is to deny the importance of law. We can prosecute those who incite illegal acts or racist behaviour; we can sue those who libel. But vulgar abuse? Bring it on. Let's learn to treat it with contempt.

There's a great truth to be learnt about an essentially open-access social media platform.
35 Cyberspace is not like a big, democratic newspaper. It's a chaos, an infinite tip, much of it rubbish, much of it wrong. There's plenty that's useful; but you must pick your way through oceans of nonsense, mountains of trivia and a good deal of poison. Unless this could be filtered, cleansed, pre-viewed and regulated — and it cannot — we make people more vulnerable, not less, by feeble attempts to render a dangerous space safer for them.

40 So bring on the fake news; bring on the slosh of sentiment; bring on the wildfires of anger and accusation. They are windows into the interior worlds of other human beings. Let us learn to see what lives there and make our own judgements. Let us learn to navigate, as we do in the spoken word, in the printed word and in our own lives. Let us learn to think for ourselves.

[END OF TEXT]

[OPEN OUT]

DO NOT WRITE ON THIS PAGE

[BLANK PAGE]

DO NOT WRITE ON THIS PAGE

National
Qualifications
2019

X824/76/21

English
Reading for Understanding,
Analysis and Evaluation — Questions

WEDNESDAY, 8 MAY
9:00 AM – 10:30 AM

Total marks — 30

Attempt ALL questions.

Write your answers clearly in the answer booklet provided. In the answer booklet, you must clearly identify the question number you are attempting.

Use **blue** or **black** ink.

Before leaving the examination room you must give your answer booklet to the Invigilator; if you do not, you may lose all the marks for this paper.

MARKS

Attempt ALL questions
Total marks — 30

Passage 1

1. Read lines 1—3.

    Identify **two** ways in which the invention of the printing press was important. Use your own words in your answer.

    2

2. Read lines 4—8.

    By referring to **at least two** examples, analyse how the writer uses language to convey her concerns about the impact of the internet.

    4

3. Read lines 9—12.

    Explain what the writer believes has happened to the idea of truth. Use your own words as far as possible in your answer.

    2

4. Read lines 13—20.

    Explain how the writer's argument about fake news is supported by the example of the Paris attack. Use your own words in your answer.

    3

5. Read lines 21—28.

    By referring to **at least two** examples, analyse how the writer uses language to criticise the way the internet is used to communicate information.

    4

6. Read lines 29—40.

    Explain fully why the writer believes that social media has a negative impact on us. Use your own words in your answer.

    3

7. Read lines 41—53.

    Analyse how the writer uses both imagery **and** sentence structure to criticise aspects of modern news.

    4

8. Read lines 54—59.

    By referring to **at least two** examples, analyse how the writer uses language to create an inspirational tone.

    3

MARKS

Question on both passages

9. Look at both passages.

The writers disagree on the challenges created by the internet.

Identify **three** key areas on which they disagree. You should support the points you make by referring to important ideas in both passages.

You may answer this question in continuous prose or in a series of developed bullet points.

5

[END OF QUESTION PAPER]

[BLANK PAGE]

DO NOT WRITE ON THIS PAGE

National
Qualifications
2019

X824/76/12

**English
Critical Reading**

WEDNESDAY, 8 MAY

11:00 AM – 12:30 PM

Total marks — 40

SECTION 1 — Scottish Text — 20 marks

Read an extract from a Scottish text you have previously studied and attempt the questions.

Choose ONE text from either

Part A — Drama   Pages 2–7
or
Part B — Prose   Pages 8–17
or
Part C — Poetry   Pages 18–28

Attempt ALL the questions for your chosen text.

SECTION 2 — Critical Essay — 20 marks

Attempt ONE question from the following genres — Drama, Prose Fiction, Prose Non-fiction, Poetry, Film and Television Drama, or Language.

Your answer must be on a different genre from that chosen in Section 1.

You should spend approximately 45 minutes on each section.

Write your answers clearly in the answer booklet provided. In the answer booklet you must clearly identify the question number you are attempting.

Use **blue** or **black** ink.

Before leaving the examination room you must give your answer booklet to the Invigilator; if you do not, you may lose all the marks for this paper.

SECTION 1 — SCOTTISH TEXT — 20 marks

Choose ONE text from Drama, Prose or Poetry.

Read the text extract carefully and then attempt ALL the questions for your chosen text.

You should spend about 45 minutes on this section.

PART A — SCOTTISH TEXT — DRAMA

Text 1 — Drama

If you choose this text you may not attempt a question on Drama in Section 2.

Read the extract below and then attempt the following questions.

The Slab Boys by John Byrne

In this extract, which is taken from Act 2 of the play, Alan is shocked by Phil and Spanky's mistreatment of Hector.

	Spanky:	How does the shirt feel? (*referring to Hector's restyled 'off-the-shoulder' shirt*)
	Hector:	'S nice and easy on my throat.
	Spanky:	Special design . . .
	Hector:	Looks all right then, Spanky?
5	Spanky:	It's a knockout, kid.
	Phil:	A knockout.
	Hector:	So you think Lucille'll bite?
	Phil:	Your maw'll be asking you whose the teethmarks are when she gives you your bath tonight. Lucille is going to flip.
10	Hector:	No kidding, Phil?
	Alan:	Hector . . .
		(*Phil holds up Parker pen out of Hector's line of vision but so that Alan can see it.*)
	Hector:	D'you like it, Alan?
	Alan:	It's . . . er . . .
15		(*Phil threatens to snap pen.*)
		. . . really gadgey, Heck.
	Hector:	Will I go now and ask her? Will I? (*Heads for door.*)
	Spanky:	(*cutting him off*) Not just yet, Hector . . . Remember you've still got to go and see Willie.
20	Hector:	Yeh, but I can do that after I've asked Lucille . . .
	Phil:	No, Spanky's right, kiddo . . . better go and see Willie first. It's important. Lucille'll not go off the boil. Here, I'll give you my coat to put on . . . (*Takes off coat.*)
	Hector:	What do I want that for? I don't mind doing a bit of swanking now that my clothes are up to date.

MARKS

25	Phil:	Yeh, but you don't want anybody else to get a preview, do you? Lessen the impact . . . know what I mean? Get the coat on. (*Forces Hector's arms into sleeves.*)
	Spanky:	(*pulling balaclava helmet from cupboard*) You better put this on and all . . . it's draughty in Willie's room. (*Pulls helmet over Hector's head.*) Cosy, eh?
	Hector:	(*slightly bamboozled*) Yeh, but will he not think I'm a bit happed up?
30	Phil:	That's just it. You've been down at Nurse. Influenza verging on pleurisy. She ordered you home but you decided to soldier on. He'll like that. Maybe not give you your . . . (*Stops.*)
	Spanky:	(*quickly*) Wireless back.
	Hector:	I'm not expecting my wireless back. You know what he's like.
35	Spanky:	Well, you can't expect it back just 'cos you've got the flu, Heck . . .
	Phil:	Triple pneumonia, Spanks.
	Hector:	I'm all mixed up . . . what've I got again?
	Spanky:	Triple pneumonia . . .
	Phil:	Double rupture . . .
40	Hector:	I'll away along, then.
	Spanky:	Good man. All the best.
	Phil:	Good luck, son . . .
		(*They shove Hector out the door.*)
		You'll need it.
45		(*They hold on to each other, laughing.*)
	Alan:	Well, I hope you're proud of yourselves . . . that was a pretty lousy trick to play!
	Spanky:	Oh was it, by jove?
	Phil:	A trick, you cad! Take that! (*Bops Alan's head a smack.*)
	Alan:	Hey, watch it! That was sore . . . Chuck it!

Questions

1. Look at lines 1–16.

    By referring to **at least two** examples, analyse how the writer's use of both stage directions **and** dialogue conveys the slab boys' (Phil and Spanky's) manipulation of other characters.   **4**

2. Look at lines 17–40.

    By referring to **at least two** examples, analyse how the writer uses language to convey different aspects of Hector's personality.   **4**

3. Look at lines 41–49.

    Analyse how the writer uses language to create a mocking tone.   **2**

4. By referring to this extract and to elsewhere in the play, discuss how the theme of deception **and/or** self-deception is developed.   **10**

OR

Text 2 — Drama

If you choose this text you may not attempt a question on Drama in Section 2.

Read the extract below and then attempt the following questions.

***The Cheviot, the Stag and the Black, Black Oil* by John McGrath**

In this extract, a group of characters discuss depopulation of the Highlands.

M.C.2:	In 1861, one hundred and sixty of the islands of the Hebrides were inhabited. In 1941, there were seventy three.
	ACADEMIC *goes to the microphone, holding a book.*

5

ACADEMIC:	All this created a mighty wilderness. In the words of the Highlands and Islands Development Board Brochure — Explore the Highlands and Islands: 'A great open lung, guaranteed to breathe new life into the most jaded . . . Overcrowding? Not in Sutherland . . . a land of solitary splendour — mountains, lochs and glens of unrivalled beauty add a sharper poignancy to the scattered stones of the ruined crofting townships.' Yes, the tragedy of the Highlands has become a saleable commodity.

10

	Enter ANDY McCHUCKEMUP, *a Glasgow Property-operator's man. He looks round, takes the mike.*
ANDY:	The motel — as I see it — is the thing of the future. That's how we see it, myself and the Board of Directors, and one or two of your local Councillors — come on now, these are the best men money can buy. So — picture it, if yous will, right there at the top of the glen, beautiful vista — The Crammem Inn, High Rise Motorcroft — all finished in natural, washable, plastic granitette. Right next door, the 'Frying Scotsman' All Night Chipperama — with a wee ethnic bit, Fingal's Caff — serving seaweed-suppers-in-the-basket, and draught Drambuie. And to cater for the younger set, yous've got your Grouse-a-go-go. I mean, people very soon won't want your bed and breakfasts, they want everything laid on, they'll be wanting their entertainment and that, and wes've got the know-how to do it and wes have got the money to do it. So — picture it, if yous will — a drive-in clachan on every hill-top where formerly there was hee-haw but scenery.

15

20

25

	Enter LORD VAT OF GLENLIVET, *a mad young laird.*
LORD VAT:	Get off my land — these are my mountains.
ANDY:	Who are you, Jimmy?
LORD VAT:	Lord Vat of Glenlivet. I come from an ancient Scotch family and I represent the true spirit of the Highlands.

30

ANDY:	Andy McChuckemup of Crammem Inn Investments Ltd., Govan, pleased for to make your acquaintance Your Worship. Excuse me, is this your fields?
LORD VAT:	You're invading my privacy.
ANDY:	Excuse me, me and wor company's got plans to develop this backward area into a paradise for all the family — improve it, you know, fair enough, eh?

35

MARKS

LORD VAT: Look here, I've spent an awful lot of money to keep this place private and peaceful. I don't want hordes of common people trampling all over the heather, disturbing the birds.

ANDY: Oh no, we weren't planning to do it for nothing, an' that — there'll be plenty in it for you . . .

40

Questions

5.   Look at lines 1–10.

   By referring to **at least two** examples, analyse how language is used to convey the negative impact of the clearances on the Highlands.   4

6.   Look at lines 11–25.

   By referring to **at least two** examples, analyse how language is used to create humour.   4

7.   Look at lines 26–40.

   Analyse how language is used to convey the differing attitudes of Andy **and** Lord Vat to the Highlands.   2

8.   By referring to this extract and to elsewhere in the play, discuss how McGrath explores the theme of exploitation.   10

[Turn over

OR

Text 3 — Drama

If you choose this text you may not attempt a question on Drama in Section 2.

Read the extract below and then attempt the following questions.

Men Should Weep by Ena Lamont Stewart

In this extract from Act 2, scene 2, Maggie is finding it increasingly difficult to cope with the demands of family life.

MAGGIE: (*screaming at him*) Look at yer new boots! (*She seizes him, shakes him and hits him*) Ye've kicked the taes oot o them again! I'll learn ye tae play fitba' in yer best boots.

Crying hysterically, she belabours Ernest who tries to get away, yelling, but she holds on

5   Whaur d'ye think I'll find the money for anither pair? Oh, I cannae staun ony mair o this . . . I cannae staun it!

She collapses in a storm of weeping. Edie joins in out of fear and sympathy, and John jumps up in alarm. He goes to calm her

              (*Shouting at John*) Leave me alane! Leave me alane! I hate ye! I hate the hale
10   lot o ye!

In a storm of tears she blunders out of the room

John gathers the two frightened children to him and sets down an arm round each

JOHN: Wheesht, wheesht, the baith o ye; wheesht. Listen. Listen tae me. Edie, Ernie, listen. I'll try tae explain. (*He sighs*) Yer mammy's no really angry at ye . . .

15   *The children's tears stop in a series of sobs and hiccoughs*

              Your mammy's just tired. She's been oot a day cleanin ither folks' hooses, and mebbe we ought tae hae helped mak things a bit easier for her.

Edie nods her head vigorously

              When women gets that tired they kind o loss their heids; ye unnerstaun?

20   EDIE: I wis feart, Daddy. I've never been feart o' ma Mammy before.

JOHN: She'll be sorry ye were feart, Edie.

ERNEST: Daddy, am I no tae get playin fitba again? I hevnae got nae ither boots; the auld yins crushed ma taes. I'm the centre-forward! Ma chinas'll kill me if I'm no in the team. Some o them's got real fitba boots. Daddy, could you no get us a pair
25   o real yins?

JOHN: I'll try, son. I'll try.

ERNEST: Bobbie Gray got his at the barras.

JOHN: (*a gleam of hope*) Oh aye there's the barras. We'll need tae see whit Mammy says.

30   ERNEST: (*a despairing cry*) Aw naw! She's a wumman; she cannae unnerstaun men!

EDIE: I'm awfu hungry, Daddy and the chips is gettin cold.

MARKS

ERNEST: (*desperate*) Wull ye try, Daddy, wull ye?

John bows his head, holds it between his hands and groans

JOHN: (*to himself*) Try. Try. As if I didnae try.

35 *Edie plucks his sleeve*

EDIE: So could we no juist hae wur tea, Daddy? Mebbe ma mammy's gone tae her bed.

JOHN: Aye. We'll hae wur tea.

The children sit at the table and dive into the chips. John slowly and painfully locates the
40 *teapot and makes tea. He sets out cups: lifts the teapot and looks at the door through*
which Maggie had disappeared plainly wondering if he dare take her a cup

The door opens and she appears, her face begrutten, but calm

MAGGIE: Well, come on then, come on! Which o yous has found the strength tae mak the tea? (*In a whisper to John*) I'm sorry. Coulnae help masel. Think I'm needin
45 something tae eat.

JOHN: (*patting her*) That's a right, lass.

Edie offers her mother the chips

MAGGIE: Naw, hen! I'm no for a chip. They gie me the heartburn. (*She sits down and stretches for bread and butter: with a piece halfway to her mouth she stops and*
50 *gives a kind of laugh*) Heartburn! I wonder whit kind o a male idiot called indigestion heartburn? Ma Goad! I could tell him whit heartburn is! Ma Goad! Couldn't I no!

Questions

9. Read lines 1—11.

   By referring to **at least two** examples, analyse how both stage directions **and** dialogue are used to convey Maggie's state of mind.　　4

10. Read lines 12—41.

    By referring to **at least two** examples, analyse how John's response to the situation reveals differing aspects of his character.　　4

11. Read lines 43—52.

    Explain why Maggie feels troubled at this point.　　2

12. By referring to this extract and to elsewhere in the play, discuss how Lamont Stewart explores the role of women.　　10

SECTION 1 — SCOTTISH TEXT — 20 marks

Choose ONE text from Drama, Prose or Poetry.

Read the text extract carefully and then attempt ALL the questions for your chosen text.

You should spend about 45 minutes on this section.

PART B — SCOTTISH TEXT — PROSE

Text 1 — Prose

If you choose this text you may not attempt a question on Prose (Fiction or Non-fiction) in Section 2.

Read the extract below and then attempt the following questions.

The Telegram **by Iain Crichton Smith**

'Don't worry, Sarah, it won't be for you. Donald only left home last week.'

'You don't know,' said the fat woman, 'you don't know.' And then she added without thinking, 'It's different for the officers.'

'Why is it different for the officers?' said the thin woman in an even voice without taking
5 her eyes from the black figure.

'Well, I just thought they're better off,' said the fat woman in a confused tone, 'they get better food and they get better conditions.'

'They're still on the ship,' said the thin woman who was thinking that the fat woman was very stupid. But then most of them were: they were large, fat and lazy. Most of them could
10 have better afforded to send their sons and daughters to university but they didn't want to be thought of as snobbish.

'They are that,' said the fat woman. 'But your son is educated,' she added irrelevantly. Of course her son didn't salute the thin woman's son if they were both home on leave at the same time. It had happened once they had been. But naturally there was the uneasiness.

15 'I made sacrifices to have my son educated,' said the thin woman. 'I lived on a pension of ten shillings a week. I was in nobody's debt. More tea?'

'No thank you,' said the fat woman. 'He's passed Bessie's house. That means it can't be Roddy. He's safe.'

For a terrible moment she realised that she had hoped that the elder would have turned in
20 at Bessie's house. Not that she had anything against either Bessie or Roddy. But still one thought of one's own family first.

The thin woman continued remorselessly as if she were pecking away at something she had pecked at for many years. 'The teacher told me to send Iain to University. He came to see me. I had no thought of sending him before he came. "Send your son to university," he said
25 to me. "He's got a good head on him." And I'll tell you, Sarah, I had to save every penny. Ten shillings isn't much. When did you see me with good clothes in the church?'

'That's true,' said the fat woman absently. 'We have to make sacrifices.' It was difficult to know what she was thinking of — the whale meat or the saccharines? Or the lack of clothes? Her mind was vague and diffused except when she was thinking about herself.

MARKS

30   The thin woman continued: 'Many's the night I used to sit here in this room and knit clothes for him when he was young. I even knitted trousers for him. And for all I know he may marry an English girl and where will I be? He might go and work in England. He was staying in a house there at Christmas. He met a girl at a dance and he found out later that her father was a mayor. I'm sure she smokes and drinks. And he might not give me anything
35   after all I've done for him.'

'Donald spends all his money,' said the fat woman. 'He never sends me anything. When he comes home on leave he's never in the house. But I don't mind. He was always like that. Meeting strange people and buying them drinks. It's his nature and he can't go against his nature. He's passed the Smiths. That means Tommy's all right.'

40   There were only another three houses before he would reach her own, and then the last one was the one where she was sitting.

'I think I'll take a cup of tea,' she said. And then, 'I'm sorry about the cow.' But no matter how you tried you never could like the thin woman. She was always putting on airs. Mayor indeed. Sending her son to university. Why did she want to be better than anyone else?
45   Saving and scrimping all the time. And everybody said that her son wasn't as clever as all that. He had failed some of his exams too. Her own Donald was just as clever and could have gone to university but he was too fond of fishing and being out with the boys.

As she drank her tea her heart was beating and she was frightened and she didn't know what to talk about and yet she wanted to talk. She liked talking, after all what else was
50   there to do? But the thin woman didn't gossip much. You couldn't feel at ease with her, you had the idea all the time that she was thinking about something else.

Questions

13.   Look at lines 1—16.

By referring to **at least two** examples, analyse how the writer's use of language reveals that **both** women are judgemental.   4

14.   Look at lines 30—35.

Analyse how the writer's use of language conveys the thin woman's disappointment concerning her son.   2

15.   Look at lines 42—51.

By referring to **at least two** examples, analyse how the writer's use of language highlights the fat woman's resentment of the thin woman at this point.   4

16.   By referring to this extract and to at least one other short story, discuss the importance of female characters in Crichton Smith's stories.   10

[Turn over

OR

Text 2 — Prose

If you choose this text you may not attempt a question on Prose (Fiction or Non-fiction) in Section 2.

Read the extract below and then attempt the following questions.

The Eye of the Hurricane by George Mackay Brown

'Courage,' said Captain Stevens, 'by God we need courage more than we need money or clothes or sleep. We need it all the time. Cradle and coffin, they're both shaped like ships — you'll have noticed that — and it's a desperate and a dangerous voyage we all have to make, from birth into death and beyond it. Even the pen-pusher who sits at a desk all day
5   with papers and ink. We all need courage.'

He paused for a minute, then said quietly, 'There is only one thing more important than courage — love.' He suddenly glared at Stony Hackland. 'Take that smirk off your face, Hackland,' he shouted.

'Sorry, sir,' said Stony Hackland.

10 'The love of women,' said Captain Stevens, 'a very precious jewel. I have known men lucky enough to possess it. They had a completeness in their lives, these lovers, everything they did seemed to be well done, faithfully done, even when it wasn't. I think of them now and I envy them bitterly, because, personally speaking, this gift of love has passed me by. I'm an old man now, I can never know what it is. (Spasms of lust, I've had them all right, but that's
15 quite another thing.) I'm not complaining, mind you. I suppose I must thank God for the one crude gift he's given me, courage. I think I may need it before this trip's over.'

'Courage,' muttered Robert Jansen, and raised his glass. We all drank, except the captain.

'At least you can depend on courage,' said Captain Stevens. 'There's no substitute for courage when the time comes. But love — what counterfeits, what frauds and imitations
20 it's given rise to! Poor Falquist — the fly-by-night he tied himself to, by God, though she was five hundred miles away at the time, she and no other held the gun to his head and pulled the trigger. And I've known worse than her, many, much worse.' He turned to me. 'You,' he said, 'what's your name again, I forget?'

'Barclay, sir,' I said.

25 'Are you married, Barclay?' he said.

'No, sir.' I said.

'Get yourself a good wife, Barclay,' he said. 'We're going through the shining eye of the hurricane. It'll only last two hours, three at the most, don't delude yourselves. . . . I want you, Barclay, to go down and have a look at the cargo and come back here and report. It'll
30 soon start blowing again and then you won't be able to go.'

He swayed and fell against the television set as if he had been axed at the knees. The box shuddered and slid to the floor and seemed to explode; valves and coils were flung all over the room. My hand was scratched by a bit of flying glass.

Stony Hackland bent over Captain Stevens and raised him by the shoulders. 'Wind's getting
35 up,' he said.

I went straight from the house into the cold starlight and down to the small house on the pier where Miriam lived with her parents.

MARKS

All the way back she only spoke once. 'You promised to look after him,' she said.

40 When Miriam and I arrived Robert Jansen and Stony Hackland had got the old man back into his bed, but only, it seemed, after a struggle. The room was a worse shambles than ever; the curtain was half ripped from the pelmet and a black star had exploded across the mirror; the only thing left standing was the photograph of Elizabeth Stevens on the bedside table. Captain Stevens didn't seem to recognize Miriam at first. She bent over him and put his lead-blue hands back under the blanket. 'No women on this ship,' he mumbled. 'Be put
45 ashore first port.'

'Yes,' said Miriam, 'and it won't be long till we're there. The storm's blowing done.'

Stony Hackland and Robert Jansen sat in the fireplace drinking the last of the rum out of cups. 'He's the decentest skipper ever I sailed with,' said Stony Hackland. 'Strict, but very fair in his dealings.'

50 'A straight shooter,' said Robert Jansen.

Miriam's lips moved soundlessly over the stiffening face on the pillow. He opened his eyes once and looked at her. 'Elizabeth,' he said.

Then blindness, silence, cold.

Miriam turned towards the two drunk men in the fireplace. 'You'll be pleased to know,' she
55 said, 'that you've killed Captain Stevens.'

Robert Jansen began to cry.

To me she said coldly, 'Get Dr Wilson.'

Questions

17. Look at lines 1—9.

    Analyse how language is used to reveal **two** aspects of Captain Stevens' character.   2

18. Look at lines 10—30.

    By referring to **at least two** examples, analyse how language is used to convey Captain Stevens' positive **and** negative views about relationships.   4

19. Look at lines 36—57.

    By referring to **at least two** examples, analyse how language is used to convey the different reactions of Miriam **and** the men to the situation.   4

20. By referring to this extract and to at least one other short story, discuss how Mackay Brown conveys the impact on his characters of intense situations **and/or** events.   10

[Turn over

OR

Text 3 — Prose

If you choose this text you may not attempt a question on Prose (Fiction or Non-fiction) in Section 2.

Read the extract below and then attempt the following questions.

The Strange Case of Dr Jekyll and Mr Hyde by Robert Louis Stevenson

In this extract, which is from The Last Night, Utterson is accompanying Poole to Jekyll's.

It was a wild, cold, seasonable night of March, with a pale moon, lying on her back as though the wind had tilted her, and a flying wrack of the most diaphanous and lawny texture. The wind made talking difficult, and flecked the blood into the face. It seemed to have swept the streets unusually bare of passengers, besides; for Mr Utterson thought he
5 had never seen that part of London so deserted. He could have wished it otherwise; never in his life had he been conscious of so sharp a wish to see and touch his fellow-creatures; for struggle as he might, there was borne in upon his mind a crushing anticipation of calamity. The square, when they got there, was all full of wind and dust, and the thin trees in the garden were lashing themselves along the railing. Poole, who had kept all the way a
10 pace or two ahead, now pulled up in the middle of the pavement, and in spite of the biting weather, took off his hat and mopped his brow with a red pocket-handkerchief. But for all the hurry of his coming, these were not the dews of exertion that he wiped away, but the moisture of some strangling anguish; for his face was white and his voice, when he spoke, harsh and broken.

15 'Well, sir,' he said, 'here we are, and God grant there be nothing wrong.'

'Amen, Poole,' said the lawyer.

Thereupon the servant knocked in a very guarded manner; the door was opened on the chain; and a voice asked from within, 'Is that you, Poole?'

'It's all right,' said Poole. 'Open the door.'

20 The hall, when they entered it, was brightly lighted up; the fire was built high; and about the hearth the whole of the servants, men and women, stood huddled together like a flock of sheep. At the sight of Mr Utterson, the housemaid broke into hysterical whimpering; and the cook, crying out 'Bless God! it's Mr Utterson,' ran forward as if to take him in her arms.

'What, what? Are you all here?' said the lawyer peevishly. 'Very irregular, very unseemly;
25 your master would be far from pleased.'

'They're all afraid,' said Poole.

Blank silence followed, no one protesting; only the maid lifted up her voice and now wept loudly.

'Hold your tongue!' Poole said to her, with a ferocity of accent that testified to his own
30 jangled nerves; and indeed, when the girl had so suddenly raised the note of her lamentation, they had all started and turned towards the inner door with faces of dreadful expectation. 'And now,' continued the butler, addressing the knife-boy, 'reach me a candle, and we'll get this through hands at once.' And then he begged Mr Utterson to follow him, and led the way to the back garden.

35 'Now, sir,' said he, 'you come as gently as you can. I want you to hear, and I don't want you to be heard. And see here, sir, if by any chance he was to ask you in, don't go.'

MARKS

Mr Utterson's nerves, at this unlooked-for termination, gave a jerk that nearly threw him from his balance; but he re-collected his courage and followed the butler into the laboratory building and through the surgical theatre, with its lumber of crates and bottles,
40 to the foot of the stair. Here Poole motioned him to stand on one side and listen; while he himself, setting down the candle and making a great and obvious call on his resolution, mounted the steps and knocked with a somewhat uncertain hand on the red baize of the cabinet door.

'Mr Utterson, sir, asking to see you,' he called; and even as he did so, once more violently
45 signed to the lawyer to give ear.

A voice answered from within: 'Tell him I cannot see anyone,' it said complainingly.

'Thank you, sir,' said Poole, with a note of something like triumph in his voice; and taking up his candle, he led Mr Utterson back across the yard and into the great kitchen, where the fire was out and the beetles were leaping on the floor.

50 'Sir,' he said, looking Mr Utterson in the eyes, 'was that my master's voice?'

'It seems much changed,' replied the lawyer, very pale, but giving look for look.

'Changed? Well, yes, I think so,' said the butler. 'Have I been twenty years in this man's house, to be deceived about his voice? No, sir; master's made away with — he was made away with, eight days ago, when we heard him cry out upon the name of God; and *who's* in
55 there instead of him, and *why* it stays there, is a thing that cries to Heaven, Mr Utterson!'

Questions

21. Look at lines 1—14.

     By referring to **at least two** examples, analyse how the writer uses language to create an unsettling atmosphere.   4

22. Look at lines 15—28.

     Analyse how the writer uses language to convey the role of Utterson.   2

23. Look at lines 29—55.

     By referring to **at least two** examples, analyse how language is used to create tension.   4

24. By referring to this extract and to elsewhere in the novel, discuss how Stevenson uses symbolism to develop the central concerns of the text.   10

[Turn over

OR

Text 4 — Prose

If you choose this text you may not attempt a question on Prose (Fiction or Non-fiction) in Section 2.

Read the extract below and then attempt the following questions.

Sunset Song by Lewis Grassic Gibbon

This extract is from Part I (Ploughing).

She'd bidden by Don all her life, mother, she'd been born in Kildrummie, her father a ploughman there, he'd got no more than thirteen shillings a week and he'd had thirteen of a family, to work things out in due ratio, maybe. But mother said they all got on fine, she was never happier in her life than those days when she tramped bare-footed the roads to
5   the little school that nestled under the couthy hills. And at nine she left the school and they packed a basket for her and she bade her mother ta-ta and set out to her first fee, no shoes on her feet even then, she hadn't worn shoes till she was twelve years old. It hadn't been a real fee that first one, she'd done little more than scare the crows from the fields of an old bit farmer and sleep in a garret, but fine she'd liked it, she'd never forget the
10 singing of the winds in those fields when she was young or the daft crying of the lambs she herded or the feel of the earth below her toes. *Oh, Chris, my lass, there are better things than your books or studies or loving or bedding, there's the countryside your own, you its, in the days when you're neither bairn nor woman.*

So mother had worked and ran the parks those days, she was blithe and sweet, you knew,
15 you saw her against the sun as though you peered far down a tunnel of the years. She stayed long on her second fee, seven or eight years she was there till the day she met John Guthrie at a ploughing-match at Pittodrie. And often once she'd tell of that to Chris and Will, it was nothing grand of a match, the horses were poor and the ploughing worse and a coarse, cold wind was soughing across the rigs and half Jean Murdoch made up her mind to
20 go home. Then it was that it came the turn of a brave young childe with a red head and the swackest legs you ever saw, his horses were laced in ribbons, bonny and trig, and as soon as he began the drill you saw he'd carry off the prize. And carry it off he did, young John Guthrie, and not that alone. For as he rode from the park on one horse he patted the back of the other and cried to Jean Murdoch with a glint from his dour, sharp eye *Jump up if you*
25 *like.* And she cried back *I like fine!* and caught the horse by its mane and swung herself there till Guthrie's hand caught her and set her steady on the back of the beast. So out from the ploughing match at Pittodrie the two of them rode together, Jean sitting upon the hair of her, gold it was and so long, and laughing up into the dour, keen face that was Guthrie's.

30 So that was beginning of their lives together, she was sweet and kind to him, but he mightn't touch her, his face would go black with rage at her because of that sweetness that tempted his soul to hell. Yet in two-three years they'd chaved and saved enough for gear and furnishings, and were married at last, and syne Will was born, and syne Chris herself was born, and the Guthries rented a farm in Echt, Cairndhu it was, and sat themselves
35 down there for many a year.

MARKS

Winters or springs, summers or harvests, bristling or sunning the sides of Barmekin, and life ploughed its rigs and drove its teams and the dourness hardened, hard and cold, in the heart of Jean Guthrie's man. But still the glint of her hair could rouse him, Chris would hear him cry in agony at night as he went with her, mother's face grew queer and
40 questioning, her eyes far back on those Springs she might never see again, dear and blithe they had been, she could kiss and hold them still a moment alone with Chris or Will. Dod came, then Alec came, and mother's fine face grew harder then. One night they heard her cry to John Guthrie *Four of a family's fine; there'll be no more*. And father thundered at her, that way he had *Fine? We'll have what God in His mercy may send to us, woman. See you to*
45 *that.*

Questions

25. Look at lines 1—13.

Analyse how the writer's use of language creates a nostalgic mood.   2

26. Look at lines 14—29.

By referring to **at least two** examples, analyse how the writer's use of language conveys the impact of Jean's first encounter with John Guthrie.   4

27. Look at lines 30—45.

By referring to **at least two** examples, analyse how the writer's use of language conveys aspects of the character of John Guthrie.   4

28. By referring to this extract and to elsewhere in the novel, discuss how Grassic Gibbon conveys the influence of **both** Jean and John Guthrie on Chris's life.   10

[Turn over

OR

Text 5 — Prose

If you choose this text you may not attempt a question on Prose (Fiction or Non-fiction) in Section 2.

Read the extract below and then attempt the following questions.

The Cone-Gatherers by Robin Jenkins

In this extract, Lady Runcie-Campbell is in the car with her children and Duror and they have seen the cone-gatherers. Roderick has greeted them from the car window.

Lady Runcie-Campbell burst out laughing; she was still astonished, but she was also fond and proud.

'Well,' she said, 'aren't you the complete democrat? But don't overdo it, please.'

'I wanted to tell them we were sorry,' he said.

5   Her astonishment sharpened into indignation.

'What!' she cried. 'If this is a joke, Roderick, I don't much admire its taste.'

'It's not a joke,' he said. 'We didn't treat them fairly.'

She frowned. Foreboding chilled her. Too weak physically to be able to attend school like other boys of his class, was he also, as his father when tipsy at midnight had once dolefully
10   declared, faulty in mind? He did not see things or people as a baronet's heir should. Certainly his tutor could not be accused of corrupting him: Mr Sorn-Wilson was more aristocratic than any duke. Yet there had been a corrupter: her own father now dead; and perhaps there still was one, herself the Christian.

With a sigh she turned again to Duror.

15   He had been standing respectfully waiting for permission to take his leave.

She found comfort and encouragement in his aloof submissiveness. Surely an order of society in which so honourable a man as Duror knew his subordinate place and kept it without grievance or loss of dignity, must be not only healthy and wise, but also sanctioned by God?

20   'Of course he knows you're coming, Duror,' she said. 'I telephoned him.'

'It was good of you, my lady.'

'I'll consider my goodness recompensed,' she said, smiling, 'when you come back with a good report.'

'I'm sure I'll be able to do that, my lady.'

25   'You'd be a hard man to convince you were ill, Duror. I don't ever remember you being ill.'

'I have never been ill, since I had the measles at ten.'

She laughed. 'Touch wood, Duror, touch wood.' She touched it for him. As she did so, she remembered her husband and brother in Africa, where men were killing one another; and she found herself wishing that the ancient superstition had virtue in it. Christ of course
30   would then be banished forever into the darkness.

She shivered.

'Well, Duror,' she said, 'you know we're going to the pictures. We'll pick you up here as soon as the show's over.'

'Very good, my lady.'

MARKS

35 'You won't keep us waiting?' She dropped her voice. 'I don't want to keep the children up any later than is necessary.'

He knew she was worried about the boy.

'I'll be here waiting for you, my lady,' he said.

An irrelevant thought occurred to her.

40 'How will those two get back?' she asked.

He knew whom she meant. 'They'll walk.'

'Walk? Dear me.' She laughed. 'I wouldn't say they look very good walkers, whatever they're like as climbers of trees. They must be very keen surely to visit Lendrick.'

'Likely they'll find it lonely in the wood, my lady.'

45 'I suppose so.' Admiring Duror for his solicitude, she indulged in a little herself. 'I suppose they're to be pitied really.'

'Why don't we offer them a lift, Mother?' asked Roderick, in the quiet voice she had learned to regard as ominous. 'We've got plenty of room.'

'Don't be absurd,' she said quickly.

50 'I don't think I'm being absurd. They can sit next to me. I don't mind.'

'Well, I do.' It was Sheila who spoke, rescuing her mother from the predicament of having to rebuke Roderick for naivety, and at the same time trying to preserve his charitable attitude towards his inferiors.

Earnestly he argued with his sister.

55 'They wouldn't have to be near you, Sheila,' he said. 'You could sit in beside Mother. They could sit at the back away from everybody.'

'My dear boy,' said his mother, laughing, 'this is no time for playing Sir Galahad.'

'We've carried dogs in the car,' he said.

'Yes, we have. It's our car, dear boy. We can please ourselves whom or what we carry.
60 You're being too quixotic for words.'

He spoke quietly, in a kind of huff. 'Human beings are more important than dogs.'

Questions

29. Look at lines 1—14.

    By referring to **at least two** examples, analyse how the writer's use of language conveys Lady Runcie-Campbell's differing emotions about her son.   4

30. Look at lines 15—46.

    By referring to **at least two** examples, analyse how the writer's use of language conveys Duror's acceptance of the class system.   4

31. Look at lines 47—61.

    Analyse how the writer's use of language creates a positive impression of Roderick.   2

32. By referring to this extract and to elsewhere in the novel, discuss how Jenkins develops the role of Lady Runcie-Campbell throughout the novel.   10

Page seventeen   [Turn over

SECTION 1 — SCOTTISH TEXT — 20 marks

Choose ONE text from Drama, Prose or Poetry.

Read the text extract carefully and then attempt ALL the questions for your chosen text.

You should spend about 45 minutes on this section.

PART C — SCOTTISH TEXT — POETRY

Text 1 — Poetry

If you choose this text you may not attempt a question on Poetry in Section 2.

Read the extract below and then attempt the following questions.

Tam O' Shanter **by Robert Burns**

The extract begins at stanza five of the poem.

     But to our tale: Ae market night,
Tam had got planted unco right,
Fast by an ingle, bleezing finely,
Wi reaming swats, that drank divinely;
5 And at his elbow, Souter Johnie,
His ancient, trusty, drouthy crony;
Tam lo'ed him like a very brither;
They had been fou for weeks thegither.
The night drave on wi' sangs and clatter;
10 And aye the ale was growing better:
The landlady and Tam grew gracious,
Wi' favours secret, sweet and precious:
The Souter tauld his queerest stories;
The landlord's laugh was ready chorus:
15 The storm without might rair and rustle,
Tam did na mind the storm a whistle.

     Care, mad to see a man sae happy,
E'en drown'd himsel amang the nappy.
As bees flee hame wi' lades o' treasure,
20 The minutes wing'd their way wi' pleasure:
Kings may be blest, but Tam was glorious,
O'er a' the ills o' life victorious!

MARKS

But pleasures are like poppies spread:
You seize the flower, its bloom is shed;
25　Or like the snow falls in the river,
A moment white—then melts for ever;
Or like the borealis race,
That flit ere you can point their place;
Or like the rainbow's lovely form
30　Evanishing amid the storm. —
Nae man can tether time nor tide,
The hour approaches Tam maun ride;
That hour, o' night's black arch the keystane,
That dreary hour he mounts his beast in;
35　And sic a night he taks the road in,
As ne'er poor sinner was abroad in.

The wind blew as 'twad blawn its last;
The rattling showers rose on the blast;
The speedy gleams the darkness swallow'd;
40　Loud, deep and lang the thunder bellow'd:
That night, a child might understand,
The Deil had business on his hand.

Weel-mounted on his gray mare, Meg,
A better never lifted leg,
45　Tam skelpit on thro' dub and mire,
Despising wind, and rain, and fire;
Whiles holding fast his guid blue bonnet,
Whiles crooning o'er some auld Scots sonnet,
Whiles glow'ring round wi' prudent cares,
50　Lest bogles catch him unawares;
Kirk-Alloway was drawing nigh,
Whare ghaists and houlets nightly cry.

Questions

33.　Look at lines 1—22.

By referring to **at least two** examples, analyse how the poet's use of language conveys the impression that the inn is a welcoming place.　4

34.　Look at lines 23—42.

By referring to **at least two** examples, analyse how the poet's use of language creates an unsettling atmosphere.　4

35.　Look at lines 43—52.

Analyse how the poet's use of language conveys **two** aspects of Tam's character.　2

36.　By referring to this extract and to at least one other poem, discuss how Burns portrays vulnerable **and/or** flawed characters.　10

OR

Text 2 — Poetry

If you choose this text you may not attempt a question on Poetry in Section 2.

Read the poem below and then attempt the following questions.

In Mrs Tilscher's Class by Carol Ann Duffy

You could travel up the Blue Nile
with your finger, tracing the route
while Mrs Tilscher chanted the scenery.
Tana. Ethiopia. Khartoum. Aswan.
5 That for an hour, then a skittle of milk
and the chalky Pyramids rubbed into dust.
A window opened with a long pole.
The laugh of a bell swung by a running child.

This was better than home. Enthralling books.
10 The classroom glowed like a sweet shop.
Sugar paper. Coloured shapes. Brady and Hindley
faded, like the faint, uneasy smudge of a mistake.
Mrs Tilscher loved you. Some mornings, you found
she'd left a good gold star by your name.
15 The scent of a pencil slowly, carefully, shaved.
A xylophone's nonsense heard from another form.

Over the Easter term, the inky tadpoles changed
from commas into exclamation marks. Three frogs
hopped in the playground, freed by a dunce,
20 followed by a line of kids, jumping and croaking
away from the lunch queue. A rough boy
told you how you were born. You kicked him, but stared
at your parents, appalled, when you got back home.

That feverish July, the air tasted of electricity.
25 A tangible alarm made you always untidy, hot,
fractious under the heavy, sexy sky. You asked her
how you were born and Mrs Tilscher smiled,
then turned away. Reports were handed out.
You ran through the gates, impatient to be grown,
30 as the sky split open into a thunderstorm.

MARKS

Questions

37. Look at lines 1—16.

    By referring to **at least two** examples, analyse how the poet's use of language conveys a sense of excitement **and/or** wonder.   **4**

38. Look at lines 17—21 ('Over . . . lunch queue').

    Analyse how the poet uses language to convey the idea that the children are growing up.   **2**

39. Look at lines 21—30 ('A rough boy . . . thunderstorm').

    By referring to **at least two** examples, analyse how the poet's use of language creates a disturbing mood.   **4**

40. By referring to this poem and to at least one other poem, discuss how Duffy uses contrast to explore central concerns.   **10**

[Turn over

OR

Text 3 — Poetry

If you choose this text you may not attempt a question on Poetry in Section 2.

Read the poem below and then attempt the following questions.

Last Supper **by Liz Lochhead**

She is getting good and ready to renounce
his sweet flesh.
Not just for lent. (For
Ever)
5   But meanwhile she is assembling the ingredients
for their last treat, the proper
feast (after all
didn't they always
eat together
10   rather more than rather well?)
So here she is tearing foliage, scrambling
the salad, maybe lighting candles even, anyway
stepping back to admire the effect of
the table she's made (and oh yes now
15   will have to lie on) the silverware,
the nicely al-
dente vegetables, the cooked goose.
He could be depended on to bring the bottle
plus betrayal with a kiss.

20   Already she was imagining it done with, this feast, and
exactly
what kind of leftover hash she'd make of it
among friends, when it was just
The Girls, when those three met again.
25   What very good soup
she could render from the bones,
then something substantial, something extra
tasty if not elegant.

Yes, there they'd be, cackling around the cauldron,
30   spitting out the gristlier bits
of his giblets;
gnawing on the knucklebone of some
intricate irony;
getting grave and dainty at the
35   petit-gout mouthfuls of reported speech.

MARKS

'That's rich!' they'd splutter,
munching the lies, fat and sizzling as sausages.
Then they'd sink back
gorged on truth
40 and their own savage integrity,
sleek on it all, preening
like corbies, their bright eyes blinking
satisfied
till somebody would get hungry
45 and go hunting again.

Questions

41. Look at lines 1—19.

By referring to **at least two** examples, analyse how the poet's use of language establishes the speaker's bitterness towards her ex-partner.   4

42. Look at lines 20—35.

By referring to **at least two** examples, analyse how the poet's use of language suggests the speaker's excitement at the prospect of revenge.   4

43. Look at lines 36—45.

Analyse how the poet's use of imagery creates a disturbing impression of the speaker and her friends.   2

44. By referring to this poem and to at least one other poem, discuss how Lochhead uses contrast to explore central concerns.   10

[Turn over

Page twenty-three

OR

Text 4 — Poetry

If you choose this text you may not attempt a question on Poetry in Section 2.

Read the poem below and then attempt the following questions.

Assisi by Norman MacCaig

The dwarf with his hands on backwards
sat, slumped like a half-filled sack
on tiny twisted legs from which
sawdust might run,
5   outside the three tiers of churches built
in honour of St Francis, brother
of the poor, talker with birds, over whom
he had the advantage
of not being dead yet.

10   A priest explained
how clever it was of Giotto
to make his frescoes tell stories
that would reveal to the illiterate the goodness
of God and the suffering
15   of His Son. I understood
the explanation and
the cleverness.

A rush of tourists, clucking contentedly,
fluttered after him as he scattered
20   the grain of the Word. It was they who had passed
the ruined temple outside, whose eyes
wept pus, whose back was higher
than his head, whose lopsided mouth
said *Grazie* in a voice as sweet
25   as a child's when she speaks to her mother
or a bird's when it spoke
to St Francis.

MARKS

Questions

45. Look at lines 1—4.

   Analyse how the poet's use of language dehumanises the beggar.   2

46. Look at lines 5—17.

   By referring to **at least two** examples, analyse how the poet's use of language
   conveys the contrast between St Francis and the priest.   4

47. Look at lines 18—27.

   By referring to **at least two** examples, analyse how the poet's use of language creates
   an effective conclusion to the poem.   4

48. By referring to this poem and to at least one other, discuss how MacCaig explores the
   connection between characters and their surroundings.   10

[Turn over

OR

Text 5 — Poetry

If you choose this text you may not attempt a question on Poetry in Section 2.

Read the extract below and then attempt the following questions.

Hallaig by Sorley MacLean

This extract is the first 33 lines of the poem.

'Time, the deer, is in the wood of Hallaig'

The window is nailed and boarded
through which I saw the West
and my love is at the Burn of Hallaig,
5   a birch tree, and she has always been

between Inver and Milk Hollow,
here and there about Baile-chuirn:
she is a birch, a hazel,
a straight, slender young rowan.

10 In Screapadal of my people
where Norman and Big Hector were,
their daughters and their sons are a wood
going up beside the stream.

Proud tonight the pine cocks
15 crowing on the top of Cnoc an Ra,
straight their backs in the moonlight —
they are not the wood I love.

I will wait for the birch wood
until it comes up by the cairn,
20 until the whole ridge from Beinn na Lice
will be under its shade.

If it does not, I will go down to Hallaig,
to the Sabbath of the dead,
where the people are frequenting,
25 every single generation gone.

They are still in Hallaig,
MacLeans and MacLeods,
all who were there in the time of Mac Gille Chaluim:
the dead have been seen alive.

30 The men lying on the green
at the end of every house that was,
the girls a wood of birches,
straight their backs, bent their heads.

MARKS

Questions

49. Look at lines 1—7.

By referring to **at least two** examples, analyse how the poet uses language to create an effective opening.

4

50. Look at lines 8—21.

By referring to **at least two** examples, analyse how the poet uses references to nature in order to convey central concerns.

4

51. Look at lines 22—33.

Analyse how the poet's use of language makes clear the lasting connection of humans to Hallaig.

2

52. By referring to this extract and to at least one other poem, discuss how MacLean develops the theme of humanity's connection to place.

10

[Turn over

MARKS

OR

Text 6 — Poetry

If you choose this text you may not attempt a question on Poetry in Section 2.

Read the poem below and then attempt the following questions.

Waking with Russell **by Don Paterson**

Whatever the difference is, it all began
the day we woke up face-to-face like lovers
and his four-day-old smile dawned on him again,
possessed him, till it would not fall or waver;
5   and I pitched back not my old hard-pressed grin
but his own smile, or one I'd rediscovered.
Dear son, I was *mezzo del cammin*
and the true path was as lost to me as ever
when you cut in front and lit it as you ran.
10 See how the true gift never leaves the giver:
returned and redelivered, it rolled on
until the smile poured through us like a river.
How fine, I thought, this waking amongst men!
I kissed your mouth and pledged myself forever.

Questions

53. Look at lines 1—4.

By referring to **at least two** examples, analyse how language is used to convey the speaker's positive feelings about the birth of his son.

4

54. Look at lines 5—9.

By referring to **at least two** examples, analyse how language is used to convey the significance of the birth in the speaker's life.

4

55. Look at lines 10—14.

Analyse how the poet uses language to create an effective conclusion.

2

56. By referring to this poem and to at least one other poem by Paterson, discuss how imagery is used to explore central concerns.

10

[END OF SECTION 1]

SECTION 2 — CRITICAL ESSAY — 20 marks

Attempt ONE question from the following genres — Drama, Prose Fiction, Prose Non-fiction, Poetry, Film and Television Drama, or Language.

Your answer must be on a different genre from that chosen in Section 1.

You should spend approximately 45 minutes on this section.

PART A — DRAMA

*Answers to questions on **drama** should refer to the text and to such relevant features as characterisation, key scene(s), structure, climax, theme, plot, conflict, setting . . .*

1. Choose a play in which a major character experiences different emotions throughout the play.

   By referring to appropriate techniques, explain how the dramatist makes you aware of these different emotions and discuss how this contributes to your appreciation of the play as a whole.

2. Choose a play in which there is a scene involving a significant discovery **or** deception **or** revelation.

   By referring to appropriate techniques, explain how the discovery **or** deception **or** revelation is presented and discuss how its impact contributes to your appreciation of the play as a whole.

3. Choose a play which portrays conflict within an individual **or** family **or** community.

   By referring to appropriate techniques, explain the nature of this conflict and discuss how it contributes to your appreciation of the play as a whole.

[Turn over

PART B — PROSE FICTION

*Answers to questions on **prose fiction** should refer to the text and to such relevant features as characterisation, setting, language, key incident(s), climax, turning point, plot, structure, narrative technique, theme, ideas, description . . .*

4. Choose a novel **or** short story in which there is a character who could be considered responsible for their own suffering **and/or** fate.

   By referring to appropriate techniques, explain the extent of the responsibility and discuss how this contributes to your appreciation of the text as a whole.

5. Choose a novel **or** short story which conveys a particularly pessimistic **or** inspiring message.

   By referring to appropriate techniques, explain the nature of the message and discuss how this contributes to your appreciation of the text as a whole.

6. Choose a novel **or** short story in which an incident is significant in relation to the central concerns of the text.

   By referring to appropriate techniques, explain why the incident is significant and discuss how it adds to your appreciation of the text as a whole.

PART C — PROSE NON-FICTION

*Answers to questions on **prose non-fiction** should refer to the text and to such relevant features as ideas, use of evidence, stance, style, selection of material, narrative voice . . .*

7. Choose a non-fiction text which presents a distinctive account of a place **or** an event **or** a person.

   By referring to appropriate techniques, discuss how the account effectively creates a sense of the place **or** the event **or** the person.

8. Choose a non-fiction text which provokes a strong reaction in the reader.

   By referring to appropriate techniques, discuss how the writer creates this reaction.

9. Choose a non-fiction text in which the writer challenges beliefs **or** assumptions **or** opinions.

   By referring to appropriate techniques, discuss how the writer presents this challenge.

PART D — POETRY

*Answers to questions on **poetry** should refer to the text and to such relevant features as word choice, tone, imagery, structure, content, rhythm, rhyme, theme, sounds, ideas . . .*

10. Choose a poem which makes effective use of a specific place **or** character **or** moment in time.

    With reference to appropriate techniques, discuss how the poet's presentation of the place **or** character **or** moment in time contributes to your appreciation of the poem as a whole.

11. Choose a poem which deals with conflict **or** change.

    With reference to appropriate techniques, discuss how the poet's presentation of the conflict **or** change contributes to your appreciation of the poem as a whole.

12. Choose a poem which is effective because of its use of contrast **and/or** imagery.

    With reference to appropriate techniques, discuss how the poet's use of these features contributes to your appreciation of the central concern(s) of the poem.

PART E — FILM AND TELEVISION DRAMA

*Answers to questions on **film and television drama*** should refer to the text and to such relevant features as use of camera, key sequence, characterisation, mise-en-scène, editing, music/sound, special effects, plot, dialogue . . .*

13. Choose a film **or** television drama in which a main character either conforms to **or** challenges a stereotype.

    With reference to appropriate techniques, explain how the film or programme makers create this character, and discuss how this adds to your appreciation of the film or television drama as a whole.

14. Choose a film **or** television drama whose soundtrack contrasts with **or** fits the scene(s) it accompanies.

    With reference to appropriate techniques, explain how the film or programme makers' use of the soundtrack contributes to your appreciation of the film or television drama as a whole.

15. Choose a film **or** television drama in which a particular scene or sequence contains tension **or** fear **or** surprise.

    With reference to appropriate techniques, explain how the film or programme makers create this effect, and discuss how this adds to your appreciation of the film or television drama as a whole.

* 'television drama' includes a single play, a series or a serial.

PART F — LANGUAGE

*Answers to questions on **language** should refer to the text and to such relevant features as register, accent, dialect, slang, jargon, vocabulary, tone, abbreviation . . .*

16. Choose the language of a particular geographical area **or** social group.

    Identify specific examples of language use and discuss their effectiveness as a means of communication.

17. Choose the language associated with music **or** sport **or** religion **or** politics.

    Identify the key features of this language and discuss its effectiveness in communicating its ideas.

18. Choose aspects of language associated with promoting a particular product **or** opinion.

    Identify specific examples and discuss to what extent the language is effective.

[END OF SECTION 2]

[END OF QUESTION PAPER]

HIGHER

Answers

HIGHER ENGLISH
2017

PAPER 1 — READING FOR UNDERSTANDING, ANALYSIS AND EVALUATION

Marking Instructions for each question

Passage 1

Question		Expected Response	Max Mark	Additional Guidance
1.	(a)	Read lines 1—12. Analyse how the writer's word choice in lines 1—3 emphasises the "conventional wisdom" that reading books is better than playing video games. 2 marks may be awarded for reference plus detailed/insightful comment; 1 mark for reference plus more basic comment; 0 marks for reference alone. Possible answers are shown in the "Additional Guidance" column. (Marks may be awarded 2 or 1 + 1)	2	Possible answers include: • "enriches" suggests that reading adds to one's knowledge, awareness; is rewarding, beneficial; improves one • "the mind" suggests reading is influencing something greater than just the brain; it influences our consciousness: thought, perception, emotions and imagination • "deadens" suggests video games make kids less aware, less sensitive, less vigorous; they make kids think less; lifeless • "zoning out" suggests video games make kids detached from people and things around them, unresponsive, unstimulated
	(b)	Explain in your own words "the question" the writer asks in line 6 about "other forms of culture". Candidates must attempt to use their own words. No marks for straight lifts from the passage. 2 marks may be awarded for detailed/insightful comment plus quotation/reference; 1 mark for basic comment plus quotation/reference; 0 marks for quotation/reference alone.	2	Possible answers include: • The writer is asking if these other forms of culture involve discrete thinking skills/have qualities which benefit, stimulate, challenge, stretch our minds in ways which are different from — but just as important as — reading
	(c)	By referring to at least two features of language in lines 8—12 ("Where ... books"), analyse how the writer emphasises the contrast between his positive view of "other forms of culture" and the negative view held by "most critics". 2 marks may be awarded for reference plus detailed/insightful comment; 1 mark for reference plus more basic comment; 0 marks for reference alone. Possible answers are shown in the "Additional Guidance" column. (Marks may be awarded 2 + 2, 2 + 1 + 1, 1 + 1 + 1 + 1)	4	Possible answers include: *Imagery* • "(progressive) story": just as a "story" is a developing, organised narrative, so the writer sees the positive influence of popular culture as gradual, logical, coherent, interesting ... • "our brains sharper": just as sharpening involves giving cutting tools a better edge, this suggests making our brains keener, more accurate ... • "we soak in": soaking in is a process of absorption, of taking in as much liquid as possible; this suggests we become immersed in popular culture, that its influence is natural, irresistible, all-consuming, profound, deep ... • "(lowbrow) fluff": fluff is light, downy material (for example, small pieces of wool); its use suggests critics believe popular culture is light, trivial, worthless, superficial, irrelevant, trifling ... • "honing": just as honing is a (refined) process of giving cutting tools a perfect edge, this suggests gradually making our brains as sharp as possible, more and more precise, accurate, productive ... *Word choice* • "allege" suggest doubt, calls the critics' views into question • "dumbing down" suggests popular culture offers people a reduced intellectual challenge **or** is responsible for making people less educated, less intelligent, more lowbrow

Question		Expected Response	Max Mark	Additional Guidance
1.	(c)	*(continued)*		• "progressive" suggests developing, advancing, moving forward steadily, leading to improvement • "steadily" suggests reliable, consistent progress • "imperceptibly" suggests change is gradual, subtle • "sharper" suggests keener, more precise, more accurate • "soak in" suggests it's not a superficial process; influence is deep; we are fully engaged, absorbed • "dismissed" suggests brushed aside, considered beneath contempt, irrelevant, unimportant, trivial • "lowbrow" suggests vulgar, anti-intellectual, uncultured, plebeian • "fluff" suggests worthless, trivial, inconsequential, superficial • "honing" suggests sharpening, perfecting, refining *Sentence structure* • Balanced structure/contrast of "Where … story" allows the writer to trump the critics' argument; this is heightened by the greater certainty of his "see" set against the dubious nature of what they "allege" • Use of colon to introduce a full development of his "progressive story" argument • Use of parenthesis "but … imperceptibly" to explain that this positive development is so gradual that it's easy for the less astute (like the critics) to miss it • Positioning of "I hope to persuade you" at the start of the final sentence alerts the reader to the fact that the writer is about to make what he believes is his most important point • Positioning of "increasingly" just before his key statement stresses that the point he is about to make is more and more relevant, true • Balanced nature of final statement, hinging on the "just as important as" comparison stresses skills developed by popular culture are of a comparable standard to the skills developed by reading
2.		By referring to lines 13–19, analyse how the writer uses both sentence structure and imagery to convey the difficulty of playing video games. For full marks there must be reference to both features. 2 marks may be awarded for reference plus detailed/insightful comment; 1 mark for reference plus more basic comment; 0 marks for mere identification of a feature of sentence structure. Possible answers are shown in the "Additional Guidance" column. (Marks may be awarded 2 + 2, 2 + 1 + 1, 1 + 1 + 1 + 1)	4	Possible answers include: *Sentence structure* • The positioning of **and/or** rhythmic/repetitive nature of "And the first and last thing" conveys the definitive 'Alpha and omega' nature of this phrase, especially when placed at the start of the sentence, suggests the difficulty of video games is a fundamental point to the writer • Use of parenthesis "the thing … hear" adds to the mystery, adds to the dramatic build-up to the final announcement of video games' difficulty • Additional phrase "sometimes maddeningly" has two functions: again adds to the build-up **and/or** ramps up the notion of extreme difficulty that "fiendishly" has introduced

Question		Expected Response	Max Mark	Additional Guidance
2.		*(continued)*		• Use of climax in the sentence "The dirty ... fun." — the somewhat awkward/unusual construction of this sentence is designed to stress the "not having fun" element of its conclusion • Repetition of the "you may be" structure stresses — and this is heightened by the use of the inclusive direct address — the variety of problems playing video games may cause • Repetition of adjectives ("frustrated", "confused", "disorientated", "stuck") — rat-a-tat run of adjectives suggests 'the sea of troubles' playing video games may involve • Anticlimax of "you may be stuck" in its definitive downbeat simplicity, it is a stark summation of the seemingly insoluble challenge these games present • Use of the continuous tense in final sentence — an argument might be made that this reflects the ongoing, nagging nature of the problems involved *Imagery* • "wrestling": just as wrestling involves close, physical combat with a single opponent, so it suggests a demanding, exhausting battle with an unforgiving enemy • "worrying a loose tooth": just as this involves the constant working away at a persistent physical annoyance, so it suggests that the difficulties presented by video games are nagging frustrations that constantly prey on one's mind • "stuck": just as to be stuck is to be fixed immovably, so it suggests being trapped in a situation which offers no escape • "dirty little secret": usually used in the realms of ethics or morality, a deliberate attempt to hide the truth, a cover-up of some sort, a hidden scandal; used in relation to the difficulty of video games, it heightens the potentially damaging nature of this feature, suggests it is a very negative feature that is deliberately glossed over
3.		Read lines 20–33. Identify three reasons why "reward" is so important to the learning process involved in playing video games. Use your own words as far as possible. Candidates must attempt to use their own words. No marks for straight lifts from the passage. (Marks awarded 1 + 1 + 1)	3	Possible answers include: • People are hard-wired to respond strongly to rewards • People find rewards a great stimulus to action, learning etc. • Video games are designed to be full of rewards • Rewards in video games are precise, with clear outcomes (explanation of "clearly defined") • The rewards are attractive • The rewards are presented in a variety of forms • Players are constantly reminded about the rewards • The rewards are vitally important to achieving success in the games • The rewards are more intense, striking, colourful than in real life • Players aren't always aware that they are learning (explanation of "without realising ...")

Question		Expected Response	Max Mark	Additional Guidance
4.		Read lines 34–47. Identify two criticisms and two defences the writer makes of video games. Candidates must attempt to use their own words. No marks for straight lifts from the passage. (Marks awarded 1 + 1 + 1 + 1) NB Maximum 2 marks awarded for criticism and 2 marks awarded for defence.	4	Possible answers include: *Criticisms* • The games may seem attractive but the attractions flatter to deceive, are rather superficial, blind one to the truth (explanation of "dazzled") • The games are addictive (explanation of "hooked") • The subject matter is infantile, petty, puerile, trivial … (explanation of "actual content … childish") • Unnecessarily threatening, unjustifiably scary (explanation of "gratuitously menacing" − but explanation of "menacing" alone: 0) • The subject matter is very limited **and/or** moves between the two extremes of violence and childish fantasy (explanation of "alternates … princess-rescuing") • The games are violent (explanation of "drive-by shooting") • The games are pure fantasy (explanation of "princess-rescuing") *Defences* • The activities involved are beneficial for mental training/development ("good for the brain") • The skills developed will be of use in other spheres ("come in handy elsewhere") • It resembles learning algebra, which might seem pointless and abstract but exercises the brain • Like chess, games might seem very basic (and aggressive in concept), but they are every bit as cerebral and mind-developing as chess; they develop strategic, tactical thinking
5.	(a)	Read lines 48–54. Explain in your own words the key distinction the writer makes between reading a novel and playing a video game. Candidates must attempt to use their own words. No marks for straight lifts from the passage. (Marks awarded 1 + 1)	2	Possible answers include: *reading a novel* • Can get us thinking in a creative way, transport us to in different situation (explanation of "activate our imagination") • Can affect our feelings, arouse passions (explanation of "conjure up powerful emotions") *playing a game* • Makes you explore, study carefully (explanation of "analyse") • Makes you weigh up options (explanation of "choose") • Makes you evaluate options (explanation of "priotitise") • Makes you reach a conclusion (explanation of "decide")

Question		Expected Response	Max Mark	Additional Guidance
5.	(b)	Analyse how the writer's use of language in lines 50—54 ("From ... strategies") conveys the contrast between what a gamer looks like from "the outside" and what is happening "inside the gamer's mind". For full marks there must be reference to both "outside" and "inside". 2 marks may be awarded for reference plus detailed/insightful comment; 1 mark for reference plus more basic comment; 0 marks for reference alone. Possible answers are shown in the "Additional Guidance" column. (Marks may be awarded 2 + 2, 2 + 1 + 1, 1 + 1 + 1 + 1)	4	Possible answers include: *the gamer from "the outside"* • "looks like" suggests this may be an unreliable perspective, a superficial, unquestioning way to approach an analysis of gamers • "fury" suggests the gamer is behaving in an impulsive, uncontrolled way; everything is being done at top speed, in a blur of unthinking activity • "clicking" suggests mindless, repetitive activity • "shooting" suggests destructive, homicidal activity • "clicking and shooting" automatic, unthinking, mechanical, robotic, repetitive ... • The general simplicity of the penultimate sentence (especially when compared to the much more complex final sentence) heightens the impression that this is a naïve, simplistic way to view gamers *the gamer on the inside* • "peer" suggests an active approach involving close examination • "turns out" suggests a sense of some kind of revelation, surprise, discovery • "another creature" suggests something mysterious, surprising, unexpected, interesting but hard to define, a new form of life we didn't know existed • Use of colon introduces a detailed description of the full range of intellectual activities involved in gaming • Balance/repetition of "some of them" stresses range of activities involved • Contrast in "snap judgements ... long-term strategies" shows range of important decision-making skills involved from quick, smart thinking to overall planning • "judgements" suggests wise, fair thinking • "strategies" suggests considered, creative thinking

Passage 2

Question	Expected Response	Max Mark	Additional Guidance
6.	Look at both passages. The writers disagree about video games. Identify three key areas on which they disagree. You should support the points by referring to important ideas in both passages. You may answer this question in continuous prose or in a series of developed bullet points. Candidates can use bullet points in this final question, or write a number of linked statements. Approach to marking is shown in the "Additional Guidance column. Key areas of disagreement are shown in the grid below. Other answers are possible.	5	The following guidelines should be used: 5 marks — identification of three key areas of agreement with detailed/insightful use of supporting evidence 4 marks — identification of three key areas of agreement with appropriate use of supporting evidence 3 marks — identification of three areas of agreement 2 marks — identification of two key areas of agreement 1 mark — identification of one key area of agreement 0 marks — failure to identify any key areas of agreement and/or misunderstanding of the task NB A candidate who identifies only two key areas of agreement may be awarded up to a maximum of 4 marks, as follows • 2 marks for identification of two key areas of agreement plus **either** • a further mark for appropriate use of supporting evidence to a total of 3 marks **or** • a further 2 marks for detailed/insightful use of supporting evidence to a total of 4 marks A candidate who identifies only one key area of agreement may be awarded up to a maximum of 2 marks, as follows: • 1 mark for identification of one key area of agreement • a further mark for use of supporting evidence to a total of 2 marks

	Area of Disagreement	Steven Johnson	Boris Johnson
1.	General status	They are viewed as pointless, but they are not	They are harmful, narcotically addictive
2.	Intellectual benefits	They develop the brain in a number of ways	They require no thought or effort
3.	Educational benefits	High level thinking skills are developed	They may pretend to be educational but are totally lacking in educational value; a threat to literacy
4.	The challenge involved	They can appear simple but are often very complex The process is more important than the (often simplistic) content	They encourage slovenly behaviour and thinking
5.	The reward(s) involved	They are at times extremely hard unlike other entertainment, pleasure is not immediate	They offer immediate and simple pleasures

PAPER 2 – CRITICAL READING

SECTION 1 – Scottish Text

- Candidates should gain credit for their understanding, analysis and evaluation of the extract and either the whole play or novel, or other poems and short stories by the writer.
- In the final 10-mark question the candidate should answer the question in either a series of linked statements, or in bullet points.

Detailed Marking Instructions for each question

PART A – SCOTTISH TEXT – DRAMA

Text 1 – Drama – *The Slab Boys* by John Byrne

Question	Expected Answer(s)	Max Mark	Additional Guidance
1.	2 marks awarded for detailed/ insightful comment plus quotation/reference; 1 mark for more basic comment plus quotation/reference; 0 marks for quotation/ reference alone. Possible answers are shown in the "Additional Guidance" column. (Marks may be awarded 2 + 1, 1 + 1 + 1)	3	Possible answers include: • Spanky's hesitation in e.g. "We'd like to present this little ... er ...this token of ... er ..." suggests sympathy for loss of his job and awkwardness about being sincere now, due to their previously mocking behaviour towards him • "Are you going to shut your face ... Shorty?" offhand and insulting vocabulary suggest the familiar exasperation expressed towards Hector, despite current sympathy for him • Spanky's skirting around the subject/use of euphemism to describe losing his job, "We know it's come as a bit of a surprise ... you having to leave" suggests attempt to be tactful and not embarrass or hurt Hector • Phil's unsuccessful attempt to be more articulate than Spanky – "What Spanky ... och, here" suggests he, too, feels uncomfortable in the unusual role of kindness towards Hector
2.	2 marks awarded for detailed/ insightful comment plus quotation/reference; 1 mark for more basic comment plus quotation/reference; 0 marks for quotation/ reference alone. Possible answers are shown in the "Additional Guidance" column. (Marks may be awarded 2 + 2, 2 + 1 + 1, 1 + 1 + 1 + 1)	4	Possible answers include: • Hector's comical repetition of "Eh?" emphasises his lack of understanding as Phil and Spanky try to commiserate with him for the (supposed) loss of his job • Repetition of "Till you get another job" by Phil and Spanky, culminating in climax of their saying it together builds up sense of their frustration that he does not seem to understand what they are commiserating with him about • Hector's statement of "I've already got another job" is a bathetic moment, echoing their repeated statements about his needing another job • Phil's question "Is there a mobile Broo outside?" emphasises the absurdity of the idea that he might have another job already • Spanky and Phil's exclamation in unison, "What????" is a comical climax which conveys their incredulity that he has been promoted • Hector's comment that he feels unwell is echoed by Spanky, "Me too", with the contrasting meaning: Spanky is sickened that Hector should be promoted; Hector feels sick with excitement

Question	Expected Answer(s)	Max Mark	Additional Guidance
3.	2 marks awarded for detailed/ insightful comment plus quotation/reference; 1 mark for more basic comment plus quotation/reference; 0 marks for quotation/ reference alone. Possible answers are shown in the "Additional Guidance" column. (Marks may be awarded 2 + 1, 1 + 1 + 1)	3	Possible answers include: • Repetition of questions: "... guess what? ... how about that?" suggests his excitement about starting work and/or insensitivity to the fact that he is given this chance because of Phil losing his job • "Where are the gum crystals kept again?" matter of fact question suggests that he is getting started right away, with no regard for the trauma being suffered by Phil • "Oh ... message on ..." broken sentences said while looking for gum crystals suggests his offhand attitude to the message which is so important to Phil/his selfish interest in small concerns of his own rather than vital issues of others • Blunt statement of "You didn't get in" suggests his indifference to the blow this message will cause for Phil/an element of enjoyment of Phil's devastation • "... something like that ..." lack of specific detail conveys how unimportant this information is to him/dismissive approach to something so important to another person
4.	Candidates may choose to answer in bullet points in this final question, or write a number of linked statements. Possible answers are shown in the "Additional Guidance" column.	10	Up to 2 marks can be achieved for identifying elements of commonality as identified in the question, i.e. theme of opportunity. A further 2 marks can be achieved for reference to the extract given. 6 additional marks can be awarded for discussion of similar references to at least one other part of the text. <u>In practice this means:</u> Identification of commonality (2) e.g. Opportunity is not equally or fairly available: it depends on factors such as social class, education, family connections (1) Lack of real opportunity leads to feelings of cynicism and disillusion, exemplified by the attitudes of Phil and Spanky (1) From the extract: 2 marks for detailed/insightful comment plus quotation/reference; 1 mark for more basic comment plus quotation/reference; 0 marks for quotation alone. e.g. Phil, though talented, is rejected by the art college, therefore not given the opportunity to develop his talent: there is a sense that this background, from 'Feegie', and lack of formal education is held against him (2) From at least one other part of the text: as above for up to 6 marks Possible answers include: • Phil and Spanky resent the lack of opportunities open to them since joining the slab room, claiming that they would be rewarded more if they were masons • Frustration of the slab boys at being stuck in the slab room, with no desk in sight, is clear e.g. Spanky who has been in the slab room for three years and, at the end, is told he might get a desk in eighteen months • Alan, with his education, social class and family commitments has expectations of greater opportunity e.g. he is not over-impressed with his salary of £3 (which is a lot of money to the slab boys) • Opportunities in love also come to those with more money etc., shown by Lucille agreeing to go to the Staffie with Alan, as long as he picks her up in his father's car • Jack accuses Phil and Spanky of destroying Hector's opportunities by mocking him for his eagerness to learn : he wants to give Hector a chance as a designer

Text 2 — Drama — *The Cheviot, the Stag and the Black, Black Oil* by John McGrath

Question	Expected Answer(s)	Max Mark	Additional Guidance
5.	For full marks candidates should deal with both characters but not necessarily in equal measure. 2 marks awarded for detailed/insightful comment plus quotation/reference; 1 mark for more basis comment plus quotation/reference; 0 marks for quotation/reference alone. Possible answers are shown in the "Additional Guidance" column. (Marks may be awarded 2 + 2, 2 + 1 + 1, 1 + 1 + 1 + 1)	4	Possible answers include: Lady Phosphate • Reference to Queen implies personal friendship, suggesting over-inflated sense of her own importance • Repetition of "what?" affectation suggests social posturing/shallowness of character • Over-blown and clichéd language — "divine", "rugged beauty", "abound" — suggests lack of sincerity/pretentiousness • Use of literary quotation "Oh listen ... sound" to convey supposed intellectual superiority/lack of authenticity Lord Crask • "Has your ladyship sampled the salmon?" shows eagerness to ingratiate/impress • Unnecessary use of full title to stress status/joint membership of upper classes suggests his pride and arrogance • "120,000 acres ... most of it" — comical juxtaposition of large figure with comment on true extent of land suggests boastfulness
6.	2 marks awarded for detailed/insightful comment plus quotation/reference; 1 mark for more basic comment plus quotation/reference; 0 marks for quotation/reference alone. Possible answers are shown in the "Additional Guidance" column. (Marks may be awarded 2 + 2, 2 + 1 + 1, 1 + 1 + 1 + 1)	4	Possible answers include: • Lord Crask's misunderstanding of "capital" suggests the upper class's obsession with wealth and power • Comic exchange of "Wapping ... Topping ... No Wapping" mocks the upper class's/highlights their ridiculous nature • Lord Crask offers Lochinver when Lady Phosphate asks for "a small port", demonstrating his limited understanding/lack of thought for the local population • Lord Crask offers a bush as toilet facilities suggesting that the sophistication of the upper classes is just a veneer/they are no different from anyone else • Reference to Lady Phosphate's "sten gun" — inappropriately over the top for grouse shooting — suggests her lack of regard for the natural environment • Ironic understatement "Thon was a nice wee boy" suggests complete disregard for human life
7.	1 mark for comment plus quotation/reference (x2); 0 marks for quotation/reference alone. Possible answers are shown in the "Additional Guidance" column. (Marks may be awarded 1 + 1)	2	Possible answers include: Local people • Repetition of "We'll clear" suggests their determination to let nothing stand in their way/not to be stopped or criticised • Derogatory use of plural — "the locals" — suggests dismissive/superior attitude to the community Environment • Juxtaposition of "ni-i-ice" with killing of various creatures suggest selfish lack of concern for environment • Pronunciation of "grice" and "trite" suggests unwillingness to learn about the environment

Question	Expected Answer(s)	Max Mark	Additional Guidance
8.	Candidates may choose to answer in bullet points in this final question, or write a number of linked statements. Possible answers are shown in the "Additional Guidance" column.	10	Up to 2 marks can be achieved for identifying elements of commonality as identified in the question, i.e. how the writer explores the issue of social class and its effects. A further 2 marks can be achieved for reference to the extract given. 6 additional marks can be awarded for discussion of similar references to at least one other part of the text. <u>In practice this means:</u> Identification of commonality (2) e.g. land-owning classes in the Scottish Highlands exhibit selfish and exploitative behaviour (1) leading to suffering and destitution of the poor (1) From the extract: 2 marks for detailed/insightful comment plus quotation/reference; 1 mark for more basic comment plus quotation/reference; 0 marks for quotation/reference alone. e.g. the callous killing of the little boy reveals the contemptuous attitude of the upper classes to the local population (2) From at least one other part of the text: as above for up to 6 marks Possible answers include: • Sellar evicts lower classes from their homes and destroys their livelihood, callously referring to them as "a set of savages" • International developers are encouraged as long as they adhere to the laws of capitalism, where the end justifies the means, despite the suffering of the poor in the name of 'progress' • Lord Selkirk, a member of the aristocracy, has a plan to exploit, develop and maximise profits with no regard for the consequences to the local people • Collective solidarity by the dispossessed against the upper classes has met with varying success, particularly at "The Battle of the Braes", emphasising that ultimately they are powerless • Many of the indigent characters are known only by their employment or gender — Ghillie, Aberdonian Rigger, First woman — contrasting with the use of titles and individual names of the upper class characters, showing the anonymity of and disregard for the poor

Text 3 — Drama — *Men Should Weep* by Ena Lamont Stewart

Question	Expected Answer(s)	Max Mark	Additional Guidance
9.	For full marks, both stage directions and dialogue should be covered but not necessarily in equal measure. 2 marks awarded for detailed/insightful comment plus quotation/reference; 1 mark for a more basic comment plus quotation/reference; 0 marks for quotation/reference alone. Possible answers are shown in the "Additional Guidance" column. (Marks may be awarded 2 + 2, 2 + 1 + 1, 1 + 1 + 1 + 1)	4	Possible answers include: Stage directions • "a hard-faced harridan" suggests Lizzie is a mean, cold, aggressive woman • "ignoring the others" suggests Lizzie has no time for social niceties or being pleasant to people • "Mrs Bone goes to help her" suggests Lizzie is quite happy for Granny to struggle on her own whereas Mrs Bone sees the need to lend a hand • "taking the pension book from Mrs Bone" suggests Lizzie's aggressive, greedy personality • "They both stare hard at Lizzie, then shake their heads at each other" suggests their general disbelief/incredulity at Lizzie's attitude towards life Dialogue • "An yer pension book?"/"See's a look at it."/"Ye got the money?" suggests Lizzie's mercenary outlook on life • "Well, it's no Maggie's, it's mines" suggests Lizzie's utterly selfish attitude • "If ye're comin tae bide wi me, ye're no comin tae bide *aff* me" suggests Lizzie's greed and/or her determination not to be taken advantage of • "And whit does she think you're gonna live on for the next week? Air?" aggressive questioning reveals her hard-hearted outlook • "Ach, leave ... tae feed." Mrs Harris' speech underlines how lacking in compassion or humanity Lizzie is • "I'm no takin ... no room in ma hoose" — suggests Lizzie's cold hearted, uncompromising nature • "That's jist whit I said: *anything human*" emphasises that Mrs Bone feels Lizzie is so lacking in compassion and pity that she is scarcely human
10.	2 marks awarded for detailed/insightful comment plus quotation/reference; 1 mark for a more basic comment plus quotation/reference; 0 marks for quotation/reference alone. Possible answers are shown in the "Additional Guidance" column. (Marks may be awarded 2 + 2, 2 + 1 + 1, 1 + 1 + 1 + 1)	4	Possible answers include: • "ye aul miser"/"at fifty percent" suggests outrage at Lizzie's obsession with making money • "A bargain? Frae you?" suggests incredulity that Lizzie could act in a generous manner • "Veloory hat ... bird on tap" mockery suggests their contempt for Lizzie's pretensions • "A bit whit? Pinchin?" suggests recognition of Lizzie's true nature • "No roon aboot here ye couldnae. They a ken ye." conveys a contemptuous awareness of Lizzie's reputation
11.	2 marks awarded for a detailed/insightful explanation; 1 mark for a more basic explanation; 0 marks for quotation/reference alone. Possible answers are shown in the "Additional Guidance" column. (Marks may be awarded 2, 1 + 1)	2	Possible answers include: • Granny represents the older generation who are dependent on others • Granny's situation highlights the poverty which often accompanied old age at that time • As a woman, she has no status or independence in the society of the time • She represents the vulnerable in a harsh world as she moves from household to household • Her lack of autonomy highlights the devastating effects of poverty • She represents the difficulty of family responsibility e.g. there is no room for her when Isa and Alec are made homeless

Question	Expected Answer(s)	Max Mark	Additional Guidance
12.	Candidates may choose to answer in bullet points in this final question, or write a number of linked statements. Possible answers are shown in the "Additional Guidance" column.	10	Up to 2 marks can be achieved by identifying elements of commonality as identified in the question, i.e. how the writer develops the theme of community. A further 2 marks can be achieved for reference to the extract given. 6 additional marks can be awarded for discussion of similar references to at least one other part of the text. <u>In practice this means:</u> Identification of commonality (2) e.g. community is important in this society because of the support and compassion people offer each other (1) although they can also be judgmental, opinionated, intrusive (1) From the extract: 2 marks for detailed/insightful comment plus quotation/reference; 1 mark for more basic comment plus quotation/reference; 0 marks for quotation/reference alone. e.g. Mrs Bone and Mrs Harris support Maggie by sitting with Granny while she is waiting to be collected/by defending Maggie from attack by Lizzie and are not afraid to openly pass judgement on Lizzie's behaviour and morals (2) From elsewhere in the text: as above for up to 6 marks Possible answers include: • Maggie's neighbours often help her with Granny, with baby-sitting and the support neighbours offer each other is an integral part of how this impoverished society operates. Maggie says, "Folks like us hev tae depend on their neighbours when they're needin help." • Maggie's neighbours are mostly compassionate and kind: they really worry about Bertie's serious illness; they keep up Granny's spirits; they take pleasure in Maggie's improved fortunes in the final act. As Maggie says, "Oh, they're no bad — they're coorse but kind." • Women play a central role in this community and there is a sense that they share lives which men do not understand or in which men contribute to women's problems • Members of the community are quite open in passing judgements and voicing criticisms of their husbands, of the younger generation, even of Maggie's new hat: "Whit the hell made ye tak *red*?" • Maggie and John worry about community opinions, whereas the younger generation, such as Jenny and Isa, are happy to flout the traditional values that their neighbours largely represent. Jenny says to her father, "Whit do I care whit the neighbours thinks?"

PART B — SCOTTISH TEXT — PROSE

Text 1 — Prose — *The Red Door* by Iain Crichton Smith

Question	Expected Answer(s)	Max Mark	Additional Guidance
13.	For full marks, candidates must deal with both the door and the surroundings, but not necessarily in equal measure. 2 marks awarded for detailed/insightful comment plus quotation/reference; 1 mark for more basic comment plus quotation/reference; 0 marks for quotation/reference alone. Possible answers are shown in the "Additional Guidance" column. (Marks may be awarded 2 + 2, 2 + 1 + 1, 1 + 1 + 1 + 1)	4	Possible answers include: Door • "painted very lovingly" suggests care had been taken to ensure the door looked beautiful and was not just functional • "shone with a deep inward shine" suggests that the door stood out against its backdrop/had an alluring quality which radiated from within • "looked like a picture/work of art" suggests the door was attractive and now had an importance of its own • "stood out" suggests the door was striking/out of the ordinary Surroundings • "wasn't at all modern/old" suggests the house was dated/behind the times • "intertwined ... rusty pipes like snakes" conveys the idea that the house was in need of maintenance/had been neglected • Imagery "intertwined/snake" suggests the house was constricting/restraining its occupant • "drab landscape" implies that it was uninspiring/dull/gloomy set against the brightness of the door • Dismissal of more harmonious colours "blue/green" highlights the surroundings were now tedious/uninspiring to Murdo
14.	2 marks awarded for detailed/insightful comment plus quotation/reference; 1 mark for more basic comment plus quotation/reference; 0 marks for quotation/reference alone. Possible answers are shown in the "Additional Guidance" column. (Marks may be awarded 2 + 2, 2 + 1 + 1, 1 + 1 + 1 + 1)	4	Possible answers include: • "morning was breaking/blue smoke was ascending" symbolises that the new day for the villagers was a new beginning for Murdo • "a cock was crowing" biblical allusion to signal Murdo's 'betrayal' of his current way of life • "belligerent and heraldic ... metallic breast" military connotations suggest that a new assertive/combative spirit had been awakened in Murdo • "oriental and strange" suggests that this feeling was foreign and unfamiliar to him • Murdo's inner dialogue "I have always/I go/I do ..." conveys his admission of his disillusionment with his life up to this point • "never had the courage ... coloured waistcoat/jacket" reveals Murdo's realisation of his long held desire to be an individual/be different from others/stand out from the crowd • "whiteness of the frost ... glimmerings of snow" contrast emphasises the striking physical impact of the door and the symbolic significance of a new beginning for Murdo • "seemed to have its own courage" personification represents Murdo's inner thoughts and wishes

Question	Expected Answer(s)	Max Mark	Additional Guidance
15.	2 marks awarded for detailed/insightful comment plus quotation/reference; 1 mark for more basic comment plus quotation/reference; 0 marks for quotation/reference alone. Possible answers are shown in the "Additional Guidance" column. (Marks may be awarded 2, 1 + 1)	2	Possible answers include: • Use of the question "was he happy?" highlights his uncertainty/doubts about his current way of life • Repetition of "he didn't like" emphasises the level of his discontent/frustration with his situation • "had to keep...smiling face" conveys his inner conflict over the image he projected to others • Climactic nature of "hated them" reveals the strength and depth of his true feelings
16.	Candidates may choose to answer in bullet points in this final question, or write a number of linked statements.	10	Up to 2 marks can be achieved by identifying elements of commonality as identified in the question, i.e. Crichton Smith's exploration of the conflict between individuality and conformity. A further 2 marks can be achieved for reference to the extract given. 6 additional marks can be awarded for discussion of similar references to at least one other short story by Crichton Smith. In practice this means: Identification of commonality (2) e.g. Crichton Smith shows that the impact of trying to fit in with one's surroundings (1) can cause some to suffer and deny their true feelings whilst others find the courage to break free (1) From the extract: 2 marks for detailed/insightful comment plus quotation/reference; 1 mark for more basic comment plus quotation/reference; 0 marks for quotation/reference alone. e.g. the discovery of the red door acts as a catalyst for Murdo to begin a new life where he can be true to himself (2) From at least one other text: as above for up to 6 marks Possible comments include: • *The Telegram* the thin woman has lived in the village for many years yet she is isolated by others as she does not make the same choices as them • *The Painter* William challenges the conventions of the village by painting a realistic picture of the fight and is ostracised as a result • *Mother and Son* John feels trapped by his overbearing, critical mother but is compelled by a sense of duty to stay with her thus denying his true self • *In Church* the 'priest' is a deserter who becomes a murderer as he could not conform to the expectations of war • *The Crater* the need to conform to the expected nature of an officer leads Robert to conceal his fears on the battlefield

Text 2 — Prose — *Tartan* by George Mackay Brown

Question	Expected Answer(s)	Max Mark	Additional Guidance
17.	2 marks awarded for detailed/ insightful comment plus quotation/ reference; 1 mark for more basic comment plus quotation/reference; 0 marks for quotation/reference alone. Possible answers are shown in the "Additional Guidance" column. (Marks may be awarded 2 + 2, 2 + 1 + 1, 1 + 1 + 1 + 1)	4	Possible answers include: • "muttering and sighing" suggests ongoing nature of deep grief/despair at loss of the future • Contrast between Kol's energy "leapt ... loud beserk yell" and the stillness and quiet in the room • "might have been a fly buzzing ... paid to him" comparison with "fly buzzing" conveys how completely unimportant/ irrelevant the Viking raid — normally an event of fear and danger — is in comparison to loss of child • Parallel structure of the old woman's sentences "I thought to see you a shepherd ... Or maybe you would be a man ... Or you might have been a holy priest" suggests repetitive chant to convey the primal sense of grief • "... shepherd ... fisherman ... man with lucky acres ... holy priest" conveys the range of possible futures/hope which have been destroyed by the child's death • "cross ... tangled in his cold fingers" conveys bleak finality of the human loss by creating a picture of the child's fingers, already cold • "crossed themselves in the door": simple description of the Vikings' action conveys the sense that even they are awed and moved by his death • "slunk out like a dog" suggests Kol's shame at the inappropriateness of his leap into the room
18.	2 marks awarded for detailed/ insightful comment plus quotation/ reference; 1 mark for more basic comment plus quotation/reference; 0 marks for quotation/reference alone. Possible answers are shown in the "Additional Guidance" column. (Marks may be awarded 2 + 2, 2 + 1 + 1, 1 + 1 + 1 + 1)	4	Possible answers include: • "Strangers from the sea ... you are welcome ... I ask you to accept ale" exaggerated nature of welcome, under the circumstances i.e. they are Viking raiders, suggests insincerity/attempt to manipulate them • "They are good people here, except for the man who lives ..." use of "they" distances himself from the other people of Durness/sees himself as superior and in a position to judge the others • "he will not pay me for the cloth I wove for him last winter" accusatory tone by which he attempts to gain the support of the Vikings against one of his own community • "he and his wife and his snovelly-nosed children" dismissive and distasteful description of Duncan's family suggests his feelings of superiority towards them • "Take it, take it by all means" repetition of "take it" suggests his eagerness to please the Vikings, to ingratiate himself with them • "John has been on the hill all week ... I think she is lonely" apparently simple statement of facts suggests her isolation and vulnerability and even hints at the idea that she is sexual prey, indicating how low and disloyal his attitude is
19.	1 mark for comment plus quotation/ reference (x2); 0 marks for quotation/reference alone. Possible answers are shown in the "Additional Guidance" column. (Marks awarded 1 + 1)	2	Possible answers include: • Havard's 'retrospective' threat to Malcolm: "If it (the ale) had been sour, we would have stretched you ..." suggests his aggression/bullying quality (though perhaps said in a jocular way) • Arnor's decision to "settle matters" with Duncan on behalf of Malcolm, along with "Now we need our cups filled again" suggests his desire to be seen as in command • Kol's staggering, combined with his bravado claim "Doubtless somebody will pay for this" suggests his boastful and belligerent attitude • Sven's reply to Malcolm's offer of the tartan cloth: "We were going to take it in any case" suggests his determination to show Malcolm who is in charge, despite Malcolm's attempts to manipulate/be courteous

Question	Expected Answer(s)	Max Mark	Additional Guidance
20.	Candidates may choose to answer in bullet points in this final question, or write a number of linked statements. Possible answers are shown in the "Additional Guidance" column.	10	Up to 2 marks can be achieved for identifying elements of commonality as identified in the question, i.e. the relationship between the individual and the community. A further 2 marks can be achieved for reference to the extract given. 6 additional marks can be awarded for discussion of similar references to at least one other short story by Mackay Brown. <u>In practice this means:</u> Identification of commonality (2) e.g. Individuals will usually show loyalty and commitment to the community (1) though some will rebel against or betray the community values to achieve their own fulfilment/achieve their own ends (1) From the extract: 2 marks for detailed/insightful comment plus quotation/reference; 1 mark for more basic comment plus quotation/reference; 0 marks for quotation alone. e.g. Malcolm the weaver attempts to exploit the Viking raid for his own selfish aims to settle old scores within the community, such as the non-payment for cloth, to gain favour with the raiders (2) From at least one other text: as above for up to 6 marks Possible answers include: • *A Time to Keep* loyalty to the community can mean suspicion of 'outsiders' such as Inge (from just over the hill) and Bill (a whaler). Bill's sense of their 'separateness' contributes to the negative relationship he has with the other men in the community • *A Time to Keep* Bill is appalled by the community taking charge of his wife's death, represented by the women's show of grief expressed in "litany of the dead person's virtues ... most of them lies", and the minister's comments. He rejects their sentimental clichés about going to "a better place" • *The Bright Spade* seven men show loyalty and heroism in setting off into the storm to look for food for the community- but the sacrifice of their lives in fact helps no one • *The Wireless Set* Howie feels he is bringing progress and development to the 'backward' community by bringing home the wireless set; his attitude contrasts with that of his parents, who uphold the traditional values of the community and view the outside world with suspicion • *The Eye of the Hurricane* Barclay's initial sense of superiority and objectification of the community ("simple uncomplicated people") gives way to genuine involvement in the face of Cpt. Stevens' suffering and flawed but heroic humanity

Text 3 — Prose — *The Trick is to Keep Breathing* by Janice Galloway

Question	Expected Answer(s)	Max Mark	Additional Guidance
21.	2 marks awarded for detailed/insightful comment plus quotation/reference; 1 mark for more basic comment plus quotation/reference; 0 marks for quotation/reference alone. Possible answers are shown in the "Additional Guidance" column. (Marks may be awarded 2 + 2, 2 + 1 + 1, 1 + 1 + 1 + 1)	4	Possible answers include: • "protection against witches" suggests something evil/sinister about the place • "well outside the place ... be part of" use of irony emphasises the sense of isolation/remoteness • "undesirables"/"difficult tenants"/"shunters"/"overspill" suggests the inhabitants are unwanted in the main town • Contrast between how it is meant to appear/idyllic setting eg "wild currant bushes"/"tiny, twisty roads" and what it is like in reality eg "pubs with plastic beer glasses"/"kids use the bends to play chicken" • "lying low"/"leaping out" suggests children are wild/out of control • "buses go slow"/"infrequent" emphasises remoteness/isolation • "graffiti" — vandalism indicates neglect • "It rains a lot." short sentence highlights the sense of misery emphasised by the weather
22.	2 marks awarded for detailed/insightful comment plus quotation/reference; 1 mark for more basic comment plus quotation/reference; 0 marks for quotation/reference alone. Possible answers are shown in the "Additional Guidance" column. (Marks may be awarded 2 + 2, 2 + 1 + 1, 1 + 1 + 1 + 1)	4	Possible answers include: • "never surrenders first time" personification suggests that the key refuses to be found easily • "rummage" suggests frantic search/desperation • "as though begging to be mugged" comparison suggests Joy's feelings of vulnerability • "Not mine." minor sentence emphasises her lack of belonging/ownership • "grit"/"litter" emphasises how Joy finds the place unwelcoming/unhomely • "withered leaves" suggests Joy's obsession with death/decay • "slaters run frantic"/"insects make me sick"/"disgust me" emphasises Joy's irrationality/neurotic nature • "fight my way inside" emphasises Joy's desperation to escape the outside world. • "gritty little packets"/"skeletons outside"/"too many eyes"/"unpredictable legs" suggests Joy's fear
23.	2 marks awarded for detailed/insightful comment plus quotation/reference; 1 mark for more basic comment plus quotation/reference; 0 marks for quotation/reference alone. Possible answers are shown in the "Additional Guidance" column. (Marks may be awarded 2, 1 + 1)	2	Possible answers include: • "Try to feel (the other continent)" suggests her desperation to escape • "I find the bottle ... I put an envelope ... sitting the bottle aside ... reshape the cushions ..." list of activities suggests she is trying to impose order/structure on her own situation • "But things have to be set in place." short sentence emphasises her desire for control • "Stillness helps ..."/"It keeps me contained" short sentences emphasise her attempts at self-control/order

Question	Expected Answer(s)	Max Mark	Additional Guidance
24.	Candidates may choose to answer in bullet points in this final question, or write a number of linked statements. Possible answers are shown in the "Additional Guidance" column.	10	Up to 2 marks can be achieved for identifying elements of commonality as identified in the question, i.e. how Galloway explores the impact of loneliness. A further 2 marks can be achieved for reference to the extract given. 6 additional marks can be awarded for discussion of similar references to at least one other part of the text. In practice this means: Identification of commonality (2) e.g. devastating life changing, destructive nature of loneliness (1) can affect mental health/ability to communicate/ability to form relationships (1) From the extract: 2 marks for detailed/insightful comment plus quotation/reference; 1 mark for more basic comment plus quotation/reference; 0 marks for quotation alone. e.g. Joy attempts to cope with loneliness by focusing on distracting herself and creating a sense of order in her surroundings: "A lot depends on stillness later and I have to get a lot of moving around out of my system now." (2) From at least one other part of the text: as above for up to 6 marks Possible answers include: • Joy tries to cope with her loneliness following Michael's death by engaging in a number of casual relationships with men • Joy distracts herself from her loneliness by engaging in a variety of mundane activities e.g. sewing, reading magazines, various rituals including bathing etc. • Joy forces herself to engage in the activities suggested by her friend Marianne, including visiting Marianne's mother, Ellen, regularly • In order to hide her loneliness from others, Joy attempts to appear upbeat and in control to others for example Tony, Myra etc. • Joy attempts to alleviate her loneliness after Michael's death by trying to re-create his physical presence e.g. spraying his aftershave

Text 4 — Prose — *Sunset Song* by Lewis Grassic Gibbon

Question	Expected Answer(s)	Max Mark	Additional Guidance
25.	2 marks awarded for detailed/insightful comment plus quotation/reference; 1 mark for more basic comment plus quotation/reference; 0 marks for quotation/reference alone. Possible answers are shown in the "Additional Guidance" column. (Marks may be awarded 2 + 1, 1 + 1 + 1)	3	Possible answers include: • "strong on Rich and Poor being Equal" suggests firmly held socialist principles; a belief that all wealth should be shared out evenly • "Broke he might be but he wasn't mean" suggests that regardless of his own financial problems, Chae is a generous host • "there was broth ..." suggests that he provides an abundance of food which clearly signifies his gratitude • "he could hold to the turnip-field" suggests Chae has a lively sense of humour which often reveals the ridiculous in his fellow man
26.	2 marks awarded for detailed/insightful comment plus quotation/reference; 1 mark for more basic comment plus quotation/reference; 0 marks for quotation/reference alone. Possible answers are shown in the "Additional Guidance" column. (Marks may be awarded 2 + 1, 1 + 1 + 1)	3	Possible answers include: • "his great lugs like red clouts hung out to dry" suggests comical physical appearance (his prominent ears compared to washing on a line) • "as though he hadn't seen food for a fortnight" gross exaggeration to convey his greedy consumption of the meal • "like a colie ta'en off its chain" overstated comparison to a ravenous dog just released • "a spree to the pair of them" sense that this is a bout of self-indulgence rather than part of a day's work • "*fair an expert getting*" condescending use of the word "expert" has the intention of belittling Chris • "*The kitchen's more her style than the College.*" patronising judgement reveals his own prejudice
27.	2 marks awarded for detailed/insightful comment plus quotation/reference; 1 mark for more basic comment plus quotation/reference; 0 marks for quotation/reference alone. Possible answers are shown in the "Additional Guidance" column. (Marks may be awarded 2 + 2, 2 + 1 + 1, 1 + 1 + 1 + 1)	4	Possible answers include: • "the yokels and clowns everlasting" suggests Chris resents the total disregard for learning displayed by those she perceives as country bumpkins and forever stupid • "dull-brained and crude" suggests Chris rejects those who have laughed as slow-witted and vulgar • "a coarse thing, learning" suggests many see no refining qualities in knowledge • "a lot of damn nonsense that put them above themselves" suggests many perceive education as valueless and will lead to a false sense of superiority in their offspring • "give you their lip" suggests many think that education leads to impudence • "to put him up level with the Rich" suggests Chae contradicts the views of others by declaring that education provides social equality • "the more of sense and the less of kirks and ministers" suggests Long Rob agrees with Chae and states that education improves a person's ability to think clearly and reject organised religion • "was shamed as she thought" suggests Chris revises her view of Chae and Long Rob whose kindness she recognises, despite their lack of possessions

Question	Expected Answer(s)	Max Mark	Additional Guidance
28.	Candidates may choose to answer in bullet points in this final question, or write a number of linked statements. Possible answers are shown in the "Additional Guidance" column.	10	Up to 2 marks can be achieved for identifying elements of commonality as identified in the question, i.e. Chris's conflicting emotions towards the community in Kinraddie. A further 2 marks can be achieved for reference to the extract given. 6 additional marks can be awarded for discussion of similar references to at least one other part of the text. <u>In practice this means:</u> Identification of commonality (2) e.g. Chris is appalled by the small-mindedness of the Speak (1), but she values the innate kindness of her neighbours in times of need (1) From the extract: 2 marks for detailed/insightful comment plus quotation/reference; 1 mark for more basic comment plus quotation/reference; 0 marks for quotation alone. e.g. Chris is angered by Munro's patronising comments, aimed to reduce her to his servant, but she also acknowledges the considerate nature of Chae and Long Rob (2) From at least one other part of the text: as above for up to 6 marks Possible answers include: • The two Chrisses are torn between love of school and learning ("you hated the land and the coarse speak of the folk") and her love of the land and its people • Chris is angered by the rumours about Will and Mollie Douglas, but she begins to learn about relationships after meeting Mollie on the road • Chris is aware of gossip about the Strachans, their financial problems and insurance money from the fire, but she also knows that she, her family and the community do all they can to assist at Peesie's Knapp • Chris is initially untroubled by the community's view of her seemingly heartless lack of sorrow at the death of her father, but she is comforted by their neighbourly concern at the graveside • Chris disregards the community's sense of outrage that she should marry Ewan so soon after her father's death, but she is delighted that so many locals should celebrate her wedding and wish both of them well

Text 5 — Prose — *The Cone-Gatherers* by Robin Jenkins

Question	Expected Answer(s)	Max Mark	Additional Guidance
29.	2 marks awarded for detailed/insightful comment plus quotation/reference; 1 mark for more basic comment plus quotation/reference; 0 marks for quotation/reference alone. Possible answers are shown in the "Additional Guidance" column. (Marks may be awarded 2, 1 + 1)	2	Possible answers include: • "indigo clouds" dark colour suggests the darkening, angry sky • "mustering" suggests soldiers gathering, and reflects the literal and metaphorical storm • "rumbles (of thunder)" onomatopoeia reflects the ominous sound of thunder • "whisked away" suggests the panic of the birds before the storm • "ominous" suggests something powerful/dangerous/frightening • "river of radiance" alliteration/metaphor emphasises the long thin streak of light, shining like water
30.	2 marks awarded for detailed/insightful comment plus quotation/reference; 1 mark for more basic comment plus quotation/reference; 0 marks for quotation/reference alone. Possible answers are shown in the "Additional Guidance" column. (Marks may be awarded 2 + 2, 2 + 1 + 1, 1 + 1 + 1 + 1)	4	Possible answers include: • "frightened and exhilarated" combination suggests tumult of emotions • "frightened" suggests scared/terrified • "exhilarated" suggests a rush of energy/his identification with natural forces • "chattered ... sense" suggests he is so overcome with excitement that it affects him physically • "dribble out" suggests he is so overwhelmed he loses control of his actions • "he raised his hand" suggests a need to join with the elements/wants physical contact with them • "meaningless chatters" suggests incoherence due to excitement • "screamed" suggests extreme/heightened reaction
31.	2 marks awarded for detailed/insightful comment plus quotation/reference; 1 mark for more basic comment plus quotation/reference; 0 marks for quotation/reference alone. Possible answers are shown in the "Additional Guidance" column. (Marks may be awarded 2 + 2, 2 + 1 + 1, 1 + 1 + 1 + 1)	4	Possible answers include: • "We'd better get down" indicates that Neil takes responsibility for their safety/makes important decisions • "But up here ... dangerous" indicates that Neil is aware of Calum's lack of understanding/takes on role of parent • "I don't like ..."/"Did you see ..."/"Was it from ..." simplicity of language shows Calum's childlike dependence on Neil • Repeated use of Neil's name suggests Calum seeks reassurance/comfort from his big brother • "Was it from heaven ...?" suggests Calum's naivety and his reliance on Neil's wisdom • Repeated questions ("In the shed...horse?/"What shed ... horse?") indicates Neil's frustration with Calum's childlike ways
32.	Candidates may choose to answer in bullet points in this final question, or write a number of linked statements. Possible answers are shown in the "Additional Guidance" column.	10	Up to 2 marks can be achieved for identifying elements of commonality as identified in the question, i.e. how the writer uses symbolism to develop the central concerns of the text. A further 2 marks can be achieved for reference to the extract given. 6 additional marks can be awarded for discussion of similar references to at least one other part of the text.

Question	Expected Answer(s)	Max Mark	Additional Guidance
32	(continued)		<u>In practice this means:</u> Identification of commonality (2) e.g. Jenkins uses characters, incidents and setting as representative of wider issues (1) such as the conflict between good and evil/devastation of war/sacrifice of innocence due to cruelty of mankind (1) From the extract: 2 marks for detailed/insightful comment plus quotation/reference; 1 mark for more basic comment plus quotation/reference; 0 marks for quotation alone. e.g. Calum's childlike interpretation of the light on the trees as coming from heaven, despite the danger of the storm, symbolises his innocence/innate goodness (2) From the rest of the text: as above for up to 6 marks Possible answers include: • The deer drive is a small version of what is happening in the outside world and represents the violence humanity is capable of • The presence of the destroyer/planes in this natural setting represent the inescapable conflict between good vs. evil • Calum's death in the tree represents the crucifixion with his blood purifying the world corrupted by Duror • Duror is often associated with a decaying tree representing the evil spreading within him • The cones represent hope for the future/re-birth as after destruction/war new life will grow

PART C — SCOTTISH TEXT — POETRY

Text 1 — Poetry — *Address to the Deil* by Robert Burns

Question	Expected Answer(s)	Max Mark	Additional Guidance
33.	2 marks awarded for detailed/insightful comment plus quotation/reference; 1 mark for more basic comment plus quotation/reference; 0 marks for quotation/reference alone. Possible answers are shown in the "Additional Guidance" column. (Marks may be awarded 2 + 2, 2 + 1 + 1, 1 + 1 + 1 + 1)	4	Possible answers include: • "whatever title suit thee" rather dismissive comment creates an informal/comic tone (especially when contrasted with the introductory quotation from Milton used by Burns) • List of epithets for the Deil (in particular, "Auld Hornie" and "Clootie") convey a slightly affectionate camaraderie between the Deil and the speaker • "cavern grim and sootie" stereotypical view of the Deil's abode is somewhat mocking of the Calvinistic view of Hell • "spairges about ... wretches!" ridiculous depiction of Satan torturing damned souls makes the concept of the Deil's actions seem quite comical • "cootie" use of homely term for the Deil's cauldron makes Satan seem domesticated rather than a great force for evil • "Hear me ..." use of imperative makes the speaker seem more powerful than Satan, so creating a tongue-in-cheek tone • "I'm sure ... gie" the speaker's unlikely camaraderie and mock understanding of the Deil's tasks/patronising attitude to the Deil creates a humorous tone

Question	Expected Answer(s)	Max Mark	Additional Guidance
33	*(continued)*		• "skelp … scaud … squeel" — alliteration highlights the ridiculousness of Satan's supposed tasks • "poor dogs like me … us squeel" the speaker's readiness to admit his sins and accept the stereotypical punishment conveys a child-like impression of small misdemeanours and punishments rather than grave sins
34.	2 marks awarded for detailed/insightful comment plus quotation/reference; 1 mark for more basic comment plus quotation/reference; 0 marks for quotation/reference alone. Possible answers are shown in the "Additional Guidance" column. (Marks may be awarded 2, 1 + 1)	2	Possible answers include: • Repetition/positioning of "great" stresses the immense power and fame of the Deil • "Far kenm'd an' noted"/"travels far" suggests that the Deil is an omnipresent being, known everywhere • "thou's neither lag … nor scaur" listing of the negative qualities which are absent from the Deil makes him seem a supremely confident being • "roarin' lion" use of the metaphor creates impression of bravery/strength/nobility • "a' holes and corners tryin'" suggests once again the Deil's omnipresence/ability to invade all places • "on the strong wind'd tempest flyin'" suggests that the Deil has the power to control/overcome the strongest forces of nature • Parallel structure of "Whyles, on … Whyles, in …" highlights the ability of the Deil to move effortlessly between the greatest and smallest places • "Unseen thou lurks" connotations of menace and threat suggest the Deil is a powerful predator
35.	2 marks awarded for detailed/insightful comment plus quotation/reference; 1 mark for more basic comment plus quotation/reference; 0 marks for quotation/reference alone. Possible answers are shown in the "Additional Guidance" column. (Marks may be awarded 2 + 2, 2 + 1 + 1, 1 + 1 + 1 + 1)	4	Possible answers include: • "I've heard my rev'rend graunie say" the speaker's introduction to this anecdotal section of the poem suggest an old wife's tale, not to be taken seriously • Burns' use of a clichéd description ("lanely glens … auld ruin'd castles … the moon … eldritch croon … dreary, windy, winter night") emphasises that these anecdotes are the stuff of folklore/unbelievable tales • "graunie … douse, honest woman" the tongue-in-cheek description of the speaker's grannie suggests he is aware of the silly nature of these stories but is determined to defend them thus making them seem even less reliable • "bummin'" use of comic vocabulary undermines the seriousness of grannie's tale • Series of anecdotes becomes progressively less believable, with the speaker suggesting a natural reason for the supposed presence of the Deil (an owl's screech, the wind in the trees, the rushes waving, a startled drake) yet still continuing with his assertions of the Deil's presence • "quaick, quaick" use of onomatopoeia adds a comic note when the speaker continues to insist that he has heard/seen the Deil

Question	Expected Answer(s)	Max Mark	Additional Guidance
36.	Candidates may choose to answer in bullet points in this final question, or write a number of linked statements. Possible answers are shown in the "Additional Guidance" column.	10	Up to 2 marks can be achieved for identifying elements of commonality as identified in the question, i.e. Burns' use of humour to explore serious issues. A further 2 marks can be achieved for the reference to the extract given. 6 additional marks can be awarded for discussion of similar references to at least one other poem by Burns. In practice this means: Identification of commonality (2), e.g. Burns' satirical/comical observations of characters/religious beliefs/social classes (1) lend power to his, often scathing, condemnation of injustices/Calvinist doctrines/hypocritical moralising (1) From the extract: 2 marks for detailed/insightful comment plus quotation/reference; 1 mark for more basic comment plus quotation/reference; 0 marks for reference alone. e.g. "Spairges about the brunstane cootie/To scaud poor wretches!" - the exaggerated depiction of Satan personally undertaking the stereotypical tortures of Hell is effective in ridiculing the Calvinistic views of eternal damnation and the punishment of sins. (2) From at least one other poem: as above for up to 6 marks Possible references include: • *A Man's A Man for A' That* Burns' humorous depictions of the aristocracy are juxtaposed with his admiration for the common man, thereby strengthening his appeal for social equality • *A Poet's Welcome* Burns' satirical comments concerning the gossiping critics of his daughter's social position show the lack of compassion and humanity within the Kirk • *Holy Willie's Prayer* the hypocrisy and bigotry revealed by Willie in his "prayer" allow Burns to satirise the Calvinist doctrine of predestination • *Tam O' Shanter* the humour created by the speaker's po-faced moralising on Tam's foolish behaviour at various points in the poem allows Burns to criticise those who take pleasure in judging others too readily • *Tam O' Shanter* comical anti-climax of final line, reference to horse losing tail serves as a reminder of human frailties

Text 2 — Poetry — *Valentine* by Carol Ann Duffy

Question	Expected Answer(s)	Max Mark	Additional Guidance
37.	2 marks awarded for detailed/insightful comment plus quotation/reference; 1 mark for more basic comment plus quotation/reference; 0 marks for quotation/reference alone. Possible answers are shown in the "Additional Guidance" column. (Marks may be awarded 2 + 2, 2 + 1 + 1, 1 + 1 + 1 + 1)	4	Possible answers include: Challenges • Isolation/bluntness of the opening line emphasises the strength of the speaker's rejection of traditional gifts • Positioning of "Not" at the start of the line intensifies the speaker's rejection of traditional symbols of love • Given the mundane connotations of "an onion" the incongruity of it as a symbol of love • Subversion of "moon" as a traditional romantic image as it is mundanely described as "wrapped in brown paper" Reinforces • "moon" traditionally associated with romantic evenings • "promises" suggests devotion/commitment/fidelity • "light" suggests something pure and life-enhancing • "undressing" suggests something seductive and sensual
38.	2 marks awarded for detailed/insightful comment plus quotation/reference; 1 mark for more basic comment plus quotation/reference; 0 marks for quotation/reference alone. Possible answers are shown in the "Additional Guidance" column. (Marks may be awarded 2 + 2, 2 + 1 + 1, 1 + 1 + 1 + 1)	4	Possible answers include: • Development of the extended image in "blind you with tears/Like a lover" highlights the pain and suffering that love brings • Imagery of "wobbling photo of grief" suggests the pain/distress caused by a failed/complex relationship • Single line stanza abrupt dismissal of more stereotypical love tokens/straightforward no nonsense approach • Alliteration of "Not a cute card or a kissogram" suggests contempt for predictable/insincere/unthinking view of love • Image of "fierce kiss" to suggest the lingering taste of the onion suggests the difficulty of escaping the relationship/an underlying threat or danger in the relationship • Word choice of "possessive" suggests the constricting/controlling nature of the relationship • Juxtaposition of "possessive" and "faithful" undermines the notion of commitment in a relationship • Bluntness/positioning of "for as long as we are" at end of verse suggests impermanence of love
39.	2 marks awarded for detailed/insightful comment plus quotation/reference; 1 mark for more basic comment plus quotation/reference; 0 marks for quotation/reference alone. Possible answers are shown in the "Additional Guidance" column. (Marks may be awarded 2, 1 + 1)	2	Possible answers include: • "Take it." Moving to an acceptance of a 'real' rather than a superficial view of love • "platinum loops … wedding-ring" the onion (mentioned earlier) becomes associated with the restrictive aspects of marriage/love • "Lethal" suggests movement towards a dark conclusion/dark view of love • "cling to your fingers" echoes earlier ideas of the negative long term effects of a broken relationship/possessiveness within a relationship • "knife" leaves the reader with final thought of love's potential to wound

Question	Expected Answer(s)	Max Mark	Additional Guidance
40.	Candidates may choose to answer in bullet points in this final question, or write a number of linked statements. Possible answers are shown in the "Additional Guidance" column.	10	Up to 2 marks can be achieved for identifying elements of commonality as identified in the question, i.e. how emotional conflict within an individual is explored. A further 2 marks can be achieved for reference to the text given. 6 additional marks can be awarded for discussion of similar references to at least one other poem by Duffy. In practice this means: Identification of commonality (2) e.g. the complexities of human experience can create emotional conflict in an individual's life (1), which can change significantly the individual's personality/outlook on life (1) From the poem: 2 marks for detailed/insightful comment plus quotation/reference; 1 mark for more basic comment plus quotation/reference; 0 marks for quotation/reference alone. e.g. the speaker is attracted to other, more positive aspects of love such as intimacy and tenderness but adopts a more realistic/cynical attitude towards love "Not a red rose … onion" (2) From at least one other text: as above for up to 6 marks Possible comments include: • *Anne Hathaway* the speaker is left bereft by the death of her husband, but by remembering the passionate nature of her relationship, she has become more resigned to her loss • *Havisham* the unresolved tension between love and hate that the speaker's rejection provokes, leads to an on-going deterioration in her mental state • *War Photographer* the emotional impact of the horrors the photographer has witnessed in his assignments abroad conflicts with the pride he feels in doing a professional job • *Originally* the unresolved emotional conflict of maintaining identity: where is home and all the emotional baggage the question entails • *Mrs Midas* the unresolved conflicting emotions she feels for her husband: the contempt she feels for his desires which brought about their separation conflicts with the physical intimacy she now misses.

Text 3 — Poetry — *For my Grandmother Knitting* by Liz Lochhead

Question	Expected Answer(s)	Max Mark	Additional Guidance
41.	For full marks both the past and the present must be dealt with, but not necessarily in equal measure. 2 marks awarded for detailed/insightful comment plus quotation/reference; 1 mark for more basic comment plus quotation/reference; 0 marks for quotation/reference alone. Possible answers are shown in the "Additional Guidance" column. (Marks may be awarded 2 + 2, 2 + 1 + 1, 1 + 1 + 1 + 1)	4	Possible answers include: **Past** • "sure and skilful hands of the fisher-girl" word choice emphasises sense of control and confidence, despite her youth • "master of your moments" — alliteration/slogan effect conveys sense that she was in charge/on top of the task • "deft and swift" monosyllables and consonance emphasise her skill and speed when gutting the fish • "slit the still-ticking quick silver fish" fast-paced rhythm and repetition of short "I" vowel sound conveys the efficiency and ease with which she tackled the task • "Hard work ... of necessity" positioning and choice of words emphasises how much her efforts were needed **Present** • "There is no need they say" — opening, blunt statement and dismissive tone convey her lack of perceived usefulness • "the needles still move/their rhythms" sense of her passivity/lack of agency emphasised by description of the needles as the active ones, rather than the grandmother • "You are old now": blunt statement positioned at start of Stanza 2, emphasises the definite nature of her plight • "grasp ... not so good" — sense of her diminishing alertness/control in the literal and metaphorical use of "grasp"
42.	1 mark for comment plus quotation/reference (x2); 0 marks for quotation/reference alone. Possible answers are shown in the "Additional Guidance" column.	2	Possible answers include: • "hands of the bride" connotations of special/romantic time when hand receives ring/holds hands • "hand-span waist" suggests that she was cherished by her husband/physically dainty and exquisite • "hands ... scrubbed his back" suggests devotion/physical closeness with her husband as they worked together in difficult circumstances • "hands ... six" suggests the multiple challenges of her life • "scraped ... necessary" list of verbs suggests her energy and ability to cope in down-to-earth way
43.	2 marks awarded for detailed/insightful comment plus quotation/reference; 1 mark for more basic comment plus quotation/reference; 0 marks for quotation/reference alone. Possible answers are shown in the "Additional Guidance" column. (Marks may be awarded 2 + 1, 1 + 1 + 1)	4	Possible answers include: • "the kids they say grandma ... already" reported speech without punctuation suggests an often-repeated 'lecture' conveying sense of isolation/lack of compassion/lack of communication • Repetition of "too much/too many" emphasises their perception of her uselessness/sense that they repeatedly remind her that her contribution is not needed • "At your window you wave ... Sunday" poignant picture of the grandmother waving goodbye conveys sense of her loneliness • "painful hands ... shrunken wrists" physical incongruity of hands on tiny wrists suggests how frail and clumsy she now is • "Swollen-jointed ... Old" list of adjectives in minor sentences building to the climax of "Old" emphasises the pitiful nature of her physical condition • "as if ... how to stop" climactic final line suggests her lack of control over her life

Question	Expected Answer(s)	Max Mark	Additional Guidance
44.	Candidates may choose to answer in bullet points in this final question, or write a number of linked statements. Possible answers are shown in the "Additional Guidance" column.	10	Up to 2 marks can be achieved by identifying elements of commonality as identified in the question, i.e. Lochhead's exploration of the theme of personal and/or social change. A further 2 marks can be achieved for reference to the poem given. 6 additional marks can be awarded for discussion of similar references to at least one other poem by Lochhead. In practice this means: Identification of commonality (2) e.g. Lochhead uses characters to represent aspects of life past/present, encouraging us to respond to their experience (1) showing that change can be either positive or negative — destroying valuable aspects of past or looking forward to a more positive future (1) From this poem: 2 marks for detailed/insightful comment plus quotation/reference; 1 mark for more basic comment plus quotation/reference; 0 marks for quotation/reference alone. e.g. the grandmother represents an older Scotland where traditional ways of life e.g. fishing or mining provided security and continuity, which is lacking in the modern world (2) From at least one other text: as above for up to 6 marks Possible comments include: • *Some Old Photographs* sense that Scotland of the past had social cohesion and predictability, e.g. 'all the dads in hats', though this certainty is undermined in "what was/never really" • *View of Scotland/Love Poem* the traditional Hogmanay, with its rituals which everyone followed, has been replaced by a more spontaneous celebration of life — "There is no time like the/present for a kiss" • *Last Supper* change reflected in membership of the 'revenge group' and/or dramatic reaction to partner's betrayal • *My Rival's House* the mother is hostile to change in the relationship with her son and fights against the necessity of his growing up and forming a new relationship • *The Bargain* the speaker's relationship, which thrived in the past but now faces an uncertain future, reflected by their inconclusive visit to the stalls

Text 4 — Poetry — *Basking Shark* by Norman MacCaig

Question	Expected Answer(s)	Max Mark	Additional Guidance
45.	2 marks awarded for detailed/insightful comment plus quotation/reference; 1 mark for more basic comment plus quotation/reference; 0 marks for quotation/reference alone. Possible answers are shown in the "Additional Guidance" column. (Marks may be awarded 2, 1 + 1)	2	Possible answers include: • "stub" onomatopoeia suggests sudden/unexpected contact • "where none should be" conveys the idea of things being out of the ordinary/out of place • "To have it (rise)" emphasises disbelief at the action • "rise" apparent action by 'rock' suggests surprise/incredulity • parenthetical aside implying the speaker does not want to repeat the experience "(too often)" • "slounge" onomatopoeic qualities suggest slow, relaxed movement of shark in its own element where he is the intruder
46.	2 marks awarded for detailed/insightful comment plus quotation/reference; 1 mark for more basic comment plus quotation/reference; 0 marks for quotation/reference alone. Possible answers are shown in the "Additional Guidance" column. (Marks may be awarded 2 + 2, 2 + 1 + 1, 1 + 1 + 1 + 1)	4	Possible answers include: • "But not (too often) — though enough." evaluative comment suggests that the speaker continues to dwell upon the experience • "I count as gain" suggests that despite initial unease, he has come to recognise the value of the experience • "displaced" word choice suggests the shift in his thinking • "shoggled" suggests shaken out of a comfortable mind-set • "decadent townee" self-derogatory comment suggests his sudden recognition of his superficiality/alienation from nature • "shook" suggests that the speaker was literally and metaphorically disturbed by the experience • "wrong branch...family tree" suggests that he is now less sure of his place in the evolutionary framework
47.	2 marks awarded for detailed/insightful comment plus quotation/reference; 1 mark for more basic comment plus quotation/reference; 0 marks for quotation/reference alone. Possible answers are shown in the "Additional Guidance" column. (Marks may be awarded 2 + 2, 2 + 1 + 1, 1 + 1 + 1 + 1)	4	Possible answers include: • Metaphor of "Swish up ... clearer" suggests the initial confusion as a result of the encounter has led to greater clarity • "I saw me ... emerging" suggests rebirth of his sense of himself/humanity • "in one fling" parenthesis emphasises the sudden epiphany • "emerging from the slime of everything" suggests a realisation of humanity's primeval origins • "So who's the monster?" question emphasises that the speaker has been forced to rethink humanity's superiority to apparently primitive beings • "made me grow pale" suggests physical shock at realisation of humanity's insignificance/depravity • "sail after sail" repetition suggests realisation of grandeur/majesty/timelessness of the shark

Question	Expected Answer(s)	Max Mark	Additional Guidance
48.	Candidates may choose to answer in bullet points in this final question, or write a number of linked statements. Possible answers are shown in the "Additional Guidance" column.	10	Up to 2 marks can be achieved for identifying elements of commonality as identified in the question, i.e. how MacCaig uses symbolism to develop central ideas in his poetry. A further 2 marks can be achieved for reference to the text given. 6 additional marks can be awarded for discussion of similar references to at least one other poem MacCaig. Under practice this means: Identification of commonality (2) e.g. MacCaig uses people/objects/places as symbols to explore important human issues/relationships (1) and in doing so makes us re-evaluate/consider our own views (1) From the poem: 2 marks for detailed/insightful comment plus quotation/reference; 1 mark for more basic comment plus quotation/ reference; 0 marks for quotation alone. e.g. the shark represents the apparently primitive aspect of nature, however MacCaig's reflections challenge our perception of our superiority (2) From at least one other text: as above for up to 6 marks Possible answers include: • *Visiting Hour* "withered hand trembles on its stalk" symbolises the fragility of human life and makes us consider our own mortality • *Assisi* the contrast between the inner spiritual beauty and the outer physical appearance of the beggar makes us reflect on appearance against reality • *Aunt Julia* she represents a lost heritage which makes us consider the importance of valuing and preserving the past • *Memorial* "the carousel of language" represents the vitality of relationships and communication he can't recapture provoking thoughts on finality/loss • *Sounds of the Day* "the bangle of ice ... numb" represents the pain and deadening effect of loss which makes us consider love as a destructive force

Text 5 — Poetry — *Heroes* by Sorley MacLean

Question	Expected Answer(s)	Max Mark	Additional Guidance
49.	2 marks awarded for detailed/insightful comment plus quotation/reference; 1 mark for more basic comment plus quotation/reference; 0 marks for quotation/reference alone. Possible answers are shown in the "Additional Guidance" column. (Marks may be awarded 2, 1 + 1)	2	• Repeated use of "not" and "nor" emphasises the point that the soldier is not one of the Gaelic/Scottish heroes listed/mentioned • "Englishman" general term sounds insignificant when set against Scottish/Gaelic heroes mentioned/listed • "poor little chap" diminutive word choice/description makes the soldier seem unheroic • "chubby cheeks" suggests soldier is young/baby-like and therefore unheroic • "knees grinding" suggests fear/clumsiness and is therefore unheroic • "pimply unattractive face" youthful, immature, unappealing, unheroic appearance
50.	2 marks awarded for detailed/insightful comment plus quotation/reference; 1 mark for more basic comment plus quotation/reference; 0 marks for quotation/reference alone. Possible answers are shown in the "Additional Guidance" column. (Marks may be awarded 2 + 2, 2 + 1 + 1, 1 + 1 + 1 + 1)	4	Possible answers include: • "notched iron splinters" extremely violent weaponry suggested by using the word "splinters" which are generally associated with wood and superficial injuries, here linked with iron and something more deadly is implied. Harsh consonant sounds underline this. • "the smoke and flame" description of hell-like environment • "the shaking and terror of the battlefield" 'shaking' here is ambiguous, could be the ground literally shaking with the force of explosions, or could refer to extreme fear felt by the soldiers • "bullet shower" bullets are 'raining down,' rapid, intense frequency • "hero briskly"/"wasn't much time he got" (soldier) has to respond to events without time to think/has to respond with unnatural speed/sense of life cut short • "bucking with tearing crashing screech" harsh violent word choice, participles suggest violent events happening simultaneously • "biff" ironically colloquial rendering of blow to his body • "put him to the ground" in battle soldier is victim of forces outwith his control • "mouth down in sand and gravel" the use of the word "mouth" here, rather than the more usual "face", suggests more brutality, perhaps conveying almost the "taste" of the battlefield and the indignity of his fall

Question	Expected Answer(s)	Max Mark	Additional Guidance
51.	2 marks awarded for detailed/insightful comment plus quotation/reference; 1 mark for more basic comment plus quotation/reference; 0 marks for quotation/reference alone. Possible answers are shown in the "Additional Guidance" column. (Marks may be awarded 2 + 2, 2 + 1 + 1, 1 + 1 + 1 + 1)	4	Possible answers include: • The "no" ... "or" ... "or" construct/structure highlights the lack of recognition afforded to the soldier and his memory and therefore creates pity • "not many of his troop alive" prevalence/victory of death among soldier's companions creates pity • "their word would not be strong" soldiers' voices seen as weak/would be ignored in terms of their accounts of the battle • image of "the mouth of the field of slaughter" pity created through awareness of the soldiers' susceptibility to the (metaphorically) greedy appetite that war has for death • "great warrior" pity created by the ironic tone created in this expression, and also genuine sense of sympathy conveyed for the soldier's fate • "poor manikin" pity created by the use of diminutive term, and this is emphasised by addition of the word 'poor' • "he took a little weeping to my eyes" reference to the traditional Gaelic expression creates genuine sense of pity for the soldier
52.	Candidates may choose to answer in bullet points in this final question, or write a number of linked statements. Possible answers are shown in the "Additional Guidance" column.	10	Up to 2 marks can be achieved by identifying elements of commonality as identified in the question, ie how the theme of destruction is explored. A further 2 marks can be achieved for reference to the text given. 6 additional marks can be awarded for discussion of similar references to at least one other poem by MacLean. Under_In practice this means:_ Identification of commonality (2) e.g. MacLean explores the destruction of community, relationships and individuals (1) challenging the readers to consider the negative impact of war, change in community, careless treatment of others in relationships (1) From the poem: 2 marks for detailed/insightful comment plus quotation/reference; 1 mark for more basic comment plus quotation/reference; 0 marks for quotation/reference alone. e.g. the ironic description of the "soldier"/"warrior" highlights his ordinary nature and encourages the reader to reflect on the impact of war on us all (2) From at least one other poem: as above for up to 6 marks Possible answers include: • _An Autumn Day_ seemingly random death of six companions highlights the futility, chaos, destruction of war • _Hallaig_ the destruction of Highland communities caused by the Clearances, and the sense of loss engendered by this • _Screapadal_ destruction caused by the forced Clearances, and by the modern world's intrusive impact on traditional ways of life • _I Gave You Immortality_ potentially destructive power of love and the pain it can cause • _Shores_ the destructive force and power of the sea and time

Text 6 — Poetry — *Nil Nil* by Don Paterson

Question	Expected Answer(s)	Max Mark	Additional Guidance
53.	2 marks awarded for detailed/insightful comment plus quotation/reference; 1 mark for more basic comment plus quotation/reference; 0 marks for quotation/reference alone. Possible answers are shown in the "Additional Guidance" column. (Marks may be awarded 2, 1 + 1)	2	Possible answers include: • "zenith" suggests that this moment is the pinnacle of the club's history • "majestic" suggests stately and magnificent, McGrandle is a grandiose figure • "golden (hair)" suggests something of great value • "sprinting the length" suggests an athletic prowess worthy of celebration • "balletic (toe-poke)" suggests great grace/poise/artfulness • "nearly bursting the roof of the net" hyperbolic statement emphasises the speaker's appreciation and effusiveness about this moment in the history of the club
54.	2 marks awarded for detailed/insightful comment plus quotation/reference; 1 mark for more basic comment plus quotation/reference; 0 marks for quotation/reference alone. Possible answers are shown in the "Additional Guidance" column. (Marks may be awarded 2 + 2, 2 + 1 + 1, 1 + 1 + 1 + 1)	4	Possible answers include: • "from here/it's all down" the phrase 'all down' suggests that there is no respite/decline is inevitable and complete • "pitch-sharing, pay-cuts, pawned silver" the list of worsening downturns emphasises the progression of the decline • "absolute sitters ballooned over open goals"/"dismal nutmegs" suggests decline in quality of the players • "(scores so) obscene" suggests defeats were becoming more humiliating/unacceptable • "nothing inhibits the fifty-year slide" suggests inevitability of long term decline • "then nobody" climax emphasises total absence of support • "stud-harrowed pitches" suggests neglect/disrepair/lack of care
55.	For full marks both the community and the pilot need to be dealt with but not necessarily in equal measure. 2 marks awarded for detailed/insightful comment plus quotation/reference; 1 mark for more basic comment plus quotation/reference; 0 marks for quotation/reference alone. Possible answers are shown in the "Additional Guidance" column. (Marks may be awarded 2 + 2, 2 + 1 + 1, 1 + 1 + 1 + 1)	4	Possible answers include: Community • "stopped swings" suggests all vibrancy has gone from the community/lack of youth • "dead shanty-town" suggests desolation/temporary nature of things • "cul-de-sac" suggests total dead end/lack of direction/aimless Pilot • "all that remains" suggests that every other physical part of the pilot is gone from existence and the stone is all that is left • "lone fighter-pilot" suggests isolation and vulnerability which contributes to the tragedy • "burn … melt … igniting" the combination of these words — all indicating heat and possible explosion — suggests danger/death • "no one around to admire …" suggests lonely nature of death

Question	Expected Answer(s)	Max Mark	Additional Guidance
56.	Candidates may choose to answer in bullet points in this final question, or write a number of linked statements. Possible answers are shown in the "Additional Guidance" column.	10	Up to 2 marks can be achieved by identifying elements of commonality as identified in the question, i.e. how poet explores the impact of loss. A further 2 marks can be achieved for reference to the extract given. 6 additional marks can be awarded for discussion of similar references to at least one other poem by Paterson. In practice this means: Identification of commonality (2) e.g. Loss can be profound and life changing (1) and is a fundamental part of human experience, e.g. love, innocence, community, identity (1) From this extract: 2 marks for detailed/insightful comment plus quotation/reference; 1 mark for more basic comment plus quotation/reference; 0 marks for quotation/reference alone. e.g. "black shell" describes the Skelly Dry Cleaners as a husk devoid of life which emphasises this once flourishing business has now failed, adding to the hopelessness of the community (2) From at least one other poem: as above for up to 6 marks Possible comments include: • *The Ferryman's Arms* inevitability of death causes speaker to lose sense of identity ("my losing opponent … left him there") leading to feelings of hopelessness/lack of control • *11:00 Baldovan* loss of innocence leads to uncertainty/insecurity about our place in the future ("I cannot know the little good it will do me") • *Waking with Russell* the speaker has lost his old self through the birth of his son and has now gained a brighter, richer future • *The Thread* the difficult circumstances around the son's birth led to a fear of loss and recognition that life is fragile • *Two Trees* separation of the trees represents a loss of security, however their continued growth/survival suggests the resilience of the human spirit

Section 2 – CRITICAL ESSAY

Supplementary marking grid

	Marks 20–19	Marks 18–16	Marks 15–13	Marks 12–10	Marks 9–6	Marks 5–0
Knowledge and understanding	thorough knowledge and understanding of the text	secure knowledge and understanding of the text	clear knowledge and understanding of the text	adequate knowledge and understanding of the text	limited evidence of knowledge and understanding of the text	very little knowledge and understanding of the text
The critical essay demonstrates:	perceptive selection of textual evidence to support line of argument which is fluently structured and expressed	detailed textual evidence to support line of thought which is coherently structured and expressed	clear textual evidence to support line of thought which is clearly structured and expressed	adequate textual evidence to support line of thought, which is adequately structured and expressed	limited textual evidence to support line of thought which is structured and expressed in a limited way	very little textual evidence to support line of thought which shows very little structure or clarity of expression
	perceptive focus on the demands of the question	secure focus on the demands of the question	clear focus on the demands of the question	adequate focus on the demands of the question	limited focus on the demands of the question	very little focus on the demands of the question
Analysis The critical essay demonstrates:	perceptive analysis of the effect of features of language/filmic techniques	detailed analysis of the effect of features of language/filmic techniques	clear analysis of the effect of features of language/filmic techniques	adequate analysis of the effect of features of language/filmic techniques	limited analysis of the effect of features of language/filmic techniques	very little analysis of features of language/filmic techniques
Evaluation The critical essay demonstrates	committed evaluative stance with respect to the text and the task	engaged evaluative stance with respect to the text and the task	clear evaluative stance with respect to the text and the task	adequate evidence of an evaluative stance with respect to the text and the task	limited evidence of an evaluative stance with respect to the text and the task	very little evidence of an evaluative stance with respect to the text and the task
Technical Accuracy The critical essay demonstrates:	few errors in spelling, grammar, sentence construction, punctuation and paragraphing the ability to be understood at first reading			significant number of errors in spelling, grammar, sentence construction, punctuation and paragraphing which impedes understanding		

HIGHER ENGLISH
2018

PAPER 1 — READING FOR UNDERSTANDING, ANALYSIS AND EVALUATION

Marking Instructions for each question

Passage 1

Question		Expected Answer(s)	Max Mark	Additional Guidance
1.	(a)	Candidates should identify two of the writer's feelings in the first paragraph. Candidates must use their own words. No marks for straight lifts from the passage. Award marks 1 + 1	2	Possible answers include: • she felt troubled, as though watching an illegal/senseless act • she felt responsible/guilty for a terrible act • she felt morally uncertain; questioned whether or not she was justified in doing this
	(b)	Candidates should analyse how the language emphasises the importance of trees. Award marks according to the quality of comment on appropriate language feature(s). Award **2 marks** for reference plus detailed/insightful comment. Award **1 mark** for reference plus more basic comment. Award **0 marks** for reference alone. Award marks 2 + 2 **or** 2 + 1 + 1 **or** 1 + 1 + 1 + 1	4	Possible answers include: *Word choice* • "ever more (precious)" suggests trees' increasing value • "precious" suggests trees are valuable, to be cherished • "a rebuke to built-in obsolescence": trees effectively criticise/stand in opposition to a world where products are designed to have only a limited life • "remnants" suggests precious remains from the past • "mammoth (limb)" suggests something on a massively impressive scale • "reassuring" suggests they offer comfort • "they will endure" suggests permanence, continuity, resilience • "the ancients" suggests trees have been considered valuable throughout the ages • "gods" suggests their almost religious significance • "ring by ring" suggests trees' natural, organic, unhurried growth • "worship" suggests our attitude should be respectful, reverent, devotional • "worse ... worship": candidates might argue that the use of alliteration adds to the impact of the concluding statement • use in general of "religious" language ("God's arm", "cathedrals", "gods", "worship") heightens trees' spiritual significance • "our living past": trees connect us to our heritage *Imagery* • "a steady point in a churning world": trees offer steadfast permanence in a fast-changing, impermanent, turbulent world • (personification of) "reaches out", "mammoth limb" suggests a majestic living creature • "like God's arm ... Rome": simile suggests majesty, beauty, spiritual significance, awesome impact • "calming like cathedrals": simile suggests their scale, majesty, spiritual quality, that they should be treated with reverence, that they are good for our inner well-being *Punctuation/sentence structure* • structure of opening sentence "I'm ... world": the two phrases at the end of the sentence (heightened by the parallel structure) serve as a powerful development of the "precious" idea

Question		Expected Answer(s)	Max Mark	Additional Guidance
1.	(b)	*(continued)*		• balanced nature of final sentence: the artful juxtaposition of the near-reverent tone of the first part of the sentence, followed by the more matter-of-fact, modern tone of the second half brings the paragraph to a quietly effective conclusion
2.		Candidates should demonstrate understanding of how the protesters differ from what might have been expected. Candidates must use their own words. No marks for straight lifts from the passage. Award marks 1 + 1	2	Possible answers include: • we might have expected the protesters to be (over)zealous environmental activists/(ultra)dedicated conservationists (explanation of "eco-warriors")/people who have rejected the conventional values of society (explanation of "hippies") • instead they are just normal people/a typical cross-section of the community/people of all ages and from all walks of life
3.		Candidates should analyse how the writer's use of language conveys her feelings of unhappiness. Award marks according to the quality of comment. For full marks there must be comment on at least two features. Award **2 marks** for reference plus detailed/insightful comment. Award **1 mark** for reference plus more basic comment. Award **0 marks** for reference alone.	3	Possible answers include: *Sentence structure* • series of three short, simple, matter-of-fact sentences at start of paragraph suggest the inevitable fate that awaits the trees and the irresistible march of the developers • positioning of "By March" at start of sentence suggests fixed, immovable timeline to destruction • structure of fourth sentence ("Local … benefits."): initial praise for efforts of local community is offset immediately by pessimistic recognition of government power; the sentence then reaches a climax with her attack on government policy • use of parenthesis "as new roads do" to emphasise the inevitable futility of government transport policy *Word choice:* • "last stand" (could be dealt with as imagery) suggests a defensive position facing inevitable defeat against insuperable odds • "only" suggests defeat itself is inevitable • "determined" suggests inflexible, unyielding nature of government policy • "market" suggests her scepticism about government policy: they are "selling" it as progress but "market" suggests this is more image than reality; suggests government is being unscrupulous, deceitful, conniving • "short-term" suggests transient, limited nature (of benefits) • "dubious" suggests deep uncertainty, unreliability (of benefits) • "fill up" suggests saturation, full to overflowing • "spanking new": hyperbole of her apparent enthusiasm could be argued to betoken her fundamental antipathy • "boarded-up" suggests the development will be to the continued detriment of an already rundown Hastings; suggests that Hastings itself needs attention *Contrast* • "spanking new" versus "boarded-up" emphasises the pointlessness of building new premises when existing ones lie empty and abandoned *Tone* • some candidates may recognise and discuss the changing tone of this paragraph, in particular the somewhat defeated, hopeless tone of the first three sentences which changes to an angry, scathing, sceptical tone in the rest of the paragraph.

Question		Expected Answer(s)	Max Mark	Additional Guidance
4.	(a)	Candidates should identify two claims the government makes about the protesters. For full marks candidates must demonstrate understanding of two claims. Award marks 1 + 1	2	Possible answers include: The government claims the protesters: • are not interested in protecting the environment • are only concerned about looking after their own (advantaged) interests • have no interest in the fate of people less well-off/less fortunate than themselves
	(b)	Candidates should analyse how at least two features of language convey the strength of the writer's belief in tree conservation. Award marks according to the quality of understanding shown of key ideas and the quality of comment on appropriate language features. Award **2 marks** for reference plus detailed/insightful comment. Award **1 mark** for reference plus more basic comment. Award **0 marks** for reference alone. Award marks 2 + 2 **or** 2 + 1 + 1 **or** 1 + 1 + 1 + 1		Possible answers include: *Word choice* • "special kind" suggests people who don't care about trees are particularly awful • "arrogance" suggests the insufferable conceit of those who don't care about trees • "bigger than history" suggests arrogance on a grand scale • (repeated) use of violent language when describing trees — felling (ie "cutting down" suggests something akin to an act of murder; "slicing into" suggests a savage, violent attack; "brutal" suggests a ruthless, crude, cruel, vicious attack; "grotesque" suggests a strange, distorted, unnatural, outrageous act; "chopping down" suggests a categorical, definitive act). • "fine" suggests the majesty, worthiness of the tree • "aching (poignancy)" suggests how deeply hurt she is when trees are cut down • writer's use of "shock tactics" in making a developed, quite visceral comparison between killing living creatures and cutting down trees: some candidates may recognise that the writer shows the strength of her feeling by developing an argument that many readers will find shocking or extreme *Imagery* • by comparing (in a very visual way) the fate of trees to the fate of whales and elephants ("mightiest mammal") the writer is associating trees with elevated concepts such as the awesome wonder of the natural world, beauty, majesty, conservation … • "enormous creature" suggests epic scale of what is being destroyed *Punctuation/sentence structure* • use of colon (line 31) introduces explanation of what this "special kind of arrogance" involves • punchy conclusion to paragraph ("Not so a tree") emphasises just how different the trees' situation is to even the most impressive or endangered of our natural creatures
5.	(a)	Candidates should identify any four reasons given for cutting down trees. Candidates should use their own words as far as possible. No marks for straight lifts from the passage. Award **1 mark** for each point made. Award marks 1 + 1 + 1 + 1	4	Possible answers include: • they may contribute to land sinking (which would affect buildings on that land) • they are regarded as potentially damaging to vehicles • they are regarded as potentially a danger to young people • they shed (twigs and leaves) and that leaves things (public spaces, houses or vehicles) looking dirty and untidy

Question		Expected Answer(s)	Max Mark	Additional Guidance
5.	(a)	*(continued)*		<ul><li>some trees are considered unfashionable (and people want to replace them with something more popular)</li><li>selling trees makes money, can boost a country's economy</li><li>they are converted into timber for commercial purposes</li></ul>
	(b)	Candidates should analyse how their chosen image emphasises the writer's opposition to cutting down trees. Award marks according to the quality of comment. Award **2 marks** for a detailed/insightful comment. Award **1 mark** for a more basic comment. Award **0 marks** for mere identification of an image. When dealing with imagery, candidates must demonstrate recognition of the literal root of the image and then explore how the writer is extending it figuratively. Award marks 2 **or** 1 + 1	2	Possible answers include:<ul><li>"butchers" suggests that municipal workers are cutting back the trees to a significant degree and that the work performed is brutal and indiscriminate</li><li>"embarrassed stumps" suggests that trees look vulnerable/exposed/self-conscious after the work has been carried out on them</li><li>"autumnal hell" hyperbolic term suggests ridicule of the wild over-reaction of those who find trees a problem at particular times of the year</li><li>"like a beautiful girl being forced to sell her hair" suggests Burma gave away part of the country's natural beauty for money</li></ul>
6.		Candidates should evaluate the final paragraph's effectiveness as a conclusion to the passage as a whole. Award marks according to the quality of comment. Award **2 marks** for appropriate attention to the idea of a conclusion. Award **1 mark** for a more basic comment.	2	Possible answers include:<ul><li>the writer concedes that inevitably trees will be cut down to make way for developments, a point she has already made in relation to the Hastings development and government policy in general</li><li>the writer returns to an argument which she has discussed throughout the passage: economic growth versus the innate value of trees. The Hastings development is an example of economic growth (very short-term in the writer's opinion), while the writer stresses at several points the value of preserving trees (for example, establishing the majesty and wonder of trees in the opening paragraphs; showing how much they mean to ordinary people protesting against the Hastings development; suggesting they are more important than creatures great and small)</li><li>the writer concludes by re-asserting how important a part of our heritage trees are: they are a link to our past ("they are our history inscribed in the natural world") and a means by which people leave their mark on society ("which rich men, planting beautiful orchards to their own glorious memory"). The link to the past idea has already been developed, for example in lines 10–11, while the idea of planting trees for posterity is explicitly discussed in lines 38–39 ("planting … loved ones").</li><li>some candidates will recognise the elevated quality of the writing in the final paragraph (quite different in tone to some of the almost brutally graphic sections of the passage) and link it to the persuasively idealistic message the writer has been trying to convey in much of the passage</li></ul>

Question		Expected Answer(s)	Max Mark	Additional Guidance
7.		Candidates should identify key areas of agreement in the two passages by referring in detail to both passages.	5	Candidates can use bullet points in this final question, or write a number of linked statements.
		There may be some overlap among the areas of agreement. Award marks according to the extent to which a candidate has covered two points or one.		Award a mark which reflects the quality of response in two areas:
				• identification of the key areas of agreement in attitude/ideas
		Candidates may include quotations in their evidence from the passage, but should support these with explanations.		• level of detail given in support
		The grid below shows key areas of agreement. Other answers are possible.		Award **5 marks** for identification of three key areas of agreement with detailed/insightful use of supporting evidence.
				Award **4 marks** for identification of three key areas of agreement with appropriate use of supporting evidence.
				Award **3 marks** for identification of three key areas of agreement.
				Award **2 marks** for identification of two key areas of agreement.
				Award **1 mark** for identification of one key area of agreement.
				Award **0 marks** for failure to identify any key area of agreement and/or misunderstanding of task.
				NB: A candidate who identifies only two key areas of agreement may be awarded up to a maximum of four marks, as follows
				• two marks for identification of two key areas of agreement **plus**:
				either
				• a further mark for appropriate use of supporting evidence to a total of three marks
				or
				• a further two marks for detailed/insightful use of supporting evidence to a total of four marks
				A candidate who identifies only one key area of agreement may be awarded up to a maximum of two marks, as follows
				• one mark for identification of one key area of agreement a further mark for use of supporting evidence to a total of two marks

	Area of agreement	Passage 1	Passage 2
1.	awe/wonder/majesty	spiritual, almost religious significance; comparison to whales, elephants	magnificence of the kauri
2.	heritage/permanence	link to previous centuries; certain feature in an uncertain world; will outlive us all	have outlasted the moa; now treated with reverence in New Zealand
3.	trees as teachers	we should question our assumption of superiority	we can learn from trees
4.	ordinary people see trees' importance	Hastings protesters; gift to posterity	New Zealand conservationists; Kenyan women (impact on quality of life)
5.	government and businesses' misguided economic priorities	government short-termism (Britain, Burma, Iceland, etc); trees considered expendable in the interests of "progress"	opposition to tree-based farming; profit-driven outlook of big businesses
6.	lack of respect	councils, officialdom, some homeowners	historical clearing; governments; companies; western desire to control nature
7.	brutality	trees are cut down or cut back quite brutally	hacking and racking continues

PAPER 2 — CRITICAL READING

SECTION 1 — Scottish Text

- Candidates should gain credit for their understanding, analysis and evaluation of the extract and either the whole play or novel, or other poems and short stories by the writer.

- In the final 10-mark question the candidate should answer the question in either a series of linked statements, or in bullet points.

Detailed Marking Instructions for each question

PART A — SCOTTISH TEXT — DRAMA

Text 1 — Drama —*The Slab Boys* by John Byrne

Question	Expected Answer(s)	Max Mark	Additional Guidance
1.	1 mark awarded for comment on Jack's attitude to the work of the slab room plus quotation/reference 1 mark awarded for comment on either Phil or Spanky's attitudes to the work of the slab room plus quotation/reference Marks awarded 1+1	2	Possible answers include: Jack • 'What the lads do, basically, is dole out …'/'dump it onto'/'Then it's just a matter of' description of slab room work in matter-of-fact list of activities suggests that the work done is unskilled, routine, unimaginative • Any one example from above list (e.g., 'dole out', 'dump it') suggests his dismissive attitude to the 'unskilled' work done in slab room • 'Bit of a diff from the studio, eh?' suggests a derogatory attitude to slab room, by comparing it unfavourably to the studio where 'real art' goes on Slab Boys • 'bile green/acne yellow' suggests sickness/revulsion for the work done in the slab room OR suggests they do not take their work seriously
2.	For full marks, answers must refer to both Jack and the slab boys, but not necessarily in equal measure 2 marks awarded for detailed/insightful comment plus quotation/reference. 1 mark for more basic comment plus quotation/reference 0 marks for quotation/reference alone. (Marks may be awarded 2+2, 2+1+1 or 1+1+1+1)	4	Possible answers include: Slab Boys • 'Why don't you vamoose, Jacky Boy?' (Spanky) despite Jack's seniority, Spanky tells him to leave; tone is contemptuous and belittling • 'Plooky Chops … them boils of yours is highly smittal' (Phil) cruel comment makes light of his skin problem and seeks to humiliate Jack by joking about it • 'Keep away from me! Hector, fling us over the Dettol!' (Phil) exaggerated mock-fear of the supposed contagion of his skin condition, requiring disinfectant as a weapon to protect himself, develops idea of humiliating Jack • Sequence of comments 'It would take … with pliers' builds up the sense of absurdity about the extreme treatment needed to cure Jack's condition, further humiliating him

Question	Expected Answer(s)	Max Mark	Additional Guidance
2.	*(continued)*		Jack • 'I'm warning you, McCann' ineffectual attempt to assert his authority over Phil indicates Jack's hostility • 'Jealousy ... on a desk' Jack assumes that Phil's hostility is due to envy and sneers at his lack of success, in comparison with his own progress • 'Don't worry, you haven't been condemned to spend the rest of the day here' by reassuring Alan that he has not been 'condemned' to spend long with the slab boys, he conveys his contempt for them and what they have to offer
3.	2 marks awarded for detailed/insightful comment plus quotation/reference. 1 mark for more basic comment plus quotation/reference. 0 marks for quotation/reference alone. (Marks may be awarded 2+2, 2+1+1 or 1+1+1+1)	4	Possible answers include: • Phil and Spanky's creation of the 'folk tale'/'plague tale' narrative, complete with villagers and red paint warnings, used to continue the mockery of Jack • Phil's deliberate refusal to call Alan by his actual name, e.g., 'Eamonn ... young Dowdalls' aims to undermine his importance and the significance of his visit • Phil's 'lesson' to Alan about slab room work: exaggerated simplicity to the point of ridiculousness 'this here is what we call a sink ... s-i-n-k' to mock Alan and ridicule the idea of having to explain to him the simple work they do • Phil and Spanky's double act of quick-fire comments/using pseudo-formal address, e.g., 'Mr Mac' asserts their control over the situation • Phil and Spanky's use of Hector as a 'visual aid' in teaching Alan about the slab room work, both humiliates Hector and continues the mockery of Alan/slab boy work e.g., 'Note the keen eye ... the firm set of the jaw' (as if he is a fine physical specimen)/'They're forced up under cucumber frames' (as if Hector is a particularly exquisite plant/flower)

Text 2 — Drama — *The Cheviot, the Stag and the Black, Black Oil* by John McGrath

Question	Expected Answer(s)	Max Mark	Additional Guidance
4.	Candidates can answer in bullet points in this final question, or write a number of linked statements.	10	Up to 2 marks can be achieved for identifying elements of commonality as identified in the question, i.e. how Byrne explores attitudes to authority.
			A further 2 marks can be achieved for reference to the extract given.
			6 additional marks can be awarded for discussion of similar references to at least one other part of the text.
			<u>In practice this means:</u>
			Identification of commonality (2) e.g. Figures of authority are regarded with disrespect, and sometimes openly with contempt, by Phil and Spanky (1)
			Promoted figures such as Curry/Jack sometimes use their authority inappropriately (1)
			From the extract:
			2 marks for detailed/insightful comment plus quotation/reference;
			1 mark for more basic comment plus quotation/reference;
			0 marks for quotation alone.
			e.g. Phil and Spanky humiliate Jack about his skin and mock his introduction of Alan to the slab room's 'intricacies' while Jack, unable to inspire genuine respect, is reduced to making ineffectual threats (2)
			From at least one other part of the text:
			as above for up to 6 marks
			Possible answers include:
			• Curry uses his authority to belittle Phil's hopes of entry to art college: he is annoyed with Phil for applying without permission, rather than being impressed by his artistic skill
			• Phil's refusal to accept the authority of those in charge shown by his fury at the suggestion that he should seek permission to apply to art college

Question	Expected Answer(s)	Max Mark	Additional Guidance
4.	*(continued)*		• Mr. Barton's position of authority is used by Curry as an unseen presence with which to threaten/reprimand the slab boys e.g. 'Mr Barton's just blown his top out there.' • Hector immediately begins to assert his authority over the slab boys when he is promoted to a desk ('I'll be expecting some smart grinding from this department in the future') despite his previous low status in the slab room • Curry's appearances in the slab room are for the purpose of reprimanding the lads e.g., 'Look at this paper ... 'S like bloody roughcast' his authority tends to express itself through negative and/or aggressive comments.
5.	For full marks candidates should deal with both Loch and the Speakers but not necessarily in equal measure. 2 marks may be awarded for detailed/insightful comment plus quotation/reference. 1 mark for more basic comment plus quotation/reference. 0 marks for quotation/reference alone. (Marks may be awarded 2 + 2, 2 + 1 + 1 or 1 + 1 + 1 + 1)	4	Possible answers include: Loch • 'The Marquis is not unaware of his responsibility' formal/grandiose tone suggests the appropriate gravity of the Marquis' attitude • 'responsibility' suggests that Marquis takes his role of wealthy man very seriously • 'lasting future interest and honour of his family' suggests that his aims are noble and grand • Parenthesis of 'as well as their immediate income' suggests that the actual money he can make is an afterthought, rather than his main motivation Speakers • 'immediate income was over £120,000' bald statement of figure emphasises the extent of his wealth and lack of need for more money • 'in those days ... quite a lot of money' ironic understatement suggests that he was immensely wealthy and did not need to clear the Highland lands • Repetition of 'inherited' emphasises just how much he gained from his family, without having to work for any of it • 'that had coal-mines on it' mentioned at the end of the sentence as a comical afterthought, suggests the immense potential for wealth • 'inherited the Bridgewater Canal' blunt statement emphasises the incongruity of one person owning a canal a vital part of the country's infrastructure • 'he acquired three quarters of a million acres of Sutherland' huge numbers emphasises the extent of his land ownership, suggesting the unfairness of a system where one man can possess so much

Question	Expected Answer(s)	Max Mark	Additional Guidance
6.	2 marks may be awarded for detailed/insightful comment plus quotation/reference. 1 mark for comment plus quotation/reference (x2). 0 marks for quotation/reference alone. (Marks awarded 2 or 1 + 1)	2	Possible answers include: • 'parcel of beggars' categorises all the people of Sutherland using the stereotype of 'beggars' because they are poor • 'cunning and lazy' stereotypes them as vicious and shows no sympathy or understanding of their plight • 'slavery to their own indolence' suggests that they, rather than the social system of the day, are to blame for their poverty • contrast between glowing picture of 'general interests ... happiness of the people' and 'the present state of Highlanders' suggests that everything about their culture is at odds with the prospect of prosperity • 'To be happy ... productive' emphatic statement indicates his simplistic view of their lives • 'worship industry or starve' simple statement of these two alternatives indicates no sense of the suffering which the people will face • 'The present enchantment ... broken' sums up their way of life as something to be destroyed, with no appreciation of its value to them
7.	For full marks candidates should deal with both the characters' apparently positive aims and their real motivation but not necessarily in equal measure. 2 marks may be awarded for detailed/insightful comment plus quotation/reference. 1 mark for more basis comment plus quotation/reference. 0 marks for quotation/reference alone. (Marks may be awarded 2 + 2, 2 + 1 + 1 or 1 + 1 + 1 + 1)	4	Possible answers include: Apparently positive aims • 'The coast of Sutherland abounds ... fish' positive tone creates sense of the 'promised land' waiting for the people • 'Not only ... herring too' suggests plenty and variety of food • 'Culgower ... Kockglass' list of apparently favourable locations suggests the extensive positive possibilities for future life • 'perfect natural harbour' suggests the beauty and harmony of the location, implying that life will be easy there • 'they are just in the state of society for a savage country ... Canada' presents forced emigration as an opportunity • 'wealth ... palpable' list of positive effects of clearing the Highlands emphasises the range of benefits for all Real motivation • 'Believe it or not ... used these words' undermines the nobility of the aims previously stated by Loch, suggesting a much more cynical aim • 'And there is said to be coal at Brora' stated as an apparent afterthought, suggests that the Highland people moved there could be exploited as miners • 'draining to your coast-line' suggests that the people are a swamp-like nuisance to be removed for the benefit of the land • 'mildewed districts cleared' suggests that the people are a disease/affliction on the land • 'swarm of dependants' dehumanises the people by suggesting they and their children are an infestation to be cleared out • The 'bargaining' exchange between Loch and Sellar, in which the rents/transport of people are included as one commodity to be negotiated emphasises their lack of humanity in considering the people's fate

Question	Expected Answer(s)	Max Mark	Additional Guidance
8.	Candidates may choose to answer in bullet points in this final question, or write a number of linked statements.	10	Up to 2 marks can be achieved for identifying elements of commonality as identified in the question i.e. how McGrath uses unusual dramatic techniques to highlight central concerns. A further 2 marks can be achieved for reference to the extract given. 6 additional marks can be awarded for discussion of similar references to at least one other part of the text by the author. In practice this means: Identification of commonality (2) e.g. by having characters step outside their roles and speak directly to the audience, McGrath undermines what the characters have said (1) and encourages the audience to consider the key issues of the play in a direct and immediate way (1) From the extract: 2 marks for detailed/insightful comment plus quotation/reference; 1 mark for more basic comment plus quotation/reference; 0 marks for quotation/reference alone. 2 marks only for discussion of extract. e.g. freezing the action during the discussion by Loch and Sellar enables the Speakers to highlight the hypocrisy of those two characters by presenting the audience with a factual account of the situation (2) From at least one other part of the text as above for up to 6 marks. Possible answers include: • The MC speaks directly to the audience in the opening, encouraging them to sing along, sets the tone of informality which encourages them to feel part of the performance and closer to the issues highlighted • Sellar's speech to the audience, 'I am not a cruel man … businessman' followed by winking encourages the audience to feel complicit in his lies, undermining any further comments he makes • Use of Readers to read out the list of atrocities carried out against the Highlanders follows the 'normal' acting out of one such incident and conveys the extent of the horror • The Company become sheep, bleating and crawling towards Harriet Beecher-Stowe, emphasising the mindlessness and herd mentality of those who believe her and others like her • Climactic ending when the Cast, in turn, speak to the audience 'out of character', comparing the past with the present/future, leaving the audience with a final sense of the play's key themes

Text 3 — Drama — *Men Should Weep* by Ena Lamont Stewart

Question	Expected Answer(s)	Max Mark	Additional Guidance
9.	2 marks awarded for detailed/insightful comment plus quotation/reference. 1 mark for more basic comment plus quotation/reference. 0 marks for quotation/reference alone. (Marks may be awarded 2+2, 2+1+1, 1+1+1+1)	4	Possible answers include: • 'Aw shut up!'/'Ye stupid fool!' suggests her aggressive dismissal of Alec • 'An I'm warnin you!' throwing Alec's words back at him with increased menace suggests her total lack of respect • 'You're no the only pebble on ma beach …' image suggests Alec's insignificance in Isa's life • 'it's time ye wis making a bit o dough again' suggests she only views Alec as a source of income • 'Aye. *Mebbe*' stress on '*Mebbe*' her sarcasm/realism in the face of Alec's desperate optimism suggests her dismissive attitude/dominance • 'Aye, an I mind the last hauf dizzen times …' cutting across Alec's reminiscence suggests she has no time for his fond memories of better times • 'Whit kind o fur? Rabbit?' sarcasm suggests sense of inadequacy as a provider • 'That's a you're guid for. Rinnin.' suggests her contempt for Alec's cowardly weakness
10.	For full marks candidates must deal with both dialogue and stage directions but not necessarily in equal measure. 2 marks awarded for detailed/insightful comment plus quotation/reference. 1 mark for more basic comment plus quotation/reference. 0 marks for quotation/reference alone. (Marks may be awarded 2+2, 2+1+1, 1+1+1+1)	4	Possible answers include: Dialogue • '…I'll kill ye! I wull! I'll kill ye!' repeated exclamations/threats suggest Alec's aggression and his need to control Isa/the fact that he is at the end of his tether • 'Did I hurt ye? I didnae mean tae hurt ye …' following 'I'll kill ye!' suggests how quickly Alec's feelings swing from murderous threats to anxiety as soon as Isa is angry with him • 'Isa, I'm sorry.' Alec's pitiful apology suggests his desperate need to pacify Isa • 'I canna see naethin but him an you tae.g. ether …' suggests Alec's overwhelming sense of inferiority/insecurity • 'I'll get ye onythin ye want …' – Alec's desperate promise reveals his anxiety about losing Isa • 'I proamise, Isa! I proamise! … if ye'll stay wi me …' Alec's pitiful pleading suggests his desperate need for her • 'I love ye, Isa; honest, I dae.' his earnest declaration suggests his desperation in the face of her cold-heartedness Stage directions • '*He gets hold of her by the throat*' violent actions against Isa indicate his frustration/desperate need to control her • '*He panics and drops her*' deep fear that he has gone too far and actually hurt her

Question	Expected Answer(s)	Max Mark	Additional Guidance
11.	2 marks awarded for detailed/insightful comment plus quotation/reference. 1 mark for more basic comment plus quotation/reference. 0 marks for quotation/reference alone. (Marks may be awarded 2, 1+1)	2	Possible answers include: • *'Love*! Hee-haw!' suggests Isa believes that love as a romantic feeling does not exist • 'There's nae sich a thing.' emphatic statement denying the possibility of love • 'There's wantin tae get intae bed wi someone ye fancy …' suggests she believes that in place of love, there is sex • 'or wantin someone'll let ye lie in yer bed an no have tae work;' suggests she believes that in place of love there is the more practical requirement to be provided for financially • 'No roon aboot here, onyway.' suggests she believes that romantic love isn't possible for people living in such straitened circumstances
12.	Candidates may choose to answer in bullet points in this final question, or write a number of linked statements.	10	Up to 2 marks can be achieved by identifying elements of commonality as identified in the question, i.e. how the theme of love is explored. A further 2 marks can be achieved for reference to the extract given. 6 additional marks can be awarded for discussion of similar references to at least one other part of the text by the writer. <u>In practice this means:</u> Identification of commonality (2) e.g. love can take many forms including that between husband/wife, parent/child, sibling etc, (1) and this can be destructive or life enriching (1) From this extract: 2 marks for detailed/insightful comment plus quotation/reference; 1 mark for more basic comment plus quotation/reference; 0 marks for quotation/reference alone. e.g., Isa's cold-hearted, mercenary attitude towards love means that she expects her husband to provide for her. She therefore rejects any warmth or affection from Alec when he fails to meet her demands (2) From elsewhere in the text: as above for up to 6 marks. Possible answers include: • Maggie believes that love (and marriage) is fulfilling, and makes a woman happy. She says to Lily, '… it's a pity ye had yon disappointment; ye might hev been real happy wi the right man and a couple weans.' • Lily is cynical about love. She does not believe that love is necessary; she is suspicious of men and prefers her independence 'Men! I'm wantin nae man's airms roon me.'

Question	Expected Answer(s)	Max Mark	Additional Guidance
12.	(continued)		• John shows his devotion for Maggie when, for once, he is able to treat her by buying her a new hat when he has a job • Jenny's attitude towards love is more practical. She acknowledges that being treated with respect is important and values the security that comes with a successful relationship: 'But I'm happy, an I'm makin him happy. We've a nice wee flat in a clean district, wi trees an wee gardens.' • Love for children is unconditional: Maggie says, 'Once they've been laid in yer airms, they're in yer heart tae the end o yer days, no matter whit way they turn oot.'

PART B – SCOTTISH TEXT – PROSE

Text 1 – Prose – *The Painter* by Iain Crichton Smith

Question	Expected Answer(s)	Max Mark	Additional Guidance
13.	For full marks differing attitudes must be dealt with but not necessarily in equal measure. 2 marks awarded for detailed/insightful comment plus quotation/reference. 1 mark for more basic comment plus quotation/reference. 0 marks for quotation/reference alone. (Marks may be awarded 2 or 1 + 1)	4	Possible answers: • 'certain responsibility' suggests desire to protect/care for him • 'maintained that ... so clever' suggests their certainty that he is too talented for his own good • 'always pointed ... pride' suggests they value his work • 'one of our greatest assets' suggests positive sense of ownership • 'wonderful artist' suggests admiration for/recognition of his skill • 'made us uncomfortable' suggests they are unsettled by his artistic vision • 'less glamorous'/'narrow and crooked'/'spindly and thin'/'confused and weird' suggests their resentment of his portrayal of the community • 'strange boy' suggests their (judgemental) view of him as different • 'slapdash manner' suggests their criticism of his bohemian disregard for convention
14.	2 marks awarded for detailed/insightful comment plus quotation/reference. 1 mark for more basic comment plus quotation/reference. 0 marks for quotation/reference alone. (Marks may be awarded 2 or 1 + 1)	2	Possible answers: • 'not a wholly harmonious place' suggests conflict in the community • 'share of barbarism' suggests uncivilised • 'violence' suggests aggression • 'quarrelled about land' suggests petty territorial disputes • 'much less often about women' suggests low status of women • 'prolonged controversy' suggests unforgiving/holding grudges • 'As is often the case ... hair' suggests stereotypical views

Question	Expected Answer(s)	Max Mark	Additional Guidance
15.	For full marks both positive and negative features should be dealt with but not necessarily in equal measure. 2 marks awarded for detailed/insightful comment plus quotation/reference. 1 mark for more basic comment plus quotation/reference. 0 marks for quotation/reference alone. (Marks may be awarded 2 or 1 + 1)	4	Possible answers: Positive • 'he spent most … shed' suggests industrious • 'when sober … very kind man' suggests potential for warmth • 'fond of his children … strong they were' suggests his pride in his family • 'in those moments … his life' suggests his feeling of temporary happiness • 'sunny-tempered … village' suggests good humoured/affability • 'singing songs happily … suggests a capacity for intense emotions/joy Negative • 'he regularly beat up' suggests he was abusive/cruel • 'when it suited him … temper' suggests unpredictable mood swings' • 'he would grow violent' suggests became aggressive • 'morose' suggests self-pitying • 'snarl' suggests savagery • 'especially the weakest and most inoffensive people' suggests bullying behaviour
16.	Candidates may choose to answer in bullet points in this final question, or write a number of linked statements.	10	Up to 2 marks can be achieved for identifying elements of commonality as identified in the question i.e. the theme of isolation. A further 2 marks can be achieved for reference to the extract given. 6 additional marks can be awarded for discussion of similar references to at least one other text. In practice this means: Identification of commonality (2) e.g. Crichton Smith creates characters/communities isolated because of their inability or unwillingness to fit in (1) leading to profound and/or life-limiting situations (1) From the extract: 2 marks for detailed/insightful comment plus quotation/reference 1 marks for more basic comment plus quotation/reference 0 marks for quotation alone e.g. 'he insisted on painting things as they were' suggests that William's uncompromising artistic vision sets him apart from the community (2)

Question	Expected Answer(s)	Max Mark	Additional Guidance
16.	*(continued)*		From at least one other text: as above for up to 6 marks Possible answers include: • *Mother and Son* John/his mother isolated as a result of their claustrophobic relationship and domestic circumstances which limit their choices and leads to a spiral of mutual destruction • *Red Door* After a lifetime of loneliness and isolation, Murdo is given the opportunity to break free from the restrictive environment • *The Telegram* The geographical remoteness of the community leads to emotional isolation which results in a failure to grasp the scale of/reasons behind the war • *In Church* The 'priest's' inability to cope with the war leads to his self-isolation and resultant loss of sanity/humanity • *The Crater* Robert is isolated from the other soldiers by the responsibilities of his role as an officer, which he finds overwhelming

Text 2 — Prose — *The Bright Spade* by George Mackay Brown

Question	Expected Answer(s)	Max Mark	Additional Guidance
17.	2 marks awarded for detailed/insightful comment plus quotation/reference. 1 mark for more basic comment plus quotation/reference. 0 marks for quotation/reference alone. (Marks may be awarded 2+2, 2+1+1 or 1+1+1+1)	4	Possible answers include: • 'That winter … island' suggests the island has suffered significant loss • 'wind squatted in the east … with her breath' metaphor/personification suggests the wind is a malevolent presence blasting the island with deadly power and destroying all life and colour by blowing on it • 'clung to life like the last tattered leaf on a branch' simile suggests the frailty of James of Moss and the desperation of his struggle to live as well as the inevitability of his death • 'lay stiff and pale as a candle' simile suggests the lifelessness and sadness/hopelessness of her death: her life snuffed out like a flame • Repetition of 'thin': 'thin harvest … ale was sour and thin' emphasises the lack of nourishment and richness in what nature produces on the island • Word choice of 'sour and thin' suggests the lack of flavour and pleasure to be had on the island

Question	Expected Answer(s)	Max Mark	Additional Guidance
18.	2 marks awarded for detailed/insightful comment plus quotation/reference. 1 mark for more basic comment plus quotation/reference. 0 marks for quotation/reference alone. (Marks may be awarded 2+2, 2+1+1 or 1+1+1+1)	4	Possible answers include: • 'This will need a deep grave' suggests that the laird's son is well-fed and privileged but this has not protected him from death, which has come to all/sense of many more relatives to follow, therefore a reminder of mortality • 'he threw up many fine white bones, the laird's ancestors, with his spade' suggests the delicate aristocratic nature of the laird's family which nonetheless receives the same rough treatment from death as do the poor • contrast between 'half a guinea' and 'nothing at all … coarse tobacco snuff' emphasises that death claims both rich and poor/death is the great 'leveller' • 'nobody expected most of the old people and sickly people to see the spring' word choice of 'nobody' and 'most of' emphasises the certainty of the extent of the deaths • '… snow and small fires the infant breathed her last' softness of 's' alliteration and vocabulary 'breathed her last' emphasises the sadness of the baby's death • 'the day after the funeral'/'never lived with Amos again' speedy departure of baby's mother/finality of 'never … again' emphasises the significance of one, 'little' human death – the baby was holding them together • 'one large grave for the foreigners' suggests the anonymity of death, when there are no loved ones to mourn
19.	1 mark awarded for each comment on two aspects of Jacob's personality, supported by reference to the extract. 0 marks for quotation/reference alone. (Marks awarded 1+1)	2	Possible answers include: • Self-indulgent when opportunity arises: 'had hardly sobered up' quickly drank all the whisky given by the widow of Moss • Decent/unselfish: prepared to bury the very poor people e.g., Samuel Ling, Jean of Ness for virtually no payment at all • Matter of fact: 'sneezed heroically for a month' suggests that the snuff was not to his taste, but he accepted it as payment because it was all there was • Demanding/stands up for himself: 'Who will pay my fee?' when asked to dig large grave for the unknown foreigners

Question	Expected Answer(s)	Max Mark	Additional Guidance
20.	Candidates can answer in bullet points in this final question, or write a number of linked statements.	10	Up to 2 marks can be achieved for identifying elements of commonality as identified in the question, i.e. Mackay Brown's use of characters as metaphorical and/or symbolic figures. A further 2 marks can be achieved for reference to the extract given. 6 additional marks can be awarded for discussion of similar references from at least one other short story. In practice this means: Identification of commonality (2) e.g. Mackay Brown uses characters to comment on significant aspects of humanity such as death, the journey through life, belonging (1) The universal nature of these characters means that all readers can relate to them (1) From the extract: 2 marks for detailed/insightful comment plus quotation/reference; 1 mark for more basic comment plus quotation/reference; 0 marks for quotation alone. e.g. Jacob represents death, who comes to rich and poor, loved and unknown alike, wielding his bright spade like a scythe, cutting down all before him (2) From at least one other text: as above for up to 6 marks Possible answers include: • *The Whaler's Return* Flaws represents flawed humanity, journeying across the island, facing challenges and trials which test his resolve/character (such as the incident with the tinkers) until he reaches the safety of home, represented by the worthy, though ugly, Peterina • *A Time to Keep* Bill is the 'everyman' character who struggles to be an individual and to have a passionate and genuine relationship in the face of community pressure and the trials of an uncaring natural world • *The Wireless Set* Howie represents the desire for change and progress: young, naive and confident, he brings the destructive outside world into the community in the form of the wireless set of which he is so proud, leading ultimately (through the war) to his own death • *The Wireless Set* the missionary represents the insensitive role of the 'outside' church, failing to understand the pain of Howie's parents or the values of their community and dismissing their reaction to their son's death as callous • *The Eye of the Hurricane* Cpt Stevens represents flawed and, at times, self-destructive, humanity, which nonetheless has a certain heroism, evidenced by the devotion of his old shipmates and their stories of his courage and determination at sea

Text 3 — Prose — *The Trick Is To Keep Breathing* by Janice Galloway

Question	Expected Answer(s)	Max Mark	Additional Guidance
21.	2 marks may be awarded for detailed/insightful comment plus quotation/reference. 1 mark for more basic comment plus quotation/reference. 0 marks for quotation reference alone. (Marks may be awarded 2+1, 1+1+1)	3	Possible answers include: • 'It never looks as good as I'd like' sentence following list of housework creates an anti-climax highlighting her efforts are perpetually fruitless/expectations are unrealistic • 'running … for the biscuits' suggests her desperation to appear as though she's coping • 'I get different ones … she will enjoy' suggests Joy is keen to please/seem hospitable • 'I can't choose in a hurry' blunt statement conveys her placing too high an importance on a trivial task/conceals her inner turmoil • 'I wait for too long … confused … wrong money' fixation on minor details conveys her frustration/negative perception • 'clutching'/'nearly drop the milk'/'flustered' suggests the futility of her intense desire to create a good impression • 'These visits are good … sends this woman out of love. He insisted.' Emphatic short sentence highlights Joy's reluctance to accept the help, signalling the likelihood that the visit will be unsuccessful
22.	2 marks may be awarded for detailed/insightful comment plus quotation/reference. 1 mark for more basic comment plus quotation/reference. 0 marks for quotation reference alone. (Marks may be awarded 2+1, 1+1+1)	3	Possible answers include: • 'I said … strangers' suggests self-doubt/fear of not coping • 'she would find me out and let me talk. *Make me* talk' sequence of verbs suggests Joy's perception of the visit as combative • 'without knocking and frightens me' suggests her lack of control and perceived invasion of her personal space • 'Tray … spoon' layout of list/list emphasises her deliberate attempt to think through what she is doing/calm herself down/appear organised • 'the biscuits the biscuits' repetition/layout of lines emphasises her panic/excessive desire to create a good impression • 'I burst … I polish … I make …' list of verbs emphasises her frantic attempts to take control • 'It sloshes' suggests physical manifestation of her nervousness/lack of control • 'still wearing my slippers dammit' Joy's thoughts reveal her disappointment in herself for not appearing perfect

Question	Expected Answer(s)	Max Mark	Additional Guidance
23.	2 marks may be awarded for detailed/insightful comment plus quotation/reference. 1 mark for more basic comment plus quotation/reference. 0 marks for quotation reference alone. (Marks may be awarded 2+2, 2+1+1, 1+1+1+1)	4	Possible answers include: • 'She does it every time.' emphatic sentence suggests that the visit follows the same pattern every time • 'thinking her way into the part' suggests they are following what seems like a rehearsed script/lack of naturalness • 'I throw a little difficulty every so often' suggests Joy's deliberate attempts to appear convincingly natural • incongruity of insertion of drama into prose text suggests their interaction resembles a rehearsed script • 'So, how are you … how's life …' suggests the same formulaic questions are repeated every visit • 'improvise' suggests that even apparently more spontaneous comments are in the context of the constraints • 'knowing I don't want her … can't talk to her' suggests both are aware of the lack of any real meaning in their interaction

Text 4 — Prose — *Sunset Song* by Lewis Grassic Gibbon

Question	Expected Answer(s)	Max Mark	Additional Guidance
24.	Candidates may choose to answer in bullet points in this final question, or write a number of linked statements.	10	Up to 2 marks can be achieved for identifying elements of commonality as identified in the question, i.e. Joy's difficulties with social interaction. A further 2 marks can be achieved for reference to the extract given. 6 additional marks can be awarded for discussion of similar references from at least one other part of the text. In practice this means: Identification of commonality (2) e.g. Joy finds it difficult to speak honestly to family, friends and colleagues (1) due to her reluctance to reveal her vulnerability/to acknowledge to herself that she is not coping. (1) From the extract: 2 marks for detailed/insightful comment plus quotation/reference; 1 mark for more basic comment plus quotation/reference; 0 marks for quotation alone. e.g. Joy struggles to express her true feelings to the Health Visitor, who is there to support her, because of her conflicted state of mind 'I don't want her to be here/that I want her to be here but I can't talk to her.' (2) From at least one other part of the text: as above for up to 6 marks Possible answers include: • Joy struggles to express her true feelings with the various doctors that she sees as she feels that they do not help or understand her

Question	Expected Answer(s)	Max Mark	Additional Guidance
24.	*(continued)*		• Joy finds it difficult to cope with Ellen's attempts to look after her and feed her because of her need to hide her anorexia • Joy conceals her feelings when replying to Marianne's suggestion about positive ways forward as she doesn't want to disappoint her; for example, her 'right choice' in seeking medical help • Joy engages in a number of problematic and meaningless relationships with men in an attempt to overcome her overwhelming grief at the loss of Michael • Uneasy relationship with her sister Myra stems from early experience of bullying, for example 'Hands like shovels. Myra left marks.'
25.	2 marks awarded for detailed/insightful comment plus quotation/reference. 1 mark for more basic comment plus quotation/reference. 0 marks for quotation reference alone. (Marks may be awarded 2+1 or 1+1+1)	3	Possible answers include: • 'carelessly' suggests lack of focus • 'breath of them rising up like a steam' suggests insubstantial quality • 'seemed fine … Spring' suggests sense of their greatness • 'their feet … behind' suggests their mythical qualities • 'looked at them over-long' suggests transfixed state • 'glimmered' suggests fleeting • 'ceased to be there' suggests sense of altered reality • 'mirages' suggests sense of unreal vision • 'dreamt by a land' suggests that they are a creation of the land • 'shook her head … daft' suggests coming out of dreamlike state
26.	2 marks awarded for detailed/insightful comment plus quotation/reference. 1 mark for more basic comment plus quotation/reference. 0 marks for quotation reference alone. (Marks may be awarded 2+1 or 1+1+1)	3	Possible answers include: • 'farming folk did well' suggests farming was highly profitable • 'drove of Irish steers' suggests plenty • 'lush green grass' suggests the land was fertile and productive • 'grew fat and round' suggests the cattle would thrive/farmers would make good money at market • 'in the shortest while' suggests a quick financial return • 'so many beasts' suggests abundance of livestock

Question	Expected Answer(s)	Max Mark	Additional Guidance
27.	2 marks awarded for detailed/insightful comment plus quotation/reference. 1 mark for more basic comment plus quotation/reference. (Marks may be awarded 2+2 or 2+1+1 or 1+1+1+1)	4	Possible answers include: • 'Chris gave a loud gasp' suggests her shock at the change in his physical appearance • 'so altered' suggests he has been profoundly changed • 'thin' suggest physical privations experienced • 'his fine eyes queered and strained' suggests he has experienced trauma • 'Even his laugh seemed different' suggests that everything about him has been altered, even the most natural responses • *'I'm not a ghost yet!'* suggests his acknowledgement of change/death he has witnessed • 'the lice … awful … some devil fair sucking and sucking the life from his skin' suggests the constant physical suffering from the conditions of war • 'his old laugh queerly crippled' suggests that beneath surface appearances, Chae has been disabled/weakened by his experiences of war • 'gey green and *feuch!*' emphatic description of decay, followed by the exclamation of disgust indicates the horror of what Chae has seen
28.	Candidates can answer in bullet points in this final question, or write a number of linked statements.	10	Up to 2 marks can be achieved for identifying elements of commonality as identified in the question — i.e. how Grassic Gibbon uses symbolism to explore the central concerns of the text. A further 2 marks can be achieved for reference to the extract given. 6 additional marks can be awarded for discussion of similar references to at least one other part of the text. In practice this means: Identification of commonality e.g. Grassic Gibbon uses characters, incidents and setting as representative of wider issues (1) such as loss of a way of life, impact of war, aspects of Scotland. (1) From the extract: 2 marks for detailed/insightful comment plus quotation/reference 1 mark for more basic comment plus quotation/reference 0 marks for quotation/reference alone e.g., Chris' vision of Rob and Ewan seeming to emerge from the land symbolises the old Scottish agricultural way of life which is ending. (2) From at least one other part of the text: as above for up to 6 marks Possible answers include: Scottish Chris represents the land and English Chris represents pursuit of education/modernity Standing stones represent continuity in human history/what has gone before

Question	Expected Answer(s)	Max Mark	Additional Guidance
27.	*(continued)*	4	The cutting down of trees represents the death of a generation of young men in the war/ change of use of the land
			John Guthrie represents the patriarchal society/grim Calvinism of the past
			Celebration of wedding represents the richness of Scottish culture and community spirit

Text 5 – *Prose* – *The Cone-Gatherers* by Robin Jenkins

Question	Expected Answer(s)	Max Mark	Additional Guidance
29.	2 marks awarded for detailed/insightful comment plus quotation/reference.	2	Possible answers include:
	1 mark for more basic comment plus quotation/ reference.		• 'his friends the finches' Calum is identified with nature, and is among those he loves/ trusts
	0 marks for quotation/reference alone.		• 'safe from the hawk' the security of the finches, hidden from predators, makes Calum feel comfortable/reassured
	(Marks may be awarded 2 or 1+1)		• 'ground of snares and stumbles was far below' suggests distance between him and danger/clumsiness on the ground, emphasising that he is in his element
			• 'seals were playing' suggests innocent/ carefree enjoyment of life
			• 'cushat doves were crooning' suggests comforting, harmonious sound
			• 'his brother ... singing' suggests pleasure in that Neil is at ease
			• 'present joy' suggests immediacy of his feeling of pleasure
			• 'nor did he see ... toppled down' suggests lack of awareness of future destruction
30.	The impact on both Calum and Neil should be dealt with, although not necessarily in equal measure.	4	Possible answers include: Calum:
	2 marks awarded for detailed/insightful comment plus quotation/reference.		• 'in agitation' suggests his anxiety at the approach of Duror
	1 mark for more basic comment plus quotation/ reference.		• 'could not concentrate' suggests he is worried/distracted by Duror's presence
	0 marks for quotation/reference alone.		• 'like an animal in danger' (simile) suggests he reacts like a frightened creature when trapped/cornered
	(Marks may be awarded 2+2, 2+1+1, 1+1+1+1)		• 'began to whimper' animal cry suggests vulnerability
			• 'panicky' suggests Calum's desperation as Duror approaches
			• 'let some cones dribble' suggests he has lost control and confidence and is making mistakes by dropping the cones
			Neil:
			• 'he would still pass by' suggests that he is thinking through Duror's probable movements
			• 'murmured to Calum' suggests a quiet calmness in Neil's voice as he tries to reassure Calum that there is no threat
			• 'felt sympathy' suggests Neil's awareness of humanity's isolation
			• 'typical of nature' suggests Neil's resentment that nature is against them as there is no camouflage from the leaves
			• 'objected to this spying' suggests Neil's heightened awareness that they are being watched

Question	Expected Answer(s)	Max Mark	Additional Guidance
31.	2 marks awarded for detailed/insightful comment plus quotation/reference. 1 mark for more basic comment plus quotation/reference. 0 marks for quotation/reference alone. (Marks may be awarded 2+2, 2+1+1, 1+1+1+1)	4	Possible answers include: • 'What's the matter with you?' question suggests Neil's irritability/impatience with Callum • 'He's just doing his work, like you and me.' explanation suggests Neil's pragmatism, his sense of needing to cope • 'He became angry' suggests annoyance with himself due to his lack of control of the situation • question 'What are you moaning for?' suggests that Neil's protectiveness expresses itself in an aggressive way • 'passion of resentment' suggests his sense of a clear injustice • tone of the final sentence indicates his cynicism in that Lady Runcie-Campbell/Duror value the trees more than the workers
32.	Candidates may answer in bullet points in this final question, or write a number of linked statements.	10	Up to 2 marks can be achieved for identifying elements of commonality as identified in the question, i.e. how Jenkins develops the theme of power. A further 2 marks can be achieved for reference to the extract given. 6 additional marks can be awarded for discussion of similar references to at least one other part of the text by the writer. <u>In practice this means:</u> Identification of commonality (2) e.g. Characters from the upper-class, such as Lady Runcie-Campbell, are seen to be powerful in the novel. Her actions have an impact on the main characters of the novel. (1) As gamekeeper, Duror wields power on the estate and is able to exploit this to intimidate Callum. (1) From the extract: 2 marks for detailed/insightful comment plus quotation/reference; 1 mark for more basic comment plus quotation/reference; 0 marks for quotation alone.

Question	Expected Answer(s)	Max Mark	Additional Guidance
32.	*(continued)*		e.g. Duror's powerful presence in the woods is enough to unsettle both Calum and Neil: Calum panics and begins to drop his collected cones, whereas Neil's bitterness and resentment build as he tries to calm his brother. (2)
			From at least one other part of the text:
			as above for up to 6 marks
			Possible answers include:
			• Duror exerts power over Calum by exploiting his love of nature: he cruelly involves him in the deer drive knowing that it would pain him to see an injured animal
			• Duror has power over his wife and can choose when he spends time with her, much to the anger and resentment of his mother-in-law
			• Duror has power over Lady Runcie-Campbell in the absence of her husband when he influences her/advises her not to let the cone-gatherers stay in the beach hut as he does not want his wood 'defiled'
			• Roderick challenges his mother's power when he disagrees with her over her failure to give the cone-gatherers a lift or to let them shelter from the storm in the beach hut
			• Neil attempts to exert some degree of power over Lady Runcie-Campbell by refusing to help Roderick when he is stuck in the tree

PART C — SCOTTISH TEXT — POETRY

Text 1 — Poetry — *A Man's A Man For A' That* by Robert Burns

Question	Expected Answer(s)	Max Mark	Additional Guidance
33.	2 marks awarded for detailed/insightful comment plus quotation/reference. 1 mark for more basic comment plus quotation/reference. 0 marks for quotation/reference alone. (Marks may be awarded 2+2, 2+1+1 or 1+1+1+1)	4	Possible answers include: • 'honest poverty' suggests being born into poverty can go together with integrity • 'coward – slave' suggests being ashamed of being poor is shameful in itself/shows a lack of courage, spirit, manliness • 'hangs his head' suggests servility/shame in response to poverty which speaker goes on vehemently to reject • 'toils obscure' suggests poverty and hard work go together; the hard work of the poor is unacknowledged • question creates a sense of disbelief that anyone would be ashamed of honest poverty • 'guinea stamp ... gowd' suggests true worth is the real substance of the man whereas wealth is a superficiality

Question	Expected Answer(s)	Max Mark	Additional Guidance
34.	2 marks awarded for detailed/insightful comment plus quotation/reference. 1 mark for more basic comment plus quotation/reference. 0 marks for quotation/reference alone. (Marks may be awarded 2+2, 2+1+1 or 1+1+1+1)	4	Possible answers include: • 'hamely fare' suggests something wholesome, unpretentious as opposed to 'wine' suggests luxurious and non-essential • 'hoddin grey' suggests sense of homeliness or ordinariness as compared to 'silks' something luxurious, for show, for creating an impression • 'fools'/'knaves' derogatory terms to underline his contempt • 'tinsel show' suggests the flashy, fancy but ultimately entirely superficial nature of luxury • contrast in idea of 'honest' 'e'er sae poor' man being a 'king o' men' – a contradiction in worldly terms • 'struts/stares' suggests one posing around, but to no effect • 'riband, star & a' that' suggests dependence on others/superficial insignia for his status • 'belted knight/marquis/duke' all mere titles/all can be created by man • 'rank'/'their dignities' man-made distinctions that have no value in themselves/are all about status/can be bought'
35.	2 marks awarded for detailed/insightful comment plus quotation/reference. 1 mark for more basic comment plus quotation/reference. 0 marks for quotation/reference alone. (Marks may be awarded 2 or 1+1)	2	Possible answers include: • 'let us pray' suggests we should unite in our desire for a fairer world • 'As come it will' suggests certainty that the day must come when the best human qualities are valued more than rank or privilege • 'o'er a' the earth' suggests such ideas will be welcomed globally/transcend national boundaries • 'Shall brothers be for a' that!' suggests universal brotherhood/humanity is coming/will change the world • Repetition/climax of 'for a' that' reinforces inevitability of change

Question	Expected Answer(s)	Max Mark	Additional Guidance
36.	Candidates can answer in bullet points in this final question, or write a number of linked statements.	10	Up to 2 marks can be achieved for identifying elements of commonality as identified in the question, i.e. Burns' use of contrast to explore central concerns.
			A further 2 marks can be achieved for reference to the extract given.
			6 additional marks can be awarded for discussion of similar references to at least one other poem by the poet.
			In practice this means:
			Identification of commonality (2)
			e.g. Burns uses contrast to ridicule people/ideas (1) to undermine their status/position within society (1)
			From this poem:
			2 marks for detailed/insightful comment plus quotation/reference
			1 mark for more basic comment plus quotation/reference
			0 marks for quotation/reference alone
			e.g the contrast between the self-importance of 'thon birkie, ca'd a lord' and the integrity of 'The man of independent mind' highlights the central concern of the value of ordinary men. (2)
			From at least one other poem:
			as above for up to 6 marks.
			Possible answers include:
			• *Address to the Deil* contrasts the stereotypical depiction of the devil with a far homelier persona to highlight the ridiculous nature of contemporary theological teachings
			• *Holy Willie's Prayer* the persona's view of himself as an epitome of righteousness contrasts with his actions which are lustful and spiteful highlighting the central concern of hypocrisy
			• *A Poet's Welcome to his Love–Begotten Daughter* contrast between his love for his daughter and the narrow-minded and judgemental moral attitudes of the time highlighting the pettiness of the prevailing social attitudes
			• *Tam O'Shanter* moralising narrative voice contrasts with energetic description of Tam's actions highlights the life-affirming tone of the poem
			• *To a Mouse* mouse's suffering being confined to the present is contrasted with the speaker's awareness of future uncertainty to highlight the fragility of life

Text 2 — Poetry — *Originally* by Carol Ann Duffy

Question	Expected Answer(s)	Max Mark	Additional Guidance
37.	2 marks awarded for detailed/insightful comment plus quotation/reference. 1 mark for more basic comment plus quotation/reference. 0 marks for quotation/reference alone. (Marks may be awarded 2 or 1 + 1)	2	Possible answers include: • 'fell through the fields' suggests the loss of control/uncertainty the speaker felt about the move • 'cried ... bawling' suggests intensity of upset/ intensity of physical reaction • *Home, Home* repetition suggests depth of longing • 'vacant rooms' suggests the emotional emptiness the speaker now feels • 'blind toy' suggests the speaker's incomprehension of the events taking place/ identification with child's helplessness • 'holding its paw' suggests the speaker's need for reassurance and comfort in the face of the events taking place
38.	2 marks awarded for detailed/insightful comment plus quotation/reference. 1 mark for more basic comment plus quotation/reference. 0 marks for quotation/reference alone. (Marks may be awarded 2 + 2, 2 + 1 + 1 or 1 + 1 + 1)	4	Possible answers include: • abruptness/word choice 'your accent wrong' emphasises her sense of exclusion • parenthesis of 'which seem familiar' suggests an unpleasant sense of disorientation brought about by her surroundings • 'unimagined' suggests a sense of trepidation/ confusion/fear • word choice/alliteration of 'big boys' suggests her sense of vulnerability when encountering local youths • word choice of 'eating worms' suggests her horror at the outlandish behaviour of the local youths • word choice of 'shouting' suggests she feels intimidated by the way the local youths spoke • word choice of 'You don't understand' suggests her sense of exclusion from the society of her peers • 'stirred like a loose tooth' suggests her nagging insecurity about the move
39.	2 marks awarded for detailed/insightful comment plus quotation/reference. 1 mark for more basic comment plus quotation/reference. 0 marks for quotation/reference alone. (Marks may be awarded 2 + 2, 2 + 1 + 1 or 1 + 1 + 1)	4	Possible answers include • 'skelf of shame' suggests that she is only mildly bothered by her brother's actions in this new environment • 'my tongue ... snake' suggests her old accent is fading, another stage in her process of assimilation • positioning of 'But' suggests a change of status, from being excluded to being accepted • sequence 'you forget ... or change' suggests the gradual process of assimilation she has gone through/an uncertainty as to how exactly the process took place • positioning at end of poem/abruptness of 'And I hesitate.' suggests a slight uncertainty about what culture she identifies with, or where she belongs

Question	Expected Answer(s)	Max Mark	Additional Guidance
40.	Candidates can answer in bullet points in this final question, or write a number of linked statements.	10	Up to 2 marks can be achieved by identifying elements of commonality as identified in the question i.e. how the poet explores concerns about identity
			A further 2 marks can be achieved for reference to the text given.
			6 additional marks can be awarded for discussion of similar references to at least one other poem by the poet.
			<u>In practice this means:</u>
			Identification of commonality (2) e.g. Duffy presents us with characters who have to face situations which prompt them to consider who they are (1); some are able to adapt their view of themselves whilst others are incapable of doing this, to their cost (1)
			From the poem:
			2 marks for detailed/insightful comment plus quotation/reference;1 mark for more basic comment plus quotation/reference;
			0 marks for quotation/reference alone.
			e.g. the speaker's sense of alienation from her new surroundings gradually subsides as she starts to become assimilated; the cost of this assimilation however, is an uncertainty about her cultural identity (2)
			From at least one other poem:
			as above for up to 6 marks
			Possible comments include:
			• *Anne Hathaway* a feature of the speaker's sense of who she is – the lover and wife – is threatened by the death of her husband; however, through her memories she can still retain a part of her previous identity
			• *Havisham* the deterioration in her state of mind due to the conflicting emotions she feels for her ex-lover leads to losing a stable sense of who she is
			• *War Photographer* his difficulty in reconciling his public identity as a professional photographer – getting on with the job – and his human response to the horror and suffering he has encountered
			• *Valentine* the speaker is unwilling to be defined by society's conventional view of romantic love which prompts her attempt to break free of e.g., romantic stereotypes and be more 'truthful', more authentic
			• *Mrs Midas* given the consequences of her husband's 'wish', she struggles with the loss of certain aspects of her previous identity – wife, lover, potential mother – due to her prioritising her own self preservation

Text 3 — Poetry — *Some Old Photographs* by Liz Lochhead

Question	Expected Answer(s)	Max Mark	Additional Guidance
41.	2 marks awarded for detailed/insightful comment plus quotation/reference. 1 mark for more basic comment plus quotation/reference. 0 marks for quotation/reference alone. (Marks may be awarded 2+2, 2+1+1 or 1+1+1+1)	4	Possible answers include: • 'weather evocative as scent' synaesthesia creates an appealing and atmospheric picture/suggests that strong/powerful/pleasant memories are stirred by the photographs • 'romance' suggests a passion/nostalgia for the moment captured in the image • 'big skies over the low wide river' assonance echoes the slow flowing river and suggest that those looking at the photographs are momentarily captivated/held by the picture • 'fabulous' suggests the images were extraordinary/almost mythical in quality • 'film-noir stills' conveys a magical, graceful impression which contrasts with the functional subject of 'Central Station' • 'freezing fog silvering the chilled, stilled parks' alliteration/assonance/consonance creates an enchanting/sentimentalised view of the city as captured in the photographs • 'silvering' suggests that the black and white images had an ethereal/otherworldly quality • 'glamorous' creates the impression that this period was enchanting/elegant/exciting to remember • imagery of 'drops on a rainmate are sequins' links the ordinary with the exotic as caught in a photograph/moment in time • repetition of 'of' phrases conveys the idea that the observer was enjoying looking quickly/flicking through the photographs • structure of lines echoes the idea of a series of memories being jogged as the photographs are browsed
42.	2 marks awarded for detailed/insightful comment plus quotation/reference. 1 mark for more basic comment plus quotation/reference. 0 marks for quotation/reference alone. (Marks may be awarded 2+2, 2+1+1 or 1+1+1+1)	4	Possible answers include: • 'your' personal address conveys intimacy and invites the reader to share the past with the speaker • 'still-lovely mother laughs' the snapshot of an earlier time conveys the joy and energy of the subject and creates a touching/sweet/tender memory • 'whipped up ... beach' reference to seaside suggests a joyous/carefree/youthful time reflected in the photograph • 'before you were even born' links to the romantic/idealistic view that the younger years are the happiest period in one's life • 'all the Dads in hats' suggests a familiar, unified crowd who represent a settled/more gentle period of time • list of weathers conveys the routine/familiar/ordinary/nature of the fathers' working lives in the past • contrast of 'dark/white' symbolises the predictable pattern of life at that time

Question	Expected Answer(s)	Max Mark	Additional Guidance
43.	2 marks awarded for detailed/insightful comment plus quotation/reference. 1 mark for more basic comment plus quotation/reference. 0 marks for quotation/reference alone. (Marks may be awarded 2 or 1+1)	2	Possible answers include: • alliteration 'starlings swarming ... perfect/permanent' signifies a change in focus from the sentimental to a more pragmatic view of the past • 'permanent cloud' suggests the photographs may conceal/obscure the reality of the past • 'what was/never really' reinforces the idea that the images belong in the past by denying their reliability • 'all the passing now' suggests that the images are merely a moment in time and should be treated as no more than this • evocation of senses 'noise/stink/smoky breath' serves as a reminder of the reality of Glasgow's industrial past
44.	Candidates may answer in bullet points in this final question, or write a number of linked statements.	10	Up to 2 marks can be achieved by identifying elements of commonality as identified in the question, i.e. , Lochhead's exploration of important aspects of life through everyday objects and/or situations. A further 2 marks can be achieved for reference to the text given. 6 additional marks can be awarded for discussion of similar references to at least one other poem by the poet. In practice this means: Identification of commonality (2) e.g. Lochhead chooses a variety of everyday/commonplace situations/objects as representations such as meetings, buildings, household furnishings (1) to illustrate her reflections on the complexities of human interaction. (1) From the poem: 2 marks for detailed/insightful comment plus quotation/reference; 1 mark for more basic comment plus quotation/reference; 0 marks for quotation/reference alone. e.g. The photographs present an idealised picture of the past which illuminates her views on the transient/fleeting nature of time.(2) From at least one other poem: as above for up to 6 marks Possible comments include: • *View of Scotland/Love Poem* 'dusted mantelshelves' represents the true value she places on the hospitable/generous nature of others much more so than material wealth • *For my Grandmother Knitting* the knitting needles represent the care and effort she placed in ensuring that her children/grandchildren were cherished and loved which seems not to be valued anymore

Question	Expected Answer(s)	Max Mark	Additional Guidance
44.	*(continued)*		• *The Bargain* what seems like an ordinary shopping trip is actually used as an opportunity to reflect on the past in order to make sense of the present • *My Rival's House* the visit to her boyfriend's mother highlights the destructive impact of emotional manipulation • *Last Supper* the simple preparations for a meal provide the opportunity to reflect on the intense nature of betrayal

Text 4 — Poetry — *Sounds of the Day* by Norman MacCaig

Question	Expected Answer(s)	Max Mark	Additional Guidance
45.	2 marks awarded for detailed/insightful comment plus quotation/reference. 1 mark for more basic comment plus quotation/reference. 0 marks for quotation/reference alone. (Marks may be awarded 2+2, 2+1+1, 1+1+1+1)	4	Possible answers include: • repetition of 'When a … it was' build up of 'puzzles' and answers creates a sense of the unknown • inversion delays the explanation for the sounds thus creating anticipation • 'clatter' (onomatopoeia) discordant sound suggesting unease • 'creaked' suggests disturbance/eerie mood • 'lapwing … premises' suggests a change in circumstances • 'snuffling puff' (onomatopoeia/assonance) suggests quiet sound before build-up of tension • 'black drums rolled' suggests ominous hint of event to follow • 'water falling sixty feet into itself' suggests disturbing/destructive force
46.	2 marks awarded for detailed/insightful comment plus quotation/reference. 1 mark for more basic comment plus quotation/reference. 0 marks for quotation/reference alone. (Marks may be awarded: 2 or 1+1)	2	Possible answers include: • 'When the door scraped shut' sound of closing door is a metaphor for the end of the relationship • onomatopoeia of 'scraped shut' creates harsh sound which contrasts with silence to follow/the natural sounds earlier in the poem • the sentence structure/inversion of the previous stanza is reversed with object mentioned before sound 'door … scraped shut,' • the hyperbole of 'it was the end/of all the sounds there are.' emphasises the significance of the moment

Question	Expected Answer(s)	Max Mark	Additional Guidance
47.	2 marks awarded for detailed/insightful comment plus quotation/reference. 1 mark for more basic comment plus quotation/reference. 0 marks for quotation/reference alone. (Marks may be awarded 2+2, 2+1+1, 1+1+1+1)	4	Possible answers include: Tone • direct/monosyllabic language 'You left me' creates bitter tone • hyperbole of 'quietest fire in the world' creates tone of despair • 'the whole hand goes numb' creates tone of hopelessness/finality Imagery • 'quietest fire in the world' suggests the contrast between the previous love/passion of the relationship and the absolute devastation/loss of the separation • 'plunge' suggests total immersion in relationship/resulting in grief/shock • 'bangle of ice' suggests the restriction/coldness of losing love • 'the whole hand goes numb' suggests inescapable/overwhelming/debilitating effect of loss of love
48.	Candidates may choose to answer in bullet points in this final question, or write a number of linked statements.	10	Up to 2 marks can be achieved for identifying elements of commonality as identified in the question i.e. how relationships are used to develop key themes. A further 2 marks can be achieved for reference to the text given. 6 additional marks can be awarded for discussion of similar references to at least one other poem by MacCaig. In practice this means: Identification of c ommonality (2) e.g. MaCaig presents relationships in which there is a crisis/difficulty of some kind (1) to explore the impact of loss/suffering/death/isolation etc. (1) From the poem: 2 marks for detailed/insightful comment plus quotation/reference; 1 mark for more basic comment plus quotation/reference; 0 marks for quotation/reference alone. e.g. the end of the relationship has affected the speaker so badly that he is no longer aware of/he is unable to appreciate the sounds of nature all around him 'It was the end of all sounds' emphasising the profound impact of loss (2) From at least one other text: as above for up to 6 marks

Question	Expected Answer(s)	Max Mark	Additional Guidance
48.	*(continued)*		Possible answers include: • *Aunt Julia* the speaker regrets the opportunities for communication missed as a result of her death and sees this as part of Scotland's heritage being lost • *Memorial* the speaker is haunted by the death of a loved one to such an extent that he can no longer enjoy visiting places where they had once been together and this conveys the universal and life-changing nature of loss • *Visiting Hour* the speaker's relationship with a dying relative and his inability to come to terms with the inevitability of their death • *Basking Shark* the speaker's chance encounter with the shark makes him reconsider humanity's destructive relationship with nature 'So who's the monster?' • *Assisi* the speaker reflects on society's relationship with vulnerable people represented by the beggar 'It was they who had passed the ruined temple' suggesting themes of lack of compassion, self-interest

Text 6 — Poetry — *The Ferryman's Arms* by Don Paterson

Question	Expected Answer(s)	Max Mark	Additional Guidance
49.	Both sides of the contrast must be dealt with for full marks but not necessarily in equal measure. 2 marks awarded for detailed/insightful comment plus quotation/reference. 1 mark for more basic comment plus quotation/reference. 0 marks for quotation/reference alone. (Marks may be awarded 2+2, 2+1+1 or 1+1+1+1)	4	Possible answers include: Atmosphere at beginning of the specified lines – the atmosphere of wonder/calm/security suggested by: • 'Screapadal in the morning/facing Applecross and the sun' or 'Screapadal that is so beautiful' Direct, descriptive simplicity of the language suggests calm/serenity/wonder • 'No words can be put …' and/or 'no picture, music or poem made for it' suggest the inexpressible wonder of Screapadal • 'Screapadal the sheep-pen and the cattle-fold' suggests that Screapadal is a world in itself, peaceful, self-contained • reference to 'Sanctuary' suggests a place of peace, shelter/respite, security, holy place Atmosphere towards the end of the specified lines –The atmosphere of threat/destruction/forced hardship suggested by: • 'half-dead'/'dead' repetition of references to death is unsettling, suggests threat • 'Rainy' reference to an individual who is associated with the forced movement of people out of Screapadal • 'put off the land' suggests forced removal of people, inhuman treatment • 'castle' and/or the associated word 'violence' suggests a place of threat/defence/aggression

Question	Expected Answer(s)	Max Mark	Additional Guidance
50.	2 marks awarded for detailed/insightful comment plus quotation/reference. 1 mark for more basic comment plus quotation/reference. 0 marks for quotation/reference alone. (Marks may be awarded 2 or 1+1)	2	Possible answers include: • Reference to 'green, red-rocked, yellow, light-grey, whiteness' many (and varied) adjectives of colour suggests that the place is bright/vibrant, etc. • Repetition of 'green' and 'light-grey' suggest that these colours stand out, and that the place is bright/vibrant • 'towers, columns and steeples,' comparing them to these man-made structures suggests the vastness/perpendicular height of the rocks • 'speckled light-grey' and/or 'whiteness in the sun' suggests that the place is lit/made bright/almost favoured by the sun
51.	2 marks awarded for detailed/insightful comment plus quotation/reference. 1 mark for more basic comment plus quotation/reference. 0 marks for quotation/reference alone. (Marks may be awarded 2+2, 2+1+1 or 1+1+1+1)	4	Possible answers include: • 'the Church of Falsehood' creates sympathy for the people in the suggestion (historical reference) that they might have been deceived by the Church at the time of the Clearances • 'high water'/'spring tide' suggests danger of flooding, and therefore creates sympathy for the people in that they were 'swept off' the land by the Clearances • 'lies' suggests deliberate deception • 'betrayed' creates sympathy in that the people were let down (historically) • 'the great pietist (Rainy)' bitter irony of the word 'pietist' (the opposite being suggested) creates sympathy for the people • 'without ... no ... only' accumulation of absences highlights the loss of a way of life
52.	Candidates may choose to answer in bullet points in this final question, or write a number of linked statements.	10	Up to 2 marks can be achieved for identifying elements of commonality as identified in the question, i.e. in how MacLean explores change in relation to people and/or places. A further 2 marks can be achieved for reference to the text given. 6 additional marks can be awarded for the discussion of similar references to at least one other poem by the poet. In practice this means: Identification of commonality (2) e.g. MacLean explores change in relation to individuals through the impact of traumatic circumstances/experiences (1) and change to communities due to wider world events/the passage of time (1) From the poem: 2 marks for detailed/insightful comment plus quotation/reference; 1 mark for more basic comment plus quotation/reference; 0 marks for quotation/reference alone. e.g. Reference to 'the great pietist Rainy' – ironic comment on his betrayal of local people in clearing the communities from Screapadal, which has left it desolate and uninhabited (2) From at least one other text: as above for up to 6 marks

Question	Expected Answer(s)	Max Mark	Additional Guidance
52.	*(continued)*		Possible comments include: • *Hallaig* a way of life/community changed/destroyed by the actions of man (specifically the impact of the Clearances) • *An Autumn Day* change brought by war (chaos, death) • *Heroes* individuals changed/altered by war • *I Gave You Immortality* changes caused by love and by the impact of time passing • *Shores* the speaker expresses a wish or desire for things not to change, however has to acknowledge that the only thing which lasts is the landscape
53.	2 marks awarded for detailed/insightful comment plus quotation/reference. 1 mark for more basic comment plus quotation/reference. 0 marks for quotation/reference alone. (Marks may be awarded 2+2, 2+1+1, 1+1+1+1)	4	Possible answers include: • 'I was magnetized' suggests lack of control/influence of fate • 'remote' conveys the sense that there is something distant and isolated • 'drawn (like a moth)' suggesting persona is pulled involuntarily away • 'darkened (back room)' connotations of the unseen and unknown/mystery • 'hummed to itself' suggests the pool table is a living/threatening presence • 'whole place deserted' suggests abandonment/isolation • 'I stood with my back turned' suggests vulnerability/lack of control • 'abrupt intestinal rumble' suggests discomfort/monstrous qualities • 'batted awake' suggests that inanimate object has life of its own • 'dusty green cowl' allusion to grim reaper
54.	2 marks awarded for detailed/insightful comment plus quotation/reference. 1 mark for more basic comment plus quotation/reference. 0 marks for quotation/reference alone. (Marks may be awarded 2 or 1+1)	2	Possible answers include: • 'screw back the globe' suggests a sense of absolute power/ability to control the world/turn back time • 'As physics ... negotiable' suggests the ability to exist outside the normal laws of the universe/control your own destiny • 'miracles' suggests winning outcome against all the odds • 'I went on to make' suggests active intervention of the speaker in own fate • 'immaculate clearance' suggests sense of perfection/pride in taking control • 'wee dab of side' suggests light-hearted confidence
55.	2 marks awarded for detailed/insightful comment plus quotation/reference. 1 mark for more basic comment plus quotation/reference. 0 marks for quotation/reference alone. (Marks may be awarded 2+2, 2+1+1, 1+1+1+1)	4	Possible answers include: • 'boat' allusion to ferry across the River Styx suggests transit from life to death • 'without breaking the skin of the water' the silent gliding of the ferry suggests death is unpredictable/can arrive unannounced • 'stretching' suggests endlessness of eternity • 'as black as my stout' emphasis on intensity of darkness suggests death is a mysterious presence

Question	Expected Answer(s)	Max Mark	Additional Guidance
55.	*(continued)*		• 'read and re-read the shoreline' repeated attempts to decipher his bearings suggests confusion/lack of control of direction in life • 'my losing opponent' reference to another part of himself suggests the divisions which exist within us • 'stuck in his tent of light' a moment frozen in time suggests that we can't eradicate our past/death
56.	Candidates may choose to answer in bullet points in this final question, or write a number of linked statements.	10	Up to 2 marks can be achieved by identifying elements of commonality as identified in the question, i.e. how Paterson explores the challenges of human experience. A further 2 marks can be achieved for reference to the text given. 6 additional marks can be awarded for discussion of similar references to at least one other poem by the poet. <u>In practice this means:</u> Identification of commonality (2) e.g., Paterson presents challenging experiences such as birth, growing up, relationships, death (1) to show how these shape our perception of the world and ourselves (1) From the poem: 2 marks for detailed/insightful comment plus quotation/reference; 1 mark for more basic comment plus quotation/reference; 0 marks for quotation/reference alone e.g. While waiting for the ferry, the speaker's pool game with himself forces him to confront his own mortality/accept that death is an inevitable part of life (2) From at least one other poem: as above for up to 6 marks Possible comments include: • *Nil Nil* through the deteriorating fortunes of the football team and the community, the speaker is forced to consider the inevitability of decline and death • *11:00 Baldovan* the negative effects of the passage of time are explored through the boys' altered perceptions after the bus journey • *Waking with Russell* the challenges of becoming a father allow the poet to explore how the direction of our lives can be altered by love • *The Thread* the poet deals with the difficulties of Jamie's birth, allowing him to reflect on the fragility of life • *Two Trees* the metaphor of the separation of the trees is used to explore the challenges in relationships/significance of human aspirations

Section 2 — CRITICAL ESSAY

Please see the assessment criteria for the Critical Essay on Page 171.

HIGHER ENGLISH
2019

PAPER 1 — READING FOR UNDERSTANDING, ANALYSIS AND EVALUATION

Marking instructions for each question

Passage 1

Question	Expected response	Max Mark	Additional Guidance
1.	For full marks two reasons must be identified. Candidates must attempt to use their own words. No marks for straight lifts from the passage. Award marks 1+1	2	Possible answers include: • the fact that this medium lasted for so long ('For the next 500 years') • most widely used method (of conveying facts) ('main form') • the facts were presented in a set layout ('fixed format') • it helped people to accept that objective facts existed ('stable and settled truths')
2.	For full marks there should be comment on at least two examples. Award **2 marks** for detailed/insightful comment plus quotation/reference. Award **1 mark** for more basic comment plus quotation/reference. Award **0 marks** for quotation/reference alone. Award marks 2+2, 2+1+1, 1+1+1+1	4	Possible answers include: • 'dizzying' suggests disorientating/confusing nature of the changes, relating to the developing role of the Internet • 'caught' suggests being trapped in an inescapable situation • 'confusing' suggests how puzzling and bewildering the times are • 'battles' suggests aggressive/dangerous conflict • 'opposing forces' suggests confrontation between hostile factions • the repetition/rhythm of 'between ... and ...' emphasises the indecision/doubt when confronted by polarisation • the list of contrasts 'between truth and falsehood ... a misguided mob' suggests the variety/quantity of conflicts • 'falsehood' suggests the potential for duplicity • 'rumour' suggests the potential for misinformation • 'cruelty' suggests the potentially malign use of the Internet • the polarising emotive language used to characterise the contrasts ('truth and falsehood', 'connected ... alienated', 'open ... gated enclosure', 'informed public ... misguided mob') suggests deterioration in society • 'gated enclosures' suggests exclusivity/insularity • 'misguided (mob)' suggests the mistaken ideas shared online • '(misguided) mob' suggests the potential threat of online groups
3.	Award **2 marks** for detailed/insightful comment. Award **1 mark** for more basic comment. Candidates must attempt to use their own words. No marks for straight lifts from the passage. Award marks 2 or 1+1	2	Possible answers include: • stature of truth has been lessened ('the diminishing status of truth') • we cannot decide on what is true ('we cannot agree on what these truths are') • there is no accepted way to find out what is true ('no consensus about ... achieve this consensus') • this leads to division/lack of communication within society/social breakdown ('chaos soon follows')

Question	Expected response	Max Mark	Additional Guidance
4.	Award **2 marks** for detailed/insightful comment. Award **1 mark** for more basic comment. Candidates must attempt to use their own words. No marks for straight lifts from the passage. Award marks 2+1 **or** 1+1+1	3	Possible answers include: It supports the idea that: • a false story can cause damage ('consequences are enormous') • an untrue story is taken as fact ('rumours') • news travels at considerable pace ('speed'/'quickly') • news is widely shared ('reach') • stories can become exaggerated ('the Louvre ... Pompidou ... French President') • it is not easy to counter such stories ('difficult to correct')
5.	For full marks there should be comment on at least two examples. Award **2 marks** for detailed/insightful comment plus quotation/reference. Award **1 mark** for more basic comment plus quotation/reference. Award **0 marks** for quotation/reference alone. Award marks 2+2, 2+1+1, 1+1+1+1	4	Possible answers include: • 'panic' suggests the hysterical reaction created by online news • 'malice' suggests the vindictiveness of those who spread untruths • 'deliberate manipulation' suggests premeditation in the curating of false news • repetition of 'sometimes'/list 'panic ... malice ... manipulation' emphasises range/quantity of negative reasons for spreading false news • 'falsehoods and facts' balancing of contrasting ideas/alliteration suggests a conflation of the two • '(information) cascade' suggests an overwhelming outpouring of information • 'false, misleading or incomplete' list suggests the range/quantity of negative features of information • 'misleading' suggests the internet causes people to believe something that is not true • 'cycle' suggests recurring damaging actions • 'unstoppable' suggests the inevitability/power of the process • 'momentum' suggests the ever-increasing/uncontrollable speed/power of the process
6.	Award **2 marks** for detailed/insightful comment. Award **1 mark** for more basic comment. Candidates must attempt to use their own words. No marks for straight lifts from the passage. Award marks 2+1 **or** 1+1+1	3	Possible answers include: • we are unaware of social media manipulation ('invisibly crafted') • filter bubbles are designed to confirm our convictions ('to reinforce our pre-existing beliefs'/'designed ... want to see') • filter bubbles isolate us from alternative viewpoints ('less likely ... worldview.') • filter bubbles prevent us from experiencing information that would provide a corrective to lies ('less likely ... shared.') • technological change has increased the negative influence of filter bubbles ('has become more extreme') • we have no control over filter bubbles because they are an integral part of the workings of some social media ('hardwired')

Question	Expected response	Max Mark	Additional Guidance
7.	For full marks candidates must deal with both imagery and sentence structure, but not necessarily in equal measure. Award **2 marks** for detailed/insightful comment plus quotation/reference. Award **1 mark** for more basic comment plus quotation/reference Award **0 marks** for quotation/reference alone. Award marks 2+2, 2+1+1, 1+1+1+1	4	Possible answers include: **Imagery** • 'junk-food news' suggests the worthlessness of the news/guilty pleasures of consuming the news • 'gorged' suggests the guilty/uncontrolled consumption of these stories even though we know they are false/destructive • '(fake news) farms' suggests the large scale production of the news stories/harvesting of these stories by those who seek to use them for their own ends • 'gangs' suggests intimidatory nature/pack mentality of those involved **Sentence structure** • 'clicks, advertising or profit' list suggests the range/quantity of dubious motives behind the creation of the news • 'But' at start of sentence signals renewed criticism of modern social media • '— and often more widely —' parenthesis emphasises the extent of false news • repetition of 'or'/list using 'or' emphasises the variety/quantity of positive properties which have been lost • sequence of 'fitting ... reinforcing ... driving' suggests escalation of the problem
8.	Award **2 marks** for detailed/insightful comment plus quotation/reference. Award **1 mark** for more basic comment plus quotation/reference. Award **0 marks** for quotation/reference alone. Award marks 2+1 or 1+1+1	3	Possible answers include: • 'It need ... this.' (short, emphatic statement/positioning) suggests forceful rejection of the current situation • (repetition/elaboration of) 'struggle ... worth it.' suggests the challenge/value of achieving truth • 'must' suggests necessity to carry out her suggested programme • 'search for truth' suggests quest for something of value • 'at the heart of everything' suggests that truth is a core value • 'building' suggests creating something significant • contrast of 'informed ... powerful' with 'not ... vulnerable' suggests the virtuous effects/positive outcome of her proposal • 'embraced' suggests need to openly accept the value of how news was gathered in the past • 'celebrated' suggests need to praise the news-gathering methods of the past • list of 'reporting ... statements.' suggests the (range/number of) quality aspects of journalism open to us • 'to discover what really happened' suggests the intrinsic value of truth • 'taking responsibility'/'we' suggests that the writer encourages us to get actively involved in her vision • 'kind of world we want to live in.' suggests the obviousness/attractiveness of her alternative vision

Passage 2

Question	Expected response	Max Mark	Additional Guidance
9.	Key areas of disagreement are shown in the grid.	5	Candidates can use bullet points in this final question or write a number of linked statements. The following guidelines should be used: Award **5 marks** for identification of three key areas of disagreement with detailed/insightful use of supporting evidence. Award **4 marks** for identification of three key areas of disagreement with appropriate use of supporting evidence. Award **3 marks** for identification of three key areas of disagreement. Award **2 marks** for identification of two key areas of disagreement. Award **1 mark** for identification of one key area of disagreement. Award **0 marks** for failure to identify any key areas of disagreement and/or misunderstanding of the task. NB: A candidate who identifies only two key areas of disagreement may be awarded up to a maximum of four marks, as follows: • two marks for identification of two key areas of disagreement **plus:** **either** • a further mark for appropriate use of supporting evidence to a total of three marks **or** • a further two marks for detailed/insightful use of supporting evidence to a total of four marks A candidate who identifies only one key area of disagreement may be awarded up to a maximum of two marks, as follows: • one mark for identification of one key area of disagreement, plus a further mark for use of supporting evidence to a total of two marks

	Area of Disagreement	Passage 1	Passage 2
1.	attitude towards/threat posed by the Internet	something of immediate concern/ something we can deal with	not something to cause concern 'Bring on the fake news'
2.	our ability to control our experience online	our online experience is controlled by other factors, for example 'personalised search functions'	we can exert control by learning how to 'think for ourselves'
3.	are the challenges presented by the Internet different/unprecedented?	yes: the certainty provided by printing has been replaced by the confusion of online communication	no: each technological development has brought challenges which we have surmounted for example car, post, telephone
4.	impact on individuals	impact of social media is potentially damaging to the individual: 'attacks the vulnerable'	suggests we need to become more resilient: 'protecting people from nastiness ... learning to take no notice.'
5.	impact on society	divisions within society, caused by Internet communication, will lead to social breakdown/positive action must be taken	'impossible to predict' need to keep things in perspective/society tends to cope

	Area of Disagreement	Passage 1	Passage 2
6.	value of Internet content	comparison with 'junk-food' suggests little value in much of the online content	'there's plenty that's useful' suggests there is much to be valued; possible positive effects of gaining privileged access to the thoughts of others
7.	discernment	enticing nature/scale of fake news makes discernment impossible for many people	discernment is open to all: 'let us learn to navigate'
8.	responsibility/regulation	media organisations must prioritise search for truth/self-regulate	regulation is impossible/it is the individual's responsibility 'oceans of nonsense … good deal of poison'

PAPER 2 — CRITICAL READING

Marking instructions for each question

SECTION 1 — Scottish Text

- Candidates gain marks for their understanding, analysis and evaluation of the extract and either the whole play or novel, or other poems and short stories by the writer.
- In the final 10-mark question the candidate should answer the question in a series of linked statements, or in bullet points.

Detailed Marking Instructions for each question

PART A — SCOTTISH TEXT — DRAMA

Text 1 — Drama — *The Slab Boys* by John Byrne

Question	Expected response	Max Mark	Additional Guidance
1.	For full marks, both stage directions and dialogue should be covered but not necessarily in equal measure. Award **2 marks** for detailed/ insightful comment plus quotation/reference. Award **1 mark** for more basic comment plus quotation/ reference. Award **0 marks** for quotation/ reference alone. Award marks 2+2, 2+1+1, 1+1+1+1	4	Possible answers include: **Stage directions** • '*(Phil holds up Parker pen … Alan can see it.)*' suggests a threat to Alan's precious pen at the moment he was about to warn Hector about how ridiculous he looks. • '*(Phil threatens to snap pen.)*' a more direct threat that the pen will be destroyed unless he backs them up in their setting up of Hector. **Dialogue** • 'Special design' suggests that he will stand out for positive reasons rather than looking ridiculous. • 'It's a knockout … A knockout.' Repetition/their use of the same words shows that they conspire together to manipulate Hector into thinking he looks good. • 'Your maw'll be asking you whose the teethmarks …' humorous exaggeration of his (supposed) attractiveness to Lucille helps to convince Hector to wear the ridiculous clothes they have provided. • 'Lucille is going to flip' suggests she will be amazed when in fact she will be horrified.
2.	For full marks different aspects should be covered but not necessarily in equal measure. Award **2 marks** for detailed/ insightful comment plus quotation/reference. Award **1 mark** for more basic comment plus quotation/ reference. Award **0 marks** for quotation/ reference alone. Award marks 2+2, 2+1+1, 1+1+1+1	4	Possible answers include: • 'Will I go now and ask her? Will I?' repetition suggests his eagerness/ need for reassurance. • '*(Heads for door.)*' suggests impulsive as he has not waited for a reply. • 'I can do that after I've asked Lucille' suggests his childish enthusiasm and complete lack of awareness of the reality of his situation. • stage direction '*(slightly bamboozled)*' suggests childish confusion. • his willingness to go along with Phil and Spanky's excuses of illness suggests that he is gullible and cannot see their true motives. • 'I don't mind doing a bit of swanking now that my clothes are up to date' suggests that he is quite pleased with himself in his new outfit. • 'What do I want that for?' suggests naive self-confidence.

Question	Expected response	Max Mark	Additional Guidance
3.	Award **2 marks** for detailed/insightful comment plus quotation/reference. Award **1 mark** for more basic comment plus quotation/reference. Award **0 marks** for quotation/reference alone. Award marks **2 or 1+1**	2	Possible answers include: • 'Good man. All the best' exaggerated support as if he were going on a heroic enterprise. • 'Good luck, son …' patronising dismissal. • 'Oh was it, by jove' use of 'posh', old-fashioned language to mock Alan's outdated (in their opinion) middle class values of decency. • 'A trick, you cad! Take that!' pretending to duel, suggesting Alan's defence of Hector is ridiculous, based on out-dated attitudes, part of the luxuries of a lifestyle they do not have.
4.	Candidates can choose to answer in bullet points in this final question, or write a number of linked statements.	10	Candidates can gain up to 2 marks for identifying elements of commonality as identified in the question, i.e. the theme of deception and/or self-deception is developed. Award a further 2 marks for reference to the extract given. Award 6 additional marks for discussion of similar references from at least one other part of the text by the writer. <u>In practice this means:</u> Identification of commonality (2) for example, deception/self-deception is practised by various characters throughout the play (1) for entertainment/to gain power/as a coping mechanism (1) • from the extract: Award **2 marks** for detailed/insightful comment plus quotation/reference Award **1 mark** for more basic comment plus quotation/reference Award **0 marks** for quotation/reference alone for example, Phil and Spanky's dressing Hector up in ridiculous clothes, for example the 'Off the shoulder' shirt and telling him it's a 'Special design' indicates the cruelty of their humour against others (2) • from at least one other text/part of the text: Award **2 marks** for detailed/insightful comment plus quotation/reference Award **1 mark** for more basic comment plus quotation/reference Award **0 marks** for quotation/reference alone In comments on the rest of the play, possible references include: • Curry deceives himself and tries to deceive others about his wartime experience in order to feel more powerful/exert authority • hiding Hector in the cupboard — taking their deception of him to extremes shows their insensitivity to him • Phil's self-deception about his chances of getting into art college ultimately leads to further pain as he loses his job

Question	Expected response	Max Mark	Additional Guidance
4.	*(continued)*		• Jack's criticism of Phil and Spanky's trickery of Hector 'You nobbled him when he first started' indicates that he feels their motive is to bring Hector down to their level/to undermine him rather than just for fun • Phil and Spanky's self-deception that they will start on a desk soon faces a rude awakening when Hector is promoted showing that their coping mechanism — disrespectful humour — has destroyed their chances Many other references are possible.

Text 2 — Drama — *The Cheviot, the Stag and the Black, Black Oil* by John McGrath

Question	Expected response	Max Mark	Additional Guidance
5.	Award **2 marks** for detailed/insightful comment plus quotation/reference. Award **1 mark** for more basic comment plus quotation/reference. Award **0 marks** for quotation/reference alone. Award marks 2+2, 2+1+1, 1+1+1+1	4	Possible answers include: • Opening two lines — repetitive sentence structure/blunt statistical statement/contrast emphasises the vast scale of depopulation. • 'wilderness' suggests complete desolation. • 'A great open lung' euphemistic way of describing the emptiness of the landscape. • 'Overcrowding? Not in Sutherland ...' irony created by the question and answer format. • 'a land of solitary splendour' irony of suggestion that de-population has become attractive to tourists whilst ignoring the suffering of the former inhabitants. • 'ruined crofting townships' loss of a way of life being presented as a tourist attraction. • 'tragedy' emphasises the scale of the suffering. • 'saleable commodity' human suffering is reduced to money-making enterprise.
6.	Award **2 marks** for detailed/insightful comment plus quotation/reference. Award **1 mark** for more basic comment plus quotation/reference. Award **0 marks** for quotation/reference alone. Award marks 2+2, 2+1+1, 1+1+1+1	4	Possible answers include: • 'ANDY McCHUCKEMUP' ridiculous nature of name represents careless attitude to property development. • 'Councillors ... money can buy' suggests corruption is positive. • debasement of iconic culture for commercial gain/use of pun 'Frying Scotsman'/'Fingal's Caff'. • incongruity of modern American imports combined with traditional Scottish terms for example 'Grouse-a-go-go', 'drive-in clachan' • oxymoronic 'natural, washable, plastic'. • juxtaposition of natural and man-made/'granitette' — vocabulary invented suggests fraudulence in business practices. • juxtaposition of 'seaweed-suppers', 'draught Drambuie' highlights ridiculous nature of tourism. • incongruity of 'yous've', 'wes've', 'wes' in business setting. • 'there was hee-haw but scenery' flippant dismissal of natural beauty.

Question	Expected response	Max Mark	Additional Guidance
7.	For full marks both attitudes must be covered. Award **1 mark** for comment plus quotation/reference (x2). Award **0 marks** for quotation/reference alone. Award marks 1+1	2	Possible answers include: **Lord Vat** • he is confrontational and hostile, treating Andy as a trespasser on his property. This possessiveness is seen through the use of the personal pronoun 'my'. • the use of the imperative 'Get off my land' emphasises his proprietorial/self-centred attitude. • the reference to the popular, sentimental Scottish song 'these are my mountains' emphasises his lack of genuine interest in the Highlands and its people. • dogmatic 'You're invading my privacy' leaves no latitude for negotiation on possession/reinforces his elitist snobbery. **Andy** • dismissive of true value of the countryside, 'backward area' 'improve it' — in other words, make it more profitable. • 'paradise for all the family' — clichéd slogan effect suggests quick profit-making attitude, turning the place into tourist attraction (and therefore no longer a real 'paradise').
8.	Candidates can answer in bullet points in this final question, or write a number of linked statements.	10	Candidates can gain up to 2 marks for identifying elements of commonality as identified in the question, i.e. the exploration of the theme of exploitation. Award a further 2 marks for reference to the extract given. Award 6 additional marks for discussion of similar references to at least one other part of the text by the writer. <u>In practice this means:</u> Identification of commonality (2) for example, exploitation is explored through the use of caricature (1) to highlight the historical abuses of Scotland's landscape and people (1) • from the extract: Award **2 marks** for detailed/insightful comment plus quotation/reference Award **1 mark** for more basic comment plus quotation/reference Award **0 marks** for quotation/reference alone for example, Andy McChuckemup represents a stereotypical exploitative developer who wants to capitalise on the resources of the Highlands at the expense of cultural identity (2) • from at least one other part of the text: Award **2 marks** for detailed/insightful comment plus quotation/reference Award **1 mark** for more basic comment plus quotation/reference Award **0 marks** for quotation/reference alone

Question	Expected response	Max Mark	Additional Guidance
8.	*(continued)*		In comments on the rest of the play, possible references include: • Reference to the Marquis of Stafford's huge income highlights the scale of the exploitation by the landed gentry • Loch and Sellar's comic duet for example 'The price of a culture is counted in gold' about the clearances indicates the grasping and devious attitudes of those in power — attempting to deceive the people that moving to the coast was advantageous • Lady Phosphate's preference for gaming estates shows her desire to exploit at the expense of the welfare of her tenants • caricature of Texas Jim: brash, self-important, ignorant American entrepreneur who exemplifies the exploitation of Scotland's oil by foreign interests • Lord Polwarth being controlled as a puppet dancing on a string (by Texas Jim and Whitehall) suggests the exploitation carried out by government which pretended to create safeguards for the extraction of oil but handed over control to outside interests Many other references are possible.

Text 3 — Drama — *Men Should Weep* by Ena Lamont Stewart

Question	Expected response	Max Mark	Additional Guidance
9.	For full marks both stage directions and dialogue should be covered but not necessarily in equal measure. Award **2 marks** may be awarded for detailed/insightful comment plus quotation/reference. Award **1 mark** for more basic comment plus quotation/reference. Award **0 marks** for quotation/reference alone. Award marks 2+2, 2+1+1, 1+1+1+1	4	Possible answers include: **Stage directions** • '*(screaming at him)*' suggests that Maggie is losing control. • '*seizes him, shakes him and hits him*' suggests she is so upset she is expressing herself through violence. • '*Crying hysterically*' suggests the intensity of her pain. • '*belabours Ernest*' suggests her frustration is unbearable. • '*collapses in a storm of weeping*' suggests she is distraught. • '*in a storm of tears she blunders out of the room*' suggests she is in such despair she is no longer in control of her physical movement. **Dialogue** • 'Look at yer new boots!' — Maggie's use of the command and the exclamation mark show how angry she is and how she wants Ernest to see the full stupidity of his actions. • 'I'll learn ye tae play fitba' in yer best boots' — her tone is aggressive and threatening, again showing her anger. • 'Whaur d'ye think I'll find the money for anither pair?' — use of the question shows Maggie's despair at the impossibility of their financial state. • 'Oh, I cannae staun ony mair o this … I cannae staun it!' — heartfelt repetition emphasises the depth of her despair. • 'Leave me alane! Leave me alane! I hate ye! I hate the hale lot o ye!' — short, monosyllabic sentences and the use of repetition suggest Maggie's despair has reduced her to a state of near-inarticulate rage.

Question	Expected response	Max Mark	Additional Guidance
10.	For full marks candidates must deal with more than one aspect of John's character. Award **2 marks** awarded for detailed/insightful comment plus quotation/reference. Award **1 mark** for more basic comment plus quotation/reference. Award **0 marks** for quotation/reference alone. Award marks 2+2, 2+1+1, 1+1+1+1	4	Possible answers include: • *'John gathers the two frightened children to him and sets an arm round each'* — John's attempt to comfort the children reveals his protectiveness as a father. • 'Wheesht, wheesht, the baith o ye, wheesht … me' — repetition of commands suggests John's need for control. • 'Yer mammy's no really angry at ye …'/'Your mammy's just tired'/'She'll be sorry ye were feart' — repeated explanations for Maggie's behaviour suggests John's loyalty to her. • '… mebbe we ought tae hae helped mak things a bit easier for her.' — use of inclusive 'we' suggests recognition of his own failings as a supportive husband. • 'When women gets that tired, they kind o loss their heids, ye unnerstaun?' — John's patronising comment suggests a lack of empathy for women. • 'I'll try, son, I'll try.' — (repetition) suggests John has a lack of faith in his abilities as a father OR John is hopeful of improving the situation • *'John bows his head, holds it between his hands and groans.'* — John shows his despair in acknowledging his failure to provide for his family. • 'Try. Try. As if I didnae try.' — repetition of try suggests John's despair/self-pity. • 'Aye. We'll hae wur tea', '… *slowly and painfully locates the teapot'* — use of adverbs suggests his inability to cope with basic domestic tasks.
11.	Award **2 marks** awarded for detailed/insightful comment plus quotation/reference. Award **1 mark** for more basic comment plus quotation/reference. Award **0 marks** for quotation/reference alone. Award marks 2 or 1+1	2	Possible answers include: • Maggie feels ashamed/apologetic/aware that she has deviated from her normal, nurturing role. • at the same time feeling anguish/pain/anger/frustration because the difficulties of her life persist.
12.	Candidates can answer in bullet points in this final question, or write a number of linked statements.	10	Candidates can gain up to 2 marks for identifying elements of commonality as identified in the question, i.e. how Lamont Stewart explores the role of women. Award a further 2 marks for reference to the extract given. Award 6 additional marks for discussion of similar references from at least one other part of the text. <u>In practice this means:</u> Identification of commonality (2) for example, women bear the major responsibility for family throughout the play (1) often at great cost to themselves (1) • from the extract: Award **2 marks** for detailed/insightful comment plus quotation/reference Award **1 mark** for more basic comment plus quotation/reference Award **0 marks** for quotation/reference alone

Question	Expected response	Max Mark	Additional Guidance
12.	*(continued)*		for example, Maggie's outburst 'I hate ye! I hate ye!' is an uncharacteristic loss of control due to the constant burden of domestic responsibility and lack of support (2)
			• from at least one other part of the play:
			Award **2 marks** for detailed/insightful comment plus quotation/reference
			Award **1 mark** for more basic comment plus quotation/reference
			Award **0 marks** for quotation/reference alone
			In comments on the rest of the play, possible references include:
			• Lily's more comfortable financial situation is a result of her rejection of the traditional role of wife/mother
			• Granny represents the older generation of women left without support and she is dependent on her pension/help from her family
			• Maggie's behaviour in the opening scene — rushing around trying to deal with the needs of Granny and the hunger of her children — shows the constant struggle faced by wives and mothers
			• the support network of the women in the community helps them to endure their struggles with poverty
			• Jenny represents the modern generation of women who want independence and refuse to conform but are ultimately still reliant on men
			Many other references are possible.

Text 1 — Prose — *The Telegram* by Iain Crichton Smith

Question	Expected response	Max Mark	Additional Guidance
13.	For full marks candidates must deal with both women but not necessarily in equal measure.	4	Possible answers include:
	Award **2 marks** for detailed/insightful comment plus quotation/reference.		**Thin woman**
	Award **1 mark** for more basic comment plus quotation/reference.		• 'in an even voice … black figure' suggests she is suppressing a retort/avoiding commenting.
	Award **0 marks** for quotation/reference alone.		• 'But then most of them were … lazy' highlights her prejudices and bitterness.
	Award marks		• 'better afforded' suggests she is critical of their choices for their children.
	2+2, 2+1+1 **or** 1+1+1+1		• 'didn't want … snobbish' shows she makes generalised assumptions about the other villagers.
			• 'I made sacrifices … nobody's debt' suggests she is proud/condescending/disdainful.
			• superficial civility of 'More tea?' highlights sense of her own superiority/distrust of the other woman.
			Fat woman
			• 'without thinking' suggests her deep-rooted, unreflective prejudice.
			• 'It's different for the officers' suggests she is opinionated/prejudiced.
			• 'in a confused tone' highlights her inability to understand her own prejudice.
			• repetition of 'better' conveys her illogical thinking/uninformed views.
			• '… son is educated … irrelevantly' suggests she makes unfounded assumptions about people.
			• 'Of course her son … same time' highlights her vexation about the other son's position.

Question	Expected response	Max Mark	Additional Guidance
14.	Award **2 marks** for detailed/insightful comment plus quotation/reference. Award **1 mark** for more basic comment plus quotation/reference. Award **0 marks** for quotation/reference alone. Award marks 2 **or** 1+1	2	Possible answers include: • 'Many's the night' suggests her bitterness at the numerous hardships she endured/her resentment at the sacrifices she has made for his sake. • 'even knitted trousers' conveys the extreme lengths she went to when he was younger and her resentment that he has not acknowledged that. • 'where will I be?' question highlights her view that he is in her debt and should be taking care of her/her realisation that he is unlikely to take care of her. • 'sure she smokes and drinks' clichéd 'unladylike' habits conveys her misgivings/suspicions of his choice of partner suggests that he has not lived up to her expectations. • 'after all I've done for him' plaintive tone suggests she feels he has let her down/is ungrateful at her sacrifices.
15.	Award **2 marks** for detailed/insightful comment plus quotation/reference. Award **1 mark** for more basic comment plus quotation/reference. Award **0 marks** for quotation/reference alone. Award marks 2+2, 2+1+1 **or** 1+1+1+1	4	Possible answers include: • 'But no matter ... like the thin woman' suggests that her dislike/distrust was justified as it was a universally held opinion. • 'always putting on airs' suggests she views her as being snobbish and uppity/someone who does not fit in to the village community. • short sentence 'Mayor indeed' highlights her envy of the son's achievements. • question 'why ... anyone else' suggests she is critical of the thin woman's choices. • 'Saving and scrimping' sarcastic tone suggests she views the other woman's hardships as unnecessary. • 'own Donald just as clever' highlights her desire to dismiss the thin woman's son's position/ success. • 'heart ... beating ... frightened' conveys a rare moment of truth/acknowledgement of their mutual situation yet an inability/unwillingness to communicate. • 'she didn't know ... wanted to talk' suggests she felt unsettled/anxious/on edge in her company. • 'couldn't feel at ease with her' highlights the tension between them despite the circumstances. • 'thinking about something else' suggests she could not understand/bond with the other woman.
16.	Candidates can answer in bullet points in this final question, or write a number of linked statements.	10	Candidates can gain up to 2 marks for identifying elements of commonality as identified in the question, i.e. the role of female characters in Crichton Smith's stories. Award a further 2 marks for reference to the text given. Award 6 additional marks for discussion of similar references to at least one other short story by the writer. <u>In practice this means:</u> Identification of commonality (2) for example, women have a symbolic/pivotal function in Crichton Smith's stories (1) in order to explore central concerns such as war/place of the individual in society/isolation (1)

Question	Expected response	Max Mark	Additional Guidance
16.	*(continued)*		• from this extract: Award **2 marks** for detailed/insightful comment plus quotation/reference Award **1 mark** for more basic comment plus quotation/reference Award **0 marks** for quotation/reference alone for example, the women are both affected by war yet are still in conflict highlighting the devastating effects of prejudice/narrow-mindedness (2) • from at least one other text: Award **2 marks** for detailed/insightful comment plus quotation/reference Award **1 mark** for more basic comment plus quotation/reference Award **0 marks** for quotation/reference alone In comments on other stories, possible references include: • *Mother and Son* the mother is trapped in a bleak existence and uses familial obligation as a weapon against her son • *Mother and Son* the mother diminishes her son's aspirations by mocking his suggestions that he could leave • *The Red Door* the spinster who conforms to the expectations of the villagers is seen by Murdo as frightful and unattractive • *The Red Door* Mary who defies conventions and does not care about the opinions of others is seen by Murdo as desirable and exciting • *Home* the wife is disapproving/dismissive of the home environment her husband seeks to reconnect with Many other references are possible.

Text 2 — Prose — *The Eye of the Hurricane* by George Mackay Brown

Question	Expected response	Max Mark	Additional Guidance
17.	Award **1 mark** for appropriate comment plus quotation/reference (x2). Award **0 marks** for quotation/reference alone. Award marks 1+1	2	Possible answers include: • thoughts centre on the sea — 'cradle and coffin, they're both shaped like ships'/reinforced by alliteration. • larger than life/charismatic personality shown from his emphatic comments at the beginning of the extract — 'Courage … by God we need courage' — repetition emphasises the lack of doubt. • philosophical/thoughtful — 'a dangerous voyage … from birth into death'/'Even the pen-pusher who sits at a desk all day with papers and ink' suggests he is all-inclusive in his thoughts about courage. • commanding presence — tone of 'Take that smirk off your face, Hackland.'/respect shown by other men — 'Sorry, sir'. • softer side shown when he mentions love — he speaks 'quietly' and the word 'love' is emphasised by the use of the dash.

Question	Expected response	Max Mark	Additional Guidance
18.	For full marks candidates must deal with both positive and negative views, but not necessarily in equal measure. Award **2 marks** for detailed/insightful comment plus quotation/reference. Award **1 mark** for more basic comment plus quotation/reference. Award **0 marks** for quotation/reference alone. Award marks 2+2, 2+1+1, **or** 1+1+1+1	4	Possible answers include: **Positive** • romantic view of love as 'a very precious jewel' suggests its value/beauty/importance. • 'lucky' — idea of love as special — not everyone experiences its joy. • 'completeness in their lives' — he sees love as the vital ingredient for a happy life. • 'even when it wasn't' — conveniently ignores/allows himself to ignore love's pitfalls. • 'Get yourself a good wife' command suggests he sees relationships as essential. **Negative** • 'what counterfeits, what frauds and imitations' — sentence structure emphasises the negative/deceitful/false aspects of love. • 'counterfeits'/'frauds'/'imitations' — word choice suggests false aspects of love. • 'the fly-by-night' suggests his cynicism. • 'he tied himself to' suggests he views relationships as a potential trap. • 'she and no other ... the trigger' suggests he views relationships as potentially destructive. • 'At least you can depend on courage' — casts doubt on the dependability of love.
19.	Award **2 marks** for detailed/insightful comment plus quotation/reference. Award **1 mark** for more basic comment plus quotation/reference. Award **0 marks** for quotation/reference alone. Award marks 2+2, 2+1+1, **or** 1+1+1+1	4	Possible answers include: **Miriam** • 'lead-blue hands back under the blanket' suggests practical attitude towards the situation. • reproachful tone — 'You promised to look after him,' • 'Yes,' said Miriam ... blowing done.' Comforting words suggest her caring attitude to Captain Stevens. • 'You'll be pleased ... you've killed Captain Stevens' blunt comment suggests she holds them responsible. • 'To me she said coldly'/'Get Dr. Wilson' her attitude to the men is quite cold — brevity/brusqueness of her speech **The Men** • lack of practicality/thought — 'the room was a worse shambles than ever' suggests they didn't care about tidying up/the focus was on themselves. • they put the Captain to bed 'only, it seemed, after a struggle' — lack of ability to cope in a crisis is illustrated. • lack of resourcefulness — 'I went straight from the house' — Barclay goes to find Miriam as soon as there's a problem. • selfish/self-absorbed — they sat drinking while Miriam dealt with the crisis.
20.	Candidates can answer in bullet points in this final question, or write a number of linked statements.	10	Candidates can gain up to 2 marks for identifying elements of commonality as identified in the question, i.e. the impact on his characters of intense situations and/or events. Award a further 2 marks for reference to the extract given. Award 6 additional marks for discussion of similar references to at least one other short story by the writer.

Question	Expected response	Max Mark	Additional Guidance
20.	*(continued)*		<u>In practice this means:</u> Identification of commonality (2) for example, characters are forced to confront aspects of their past/character/own actions (1) as a result of 'big' life events such as death, birth, war, love and loss (1) • from the extract: Award **2 marks** for detailed/insightful comment plus quotation/reference Award **1 mark** for more basic comment plus quotation/reference Award **0 marks** for quotation/reference alone for example, Captain Stevens sees the end of his life as the most dangerous sea voyage and his volatile behaviour is a final struggle against the prospect of his own death (2) • from at least one other text: Award **2 marks** for detailed/insightful comment plus quotation/reference Award **1 mark** for more basic comment plus quotation/reference Award **0 marks** for quotation/reference alone In comments on other stories, possible references include: • *The Wireless Set* Hugh smashes up wireless — symbol of the outside world/war that killed his son — in the extremity of his grief • *A Time to Keep* Bill pledges himself to his son, in the depth of his grief after Ingi's death • *A Time to Keep* Bill aggressively rejects the attempt at comfort provided by the minister and community in the face of his loss • *Andrina* Torvald develops powerful feeling for Andrina in the depths of his loneliness • *Andrina* Torvald is haunted by the fact he abandoned his pregnant girlfriend Many other references are possible.

Text 3 — Prose — *The Strange Case of Dr Jekyll and Mr Hyde* by Robert Louis Stevenson

Question	Expected response	Max Mark	Additional Guidance
21.	Award **2 marks** for detailed/insightful comment plus quotation/reference. Award **1 mark** for more basic comment plus quotation/reference. Award **0 marks** for quotation/reference alone. Award marks 2+2, 2+1+1, 1+1+1+1	4	Possible answers include: • 'wild, cold, seasonable night of March' suggests sense of energy and expectation in the air. • 'pale moon ... had tilted her' suggests peculiar, other-worldly. • 'diaphanous and lawny texture' suggests mystery, as the filmy nature of the moonlight is difficult to see clearly. • 'swept ... bare of passengers' suggests isolation, tension. • 'conscious ... fellow-creatures' suggests need for security, feelings of fear. • 'crushing anticipation of calamity' suggests sense of inevitable impending tragedy. • 'thin trees ... lashing themselves along the railing' suggests wildness and self-torture of nature. • 'voice ... harsh and broken' suggests tension and fear.

Question	Expected response	Max Mark	Additional Guidance
22.	Award **2 marks** for detailed insightful comment plus quotation/reference. Award **1 mark** for more basic comment plus quotation/reference. Award **0 marks** for quotation/reference alone. Award marks 2, 1+1	2	Possible answers include: • "Amen, Poole" confirms Utterson's role in representing the stability of belief in for example, Providence in a crisis. • 'At the sight of Mr. Utterson … hysterical whimpering' the maid's reaction suggests Utterson is a reassuring figure who is capable of handling the situation. • "Bless God! It's Mr. Utterson" the cook's words emphasise their reliance on Utterson as a figure of authority, come to take charge. • Utterson rebukes the servants for gathering at the fire in an 'irregular' way, emphasising his role as representing Victorian respectability/ middle class authority.
23.	Award **2 marks** awarded for detailed/insightful comment plus quotation/reference. Award **1 mark** for more basic comment plus quotation/reference. Award **0 marks** for quotation/reference alone. Award marks 2+2, 2+1+1, 1+1+1+1	4	Possible answers include: • "Hold your tongue!" Poole's uncharacteristic outburst suggests his need to control the situation. • 'ferocity of accent … own jangled nerves' suggests his unusual revelation of his own feelings, in the extremity of the situation. • 'they had all started and turned toward the inner door' their immediate reaction in looking towards the door suggests their communal fear of what lies beyond. • 'faces of dreadful expectation' suggests the anticipation of impending calamity. • 'I want you to hear … to be heard' suggests need to avoid detection by the person hidden within. • 'if by any chance … don't go' Poole's unusual command to his 'better' suggests the immediate danger they are in. • 'Mr. Utterson's nerves … balance' suggests that even the stolid Utterson is afraid in these circumstances. • "was that my master's voice?" use of question emphasises the fact that it is not Jekyll who is inside. • (repetition) 'made away with' emphasises inevitable conclusion that Jekyll may have been murdered/there has been foul play. • 'why it stays there' use of 'it' to describe the mysterious inhabitant suggests not human.
24.	Candidates can answer in bullet points in this final question, or write a number of linked statements.	10	Candidates can gain up to 2 marks for identifying elements of commonality as identified in the question, i.e. how Stevenson uses symbolism to develop the central concerns of the text. Award a further 2 marks for reference to the extract given. Award 6 additional marks for discussion of similar references to at least one other part of text. In practice this means: Identification of commonality (2) for example, Stevenson uses characters, incidents and settings as representative of wider issues (1) such as the conflict between good and evil/honesty and hypocrisy in humanity (1)

Question	Expected response	Max Mark	Additional Guidance
24.	*(continued)*		• from the extract: Award **2 marks** for detailed/insightful comment plus quotation/reference Award **1 mark** for more basic comment plus quotation/reference Award **0 marks** for quotation/reference alone for example, the servants gathered in a huddle round the fire symbolises the breakdown of order and stability in society, in the face of Hyde's destructive excesses (2) • from at least one other part of the text: Award **2 marks** for detailed/insightful comment plus quotation/reference Award **1 mark** for more basic comment plus quotation/reference Award **0 marks** for quotation/reference alone In comments on the rest of the text, possible references include: • The relationship between Jekyll and Hyde represents duality (good versus evil) in humanity • The house which is Jekyll's at the front, but with Hyde's laboratory at the back, represents the respectable, civilised front of society, with the hidden shame • The inner cabinet where Jekyll retreats to, latterly, represents the secrecy in humanity, hiding away his shameful deeds • Utterson's predictable reliability for example, taking care of Jekyll's will represents respectability and control, on which society is built • The twitching body of Hyde surrounded by symbols of Victorian respectability for example, tea things, represents the hypocrisy at the heart of society Many other references are possible.

Text 4 – Prose – *Sunset Song* by Lewis Grassic Gibbon

Question	Expected response	Max Mark	Additional Guidance
25.	Award **2 marks** for detailed/insightful comment plus quotation/reference. Award **1 mark** for more basic comment plus quotation/reference. Award **0 marks** for quotation/reference alone. Award marks 2 or 1+1	2	Possible answers include: • 'they all got on fine' suggests her harmonious childhood. • 'never happier' suggests this was the best time in her life. • 'tramped bare-footed' suggests childish energy/enthusiasm/innocent pleasure in the simple act of walking. • 'nestled under the couthy hills' suggest feelings of comfort/security. • 'ta-ta' cheery informality suggests her happy acceptance of her situation. • 'she'd never forget the singing ... fields' suggests her memory of the evocative sounds of her childhood. • 'feel of the earth below her toes' suggests the physical immediacy of her deep connection to the land.

Question	Expected response	Max Mark	Additional Guidance
26.	Award **2 marks** for detailed/insightful comment plus quotation/reference. Award **1 mark** for more basic comment plus quotation/reference. Award **0 marks** for quotation/reference alone. Award marks 2+2, 2+1+1 **or** 1+1+1+1	4	Possible answers include: • 'a brave young childe' suggests John's powerful physical presence. • 'the swackest legs you ever saw' superlative suggests Jean's admiration of John's agile physique. • 'laced in ribbons, bonny and trig' suggests she notices the pride and care expended by John in preparing his horses. • 'as soon as he began … prize' suggests her immediate awareness of his superiority. • 'with a glint from his dour, sharp eye' suggests the immediate surreptitious attraction John feels for Jean. • 'And she cried back I like fine!' suggests her instant bond with John. • 'caught the horse … swung herself' suggests her spontaneous action/determination to be with him. • repetition of 'caught' suggest the instant harmony between them.
27.	Award **2 marks** for detailed/insightful comment plus quotation/reference. Award **1 mark** for more basic comment plus quotation/reference. Award **0 marks** for quotation/reference alone. Award marks 2+2, 2+1+1 **or** 1+1+1+1	4	Possible answers include: • 'black with rage at her' suggests the violence of John's temper/his inability to compromise. • 'tempted his soul to hell' suggests John's perception of his physical desire as sinful. • 'the dourness hardened' suggests the deepening obstinacy of John's nature. • 'the glint of her hair … him' suggests John's overwhelming physical attraction to Jean. • 'what God in His mercy may send to us' suggests John places his devotion to his beliefs before his wife's wishes. • 'See you to that' suggests John's unyielding nature.
28.	Candidates can answer in bullet points in this final question, or write a number of linked statements.	10	Candidates can gain up to 2 marks for identifying elements of commonality as identified in the question, i.e. the influence of both Jean and John Guthrie on Chris's life. Award a further 2 marks for reference to the extract given. Award 6 additional marks for discussion of similar references to at least one other part of text by the writer. <u>In practice this means:</u> Identification of commonality (2) for example, Jean and John Guthrie have exerted both a positive and negative influence on Chris (1) and continued to shape her life at key moments, even after their deaths (1). • from the extract: Award **2 marks** for detailed/insightful comment plus quotation/reference Award **1 mark** for more basic comment plus quotation/reference Award **0 marks** for quotation/reference alone for example, Chris's life is shaped by her mother's deep love for the land ('there are better things … there's the countryside your own') which endures throughout her life (2)

Question	Expected response	Max Mark	Additional Guidance
28.	*(continued)*		• from at least one other part of the text: Award **2 marks** for detailed/insightful comment plus quotation/reference Award **1 mark** for more basic comment plus quotation/reference Award **0 marks** for quotation/reference alone In comments on the rest of the novel, possible references include: • the two Chrises — the Scottish Chris, influenced by her mother's love of the land, and the English Chris, encouraged by her father to pursue her education — highlight the battle within Chris in her early life • John justifies his sexual desire by his reading of Scripture, terrifying her and turning her against him • John's tyranny after he becomes bedridden leads to Chris subjugating her own wishes and dreams • John shows his trust and appreciation of Chris by making her the sole beneficiary, providing her with the opportunity to pursue her own wishes • Jean's suicide brings about the end of Chris's childhood and propels her into an adult role Many other references are possible.

Text 5 — Prose — *The Cone-Gatherers* by Robin Jenkins

Question	Expected response	Max Mark	Additional Guidance
29.	For full marks candidates should deal with more than one emotion. Award **2 marks** for detailed/insightful comment plus quotation/reference. Award **1 mark** for more basic comment plus quotation/reference. Award **0 marks** for quotation/reference alone. Award marks 2+2, 2+1+1 **or** 1+1+1+1	4	Possible answers include: • 'fond and proud' suggests she admires Roderick's kindness/friendliness towards others (reflecting her Christianity). • 'aren't you the complete democrat?' suggests that she is laughing with him and is pleased that he is following the code that she and her father have taught him. • 'aren't you the complete democrat? But don't overdo it' can also suggest an ironic or mocking tone as she thinks he has forgotten or is choosing to ignore his social class/position in society. • 'astonished'/'astonishment sharpened into indignation' reflects her frustration/shock that he cannot be true to his social class/status and/or doesn't know where to draw the line. • 'If this is a joke, Roderick, I don't much admire its taste' she criticises him for poor humour/she tries to laugh off his comments rather than be overly critical. • she wonders whether her husband is right that Roderick may be in some way 'faulty in mind' and this explains his behaviour. • 'Foreboding chilled her' suggests she worries about his future.
30.	Award **2 marks** for detailed/insightful comment plus quotation/reference. Award **1 mark** for more basic comment plus quotation/reference. Award **0 marks** for quotation/reference alone. Award marks 2+2, 2+1+1, 1+1+1+1	4	Possible answers include: • 'standing respectfully' he does not involve himself in the dialogue between mother and son but keeps his distance. • 'waiting for permission' he knows that he has to follow instructions and cannot leave of his own accord. • '(aloof) submissiveness' — suggests he knows his place and will do as he is told.

Question	Expected response	Max Mark	Additional Guidance
30.	*(continued)*		• 'honourable' — (Lady Runcie-Campbell believes) that he carries out his duties with decorum. • 'knew his subordinate place' suggests that he recognises he is of a lower class/status than the Runcie-Campbells. • 'kept it without grievance or loss of dignity' he behaves appropriately and does not complain or protest. • he frequently addresses her as 'my lady' conveying his awareness of her elevated social status.
31.	Award **2 marks** for detailed/insightful comment plus quotation/reference. Award **1 mark** for more basic comment plus quotation/reference. Award **0 marks** for quotation/reference alone. Award marks **2 or 1+1**	2	Possible answers include: • 'Why don't we offer them a lift' suggests he sees them as equals/his friends/wants to make a kind gesture … but chooses not to/fails to recognise that this contradicts the expectations of his social class/status. • 'trying to preserve his charitable attitude towards his inferiors' he has a clear sense of equality and his mother wants him to maintain this and is proud that this side of him is dominant. • 'You could sit in beside Mother. They could sit at the back away from everybody' He suggests how his sister could be kept away from the cone-gatherers and they all could be happy. • reference to 'Sir Galahad' suggests heroic/virtuous intentions. • 'Human beings are more important than dogs' Roderick's view directly contrasts with that of his sister. NB Candidates may choose to deal with this statement as a structural device, i.e. that it acts as a climactic point in the argument, emphasising Roderick's kindness/belief in equality.
32.	Candidates can answer in bullet points in this final question, or write a number of linked statements.	10	Candidates can gain up to 2 marks for identifying elements of commonality as identified in the question, i.e. how Jenkins develops the character of Lady Runcie-Campbell throughout the novel. Award a further 2 marks for reference to the extract given. Award 6 additional marks for discussion of similar references to at least one other part of text by the writer. <u>In practice this means:</u> Identification of commonality (2) for example, Lady Runcie-Campbell is portrayed as upholding aristocratic values (1) which can create conflict with Christian ideals/her role as a mother (1) • from the extract: Award **2 marks** for detailed/insightful comment plus quotation/reference Award **1 mark** for more basic comment plus quotation/reference Award **0 marks** for quotation/reference alone for example, Lady Runcie-Campbell wishes Roderick to follow the aristocratic values of the family. However, she worries that her Christian influence may have acted as a 'corrupter', making him weak (2)

Question	Expected response	Max Mark	Additional Guidance
32.	(continued)		• from at least one other part of the text: Award **2 marks** for detailed/insightful comment plus quotation/reference Award **1 mark** for more basic comment plus quotation/reference Award **0 marks** for quotation/reference alone In comments on the rest of the novel, possible references include: • she initially wants Calum and Neil removed from the estate after the deer drive, though compassion makes her change her mind suggesting the conflict between aristocratic values and Christian beliefs • she is appalled by Calum and Neil's presence in the beach hut and thinks they should go, despite the storm, to accommodate her and her family suggesting a lack of consistency in how she exercises her values • her failure to recognise Duror's true intentions leads ultimately to the final tragedy suggesting the limitations of her moral compass • she inquires after Peggy Duror's health/visits her/insists that Duror see a doctor after his collapse at the deer drive suggesting her sense of responsibility • she is presented as symbolic of Mary/Mary Magdalen at the end of the novel when she is seen weeping at the scene of Calum's death Many other references are possible.

Text 1 — Poetry — *Tam O' Shanter, A Tale*, by Robert Burns

Question	Expected response	Max Mark	Additional Guidance
33.	Award **2 marks** for detailed/insightful comment plus quotation/reference. Award **1 mark** for more basic comment plus quotation/reference. Award **0 marks** for quotation/reference only. Award marks 2+2, 2+1+1, 1+1+1+1	4	Possible answers include: • 'planted unco right' suggests a place of comfort which was just perfect for Tam. • 'bleezing finely' suggests the warmth of the fire was well-established/the fireplace was a source of great heat. • 'reaming swats' suggests generous measures of ale were distributed. • 'drank divinely' suggests that the libations were of good quality. • 'at his elbow' suggests the inn was a place of close friendships. • 'fou for weeks thegither' suggests that the inn was always open to customers/the landlord was a tolerant individual. • 'sangs and clatter' suggests liveliness and camaraderie/a good time could be had at the inn. • 'The landlady ... precious' suggests the flirtatious presence of the landlady attracted customers. • 'queerest stories' suggests the intriguing nature of the tales. • 'ready chorus' suggests the willingness of the landlord to join in the fun. • 'minutes ... pleasure' suggests the good-natured mood of the inn.

Question	Expected response	Max Mark	Additional Guidance
34.	Award **2 marks** for detailed/insightful comment plus quotation/reference. Award **1 mark** for more basic comment plus quotation/reference. Award **0 marks** for quotation/reference only. Award marks 2+2, 2+1+1, 1+1+1+1		Possible answers include: • 'like poppies spread … shed' comparison of Tam's enjoyment with a delicate flower which has been destroyed hints at the problems to come. • 'snow falls in the river … for ever' comparing Tam's happiness to fast melting snow suggests the inevitable transience of his enjoyment. • 'Or like the rainbow's lovely form … storm' Tam's pleasure is likened to the bright and beautiful arch of the rainbow; a natural phenomenon which last but a short time before disappearing in rain clouds, as Tam's pleasure will vanish in the blast. • 'Nae man … time nor tide' suggests the inevitable nature of change, and that Tam's pleasures cannot last. • 'Tam maun ride' use of the auxiliary verb 'maun' implies that Tam has no choice/is powerless. • 'night's black arch' rather Gothic image suggesting dark/evil/brooding Powers. • 'dreary hour' reference to midnight suggests time of danger/evil. 'sic a night'/'ne'er poor sinner … in' use of emphatic modifiers highlights the unique violence of the storm. • 'blawn its last' connotations of judgement day and impending doom. • 'speedy gleams the darkness swallow'd'/'thunder bellow'd' personification suggests that the night/thunder were alive and ready to consume all light and hope. • 'a child might understand' deliberate contrast of Tam's actions with a child's understanding in order to stress Tam's foolish behaviour in exposing himself to danger. • 'The Deil had business' specific mention of Satan at work suggests that Tam will become a target for evil forces.
35.	Award **1 mark** for appropriate comment with supporting quotation/reference (x2). Award **0 marks** for quotation/reference only. Award marks 1+1	2	Possible answers include: • 'skelpit … mire' suggests Tam's fast pace over rough ground showing he is a determined character. • 'Despising … fire' suggests Tam is uncaring of the wild elements he faces showing he is foolhardy. • 'holding fast … bonnet' Tam's firm grip suggests he is careful of his possessions. • 'crooning o'er … auld Scots sonnet' Tam's gentle preoccupation with old songs suggest he is a sentimental character/drunken fool. • 'glow'ring round … unawares' Tam's wary glances suggest that he is a cautious/superstitious character.
36.	Candidates can answer in bullet points in this final question, or write a number of linked statements.	10	Candidates can gain up to 2 marks for identifying elements of commonality as identified in the question, i.e. how Burns portrays vulnerable and/or flawed characters. Award a further 2 marks for reference to the extract given. Award 6 additional marks for discussion of similar references in at least one other poem by the poet.

Question	Expected response	Max Mark	Additional Guidance
36.	*(continued)*		<u>In practice this means:</u> Identification of commonality (2) for example, Burns encourages the reader to sympathise/see through vulnerable and/or flawed characters (1) because they have been affected by their social status and/or the religious conventions of the time (1) • from the extract: Award **2 marks** for detailed/insightful comment plus quotation/reference Award **1 mark** for more basic comment plus quotation/reference Award **0 marks** for quotation/reference alone for example, 'Kings may be blest but Tam was glorious/O'er a' the ills o' life victorious' the poet's depiction of Tam as a drunken, happy buffoon, rather than a victim of his own foolishness, evokes our fondness rather than our disapproval (2) • from at least one other text: Award **2 marks** for detailed/insightful comment plus quotation/reference Award **1 mark** for more basic comment plus quotation/reference Award **0 marks** for quotation/reference alone In comments on other poems, possible references include: • *A Poet's Welcome* Burns' tender expressions of love and loyalty to his daughter, highlight the wrongness of the various critics thus encouraging understanding of the speaker • *To A Mouse* the vivid description of the bleak winter which the homeless mouse will face, allow the reader to feel sympathy for the mouse and its plight • *To A Mouse* the speaker's depiction of his own fears for the future encourages the reader to empathise with the speaker and reflect on the uncertainty of human life • *Holy Willie's Prayer* Willie's description of his own drunken and lecherous activities encourages the reader to see through his self-righteous declarations of devotion • *Holy Willie's Prayer* Willie's pettiness in encouraging God to strike his enemies ('kale and potatoes') encourages the reader to understand his hypocrisy Many other references are possible.

Text 2 – Poetry – *In Mrs Tilscher's Class* **by Carol Ann Duffy**

Question	Expected response	Max Mark	Additional Guidance
37.	Award **2 marks** for detailed/insightful comment plus quotation/reference. Award **1 mark** awarded for more basic comment plus quotation/reference. Award **0 marks** for quotation/reference alone. Award marks 2+2, 2+1+1 **or** 1+1+1+1	4	Possible answers include: • 'You could travel up the Blue Nile' – 'could' and 'Blue Nile' suggest the limitless possibilities of imagination. • 'with your finger' simplicity of statement suggests the childish thrill of this experience. • 'chanted' suggests magic/casting a spell.

Question	Expected response	Max Mark	Additional Guidance
37.	*(continued)*		• 'Tana … Aswan' list of faraway names suggests the speaker is sharing the experience of the journey through hearing the names in sequence. • 'chalky … dust' suggests the magical evocation of reality in the blackboard drawings, as perceived by the speaker. • 'laugh … child' suggests sheer, spontaneous fun and exuberance of the speaker's school day's routine. • 'This was … home' simple, emphatic statement of comparison suggests just how special the classroom experience is. • "glowed" suggests attractive/sparkling/a joyous atmosphere. • 'classroom … sweet shop' comparison suggests abundance of treats which Mrs Tilscher's teaching offered. • 'Sugar … shapes' short statements combine to evoke the range of inventive activities enjoyed. • 'a good gold star' — build-up of positive vocabulary suggests the thrill of being valued, tangibly conveyed by Mrs Tilscher. • 'scent of a pencil' references to sense of smell evokes strong sense of childhood. • 'slowly, carefully shaved' use of two adverbs suggests time taken over the task and lingering pleasure in its memory now.
38.	Award **2 marks** for detailed/insightful comment plus quotation/reference. Award **1 mark** awarded for more basic comment plus quotation/reference. Award **0 marks** for quotation/reference alone. Award marks **2 or 1+1**	2	Possible answers include: • 'inky tadpoles' changing to 'frogs' suggests the children's physical journey to maturity. • 'commas into exclamation marks' suggests development from childish acceptance to heightened sense of emotion/refusal to conform to adult expectations. • 'jumping and croaking' suggests the awkward and inarticulate self-consciousness of developing maturity. • 'away from the lunch queue' suggests the children's movement away from accepted rules of behaviour as they grow older.
39.	Award **2 marks** for detailed/insightful comment plus quotation/reference. Award **1 mark** awarded for more basic comment plus quotation/reference. Award **0 marks** for quotation/reference alone. Award marks **2+2, 2+1+1 or 1+1+1+1**	4	Possible answers include: • 'A rough boy' suggests the brutality of the adult world which destroys the speaker's innocence. • 'told you how you were born': childish vocabulary used, ironically, to convey the unsettling nature of the knowledge of sex. • 'You kicked him' — simple statement suggests the speaker's absolute rejection of the boy's horrible information. • 'stared … appalled' conveys the shock felt by the speaker as she sees her parents, previously representative of security, in a new light. • 'feverish' suggests out of control, highly charged experiences. • 'air tasted of electricity' suggests strong, elemental forces at work which the speaker could not contain. • 'always untidy, hot,/fractious' list suggests uncomfortable qualities building up a 'pressure cooker' feeling of lack of self-control.

Question	Expected response	Max Mark	Additional Guidance
39.	*(continued)*		• 'heavy, sexy sky' suggests an oppressive/ restrictive atmosphere/anxiety created by awakening sexual awareness. • 'Mrs Tilscher … away' suggests that even Mrs Tilscher fails to reassure in the relentless face of adult knowledge. • 'thunderstorm' suggests ominous/threatening power.
40.	Candidates can answer in bullet points in this final question, or write a number of linked statements.	10	Candidates can gain up to 2 marks for identifying elements of commonality as identified in the question, i.e. how Duffy uses contrast to explore central concerns. Award a further 2 marks for reference to the extract given. Award 6 additional marks for discussion of similar references in at least one other poem by the poet. <u>In practice this means:</u> Identification of commonality (2) for example, Duffy uses contrast between characters/ideas/attitudes (1) to explore themes such as identity/change over time/relationships (1) • from this poem: Award **2 marks** for detailed/insightful comment plus quotation/reference Award **1 mark** for more basic comment plus quotation/reference Award **0 marks** for quotation/reference alone for example, contrast between the exuberance and enthusiasm of the child's view 'You could travel up the Blue Nile' and the more troubled view of life experienced by the older child 'untidy, hot,/fractious' encourages the reader to consider the darker aspects of growing up (2) • from at least one other text: Award **2 marks** for detailed/insightful comment plus quotation/reference Award **1 mark** for more basic comment plus quotation/reference Award **0 marks** for quotation/reference alone In comments on other poems, possible references include: • *War Photographer* contrast between his need to be professional and his natural urge towards compassion for human beings in pain raises the question of how we should respond to suffering humanity • *Originally* contrast between the speaker's initial feelings of insecurity in her new home and her eventual assimilation into the new way of life, shown by her way of speaking 'my tongue/shedding its skin like a snake' indicates human resilience • *Valentine* contrast between the sentimentalised view of love expressed through clichés and the truer view of love shown through the speaker's gift. 'I give you an onion' encourages an honest, uncompromising view of human relationships

Question	Expected response	Max Mark	Additional Guidance
40.	*(continued)*		• *Mrs Midas* contrast between the estrangement between Mrs Midas and her husband and their former intimacy, shown in her memory of 'his warm hands on my skin' suggests the complexities of a relationship in crisis • *The Way my Mother Speaks* contrast between the happiness and sadness of the speaker who cherishes her closeness to her mother while also recognising that she is moving away from her as she matures encourages the reader to appreciate the bitter-sweet nature of changing relationships Many other references are possible.

Text 3 — Poetry — *Last Supper* by Liz Lochhead

Question	Expected response	Max Mark	Additional Guidance
41.	Award **2 marks** for detailed/insightful comment plus quotation/reference. Award **1 mark** for more basic comment plus quotation/reference. Award marks 2+2, 2+1+1, 1+1+1+1	4	Possible answers include: • 'renounce his sweet flesh' suggests an ironic dismissal of their previous relationship. • positioning/capitalisation of '(For Ever)' conveys the finality of their separation. • 'last treat' introduces the religious imagery linked to the Last Supper and the idea of betrayal. • 'tearing … salad' violence of the language echoes the anger she now feels towards him. • parenthesis of '(and oh yes now will have to lie on)' is a knowing aside, suggesting having to live with the implications/consequences of decisions made. • 'silverware' continues reference to the Last Supper with the price of betrayal. • 'cooked goose' links idea of food/cookery to betrayal being discovered. • 'betrayal with a kiss' links to Judas' treachery highlighting depth of betrayal.
42.	Award **2 marks** for detailed/insightful comment plus quotation/reference. Award **1 mark** for more basic comment plus quotation/reference. Award marks 2+2, 2+1+1, 1+1+1+1	4	Possible answers include: • positioning of 'Already' highlights her anticipation for the event. • allusion to the witches from Macbeth 'when those three met again' conveys the extent of her delight in his downfall. • 'very good soup … bones' suggests the enjoyment she would gain in dissecting his character. • 'Yes, there they'd be' positioning at beginning of line and stanza highlights her delighted anticipation. • 'cackling … cauldron' continues Macbeth reference and shows vindictive pleasure taken in their verbal attacks on ex-partner. • 'spitting out … knucklebone' conveys the idea of the perverse joy in the detailed character assassination. • 'petit-gout … speech' suggests the savouring of malicious gossip relating to the ex-partner. Candidates could comment on the effect of the extended metaphor. This is a valid approach.

Question	Expected response	Max Mark	Additional Guidance
43.	Award **2 marks** for detailed/insightful comment plus quotation/reference. Award **1 mark** for more basic comment plus quotation/reference. Award marks **2 or 1+1**	2	Possible answers include: • 'munching the lies' suggests the women take delight in their character assassination/their spreading of lies and rumours. • 'gorged on truth' suggests the self-satisfaction they feel in *revealing* the flaws of the ex-partner. • 'preening (like corbies)' suggests a sense of their superiority/smugness. • 'corbies' friends who have feasted on the 'dead relationship' compared to crows who eat carrion. • 'go hunting again' suggests the predatory nature of the group.
44.	Candidates can answer in bullet points in this final question or write a number of detailed linked statements.	10	Candidates can gain up to 2 marks for identifying elements of commonality as identified in the question, i.e. how Lochhead uses contrast to explore central concerns. Award a further 2 marks for reference to the extract given. Award 6 additional marks for discussion of similar references in at least one other poem by the poet. <u>In practice this means:</u> Identification of commonality (2) for example, Lochhead uses contrast between characters/ideas/attitudes (1) to explore themes such as jealousy/betrayal/the past and present (1) • from the extract: Award **2 marks** for detailed/insightful comment plus quotation/reference Award **1 mark** for more basic comment plus quotation/reference Award **0 marks** for quotation/reference alone for example, contrast between the fierce loyalty the women show for each other and the viciousness they display towards the ex-boyfriend illustrates the destructive nature of some relationships (2) • from at least one other text: Award **2 marks** for detailed/insightful comment plus quotation/reference Award **1 mark** for more basic comment plus quotation/reference Award **0 marks** for quotation/reference alone In comments on other poems, possible references include: • *My Rival's House* contrast between the forced politeness of the mother towards the speaker and her sincere love for her son highlights her vulnerability • *View of Scotland/Love Poem* contrast between traditional rituals of the past and the more spontaneous reference to 'the present' being the right time for a kiss highlights their love • *Revelation* contrast between the innocence and vulnerability of the speaker and the sexual power and menace of the bull explores loss of innocence • *The Bargain* contrast between the happier times of the past and the present difficulties and uncertainties in the relationship highlights the changes wrought by the passage of time • *Box Room* contrast between the speaker's initial perceptions of her relationship and her later anxiety highlights her insecurity Many other references are possible.

Text 4 — Poetry — *Assisi* by Norman MacCaig

Question	Expected response	Max Mark	Additional Guidance
45.	Award **2 marks** for detailed/insightful comment plus quotation/reference. Award **1 mark** for more basic comment plus quotation/reference. Award **0 marks** for quotation/reference alone. Award marks 2 **or** 1+1	2	Possible answers include: • 'dwarf' has connotations of reduced/diminished/undersized. • 'hands on backwards' conveys impression of an inanimate doll or puppet. • 'slumped' suggests his inability to support himself or sit upright. • 'half-filled (sack)' suggests worthlessness as it is not fully functional. • sibilance/alliteration in 'sat/slumped/sack' slows the pace to emphasise his disabilities and highlight their overwhelming impact. • alliteration in 'tiny twisted' highlights the useless nature of his legs which are too weak to fulfil their purpose. • 'sawdust' suggests that he is not flesh and blood but filled with worthless stuffing.
46.	Both sides of the contrast must be dealt with for full marks but not necessarily in equal measure. Award **2 marks** for detailed/insightful comment plus quotation/reference. Award **1 mark** for more basic comment plus quotation/reference. Award **0 marks** for quotation/reference alone. Award marks 2+2, 2+1+1 **or** 1+1+1+1	4	Possible answers include: **St Francis** • 'honour' has connotations of respect and worship conveying his character and standing. A case could also be made for MacCaig using this in an ironic way to highlight the hypocrisy of the church in relation to the teachings of St Francis. • 'brother of the poor' demonstrates his kinship and closeness with those less fortunate than himself. • 'talker with birds' highlights his humble nature. • simple language of both of these phrases is that the saint's moral values of humility and generosity meant that he would have helped the beggar. **Priest** • sarcastic tone of 'explained how clever' highlights the priest's patronising demeanour/idea of trickery/manipulation of the tourists. • reference to Giotto to demonstrate his belief that he was intellectually superior. • 'tell stories' is simplistic and childlike. Contrast to the Giotto reference conveys his self-importance/deception. • 'reveal' conveys his pompous, conceited nature and his belief that he holds an elevated position in society. • 'illiterate' has pejorative connotations suggesting these people are also unenlightened, unlike him. • 'goodness of God' is an ironic reminder of the poet's contempt for the priest's hypocrisy. • ironic use of 'suffering' suggests the priest is indifferent to the misfortune of the beggar thus highlighting his hypocrisy. • alliteration in 'goodness of God'/'suffering of His Son' creates slogan-like effect suggests devaluing of original message. • repetition of 'explanation/cleverness' creates a tone of cynicism to convey the poet's conclusions are not what the priest intended. This makes him seem devoid of humanity and, therefore, a complete contrast to St Francis.

Question	Expected response	Max Mark	Additional Guidance
47.	Award **2 marks** for detailed/insightful comment plus quotation/reference. Award **1 mark** for more basic comment plus quotation/reference. Award **0 marks** for quotation/reference alone. Award marks 2+2, 2+1+1 **or** 1+1+1+1	4	Possible answers include: • extended metaphor of chickens to describe the tourists creates the impression that they are mindless and happy to be led by others therefore they are blind to reality. NB answers may deal with only one element of the image as word choice such as 'rush, clucking, fluttered, scattered, grain'. • capitalisation of 'Word' is a biblical allusion to highlight irony of the priest who favours aesthetic beauty over righteousness. • 'passed' suggests the indifference of the tourists to the true nature of suffering, further suggesting their implicit acceptance of the church's hypocrisy. • imagery of 'ruined temple' creates sympathy for the beggar as a temple being a sacred, divine place implies that the beggar is pure and has inner beauty even though his outer appearance is ravaged. • 'eyes wept pus' is a grotesque illustration designed to shock the reader into fully appreciating the pitiful reality of the beggar's existence/examining our own reaction such as disgust, we are no better than tourists. • listing of disabilities in lines 22–24 evokes the reader's sympathy and highlights the extreme nature of the beggar's difficulties. • contrast in 'voice as sweet' has an unexpected quality due to its position immediately after the list of ailments. Serves to emphasise subject's innocence and virtue. • reference to beggar's response of 'Grazie' humbles the poet and echoes his wider belief in being grateful for life itself. • reference to bird and St Francis to conclude that in the character of the beggar we are closer to the teachings of the saint than in any of the priest's actions.
48.	Candidates can answer in bullet points in this final question, or write a number of linked statements.	10	Candidates can gain up to 2 marks for identifying elements of commonality as identified in the question, i.e. how MacCaig explores the connection between characters and their surroundings. Award a further 2 marks for reference to the extract given. Award 6 additional marks for discussion of similar references in at least one other poem by the poet. In practice this means: Identification of commonality (2) for example, MacCaig presents a variety of characters for whom specific surroundings affect their behaviour/thoughts/reactions (1) to explore central concerns such as loss/suffering/the human condition (1) • from this poem: Award **2 marks** for detailed/insightful comment plus quotation/reference Award **1 mark** for more basic comment plus quotation/reference Award **0 marks** for quotation/reference alone

Question	Expected response	Max Mark	Additional Guidance
48.	*(continued)*		for example, the placing of the beggar outside the 'three tiers of churches' to highlight the irony that the wealthy church establishment ignores his plight (2) • from at least one other text: Award **2 marks** for detailed/insightful comment plus quotation/reference Award **1 mark** for more basic comment plus quotation/reference Award **0 marks** for quotation/reference alone In comments on other poems, possible references include: • *Visiting Hour* the speaker's awareness of his surroundings 'green and yellow corridors' highlights his vain attempts to remain detached from the reality of the situation • *Visiting Hour* the professionalism of the nurses 'miraculously' dealing with death in the hospital highlights his admiration for their ability to deal with such suffering • *Aunt Julia* her connection to the land 'stained with peat' demonstrates an aspect of Scottish heritage represented by the subject • *Basking Shark* the sudden appearance of the shark next to the speaker's boat on the empty sea initiates a train of thought about humanity's place in the universe • *Brooklyn Cop* the cop's aggression in the tough environment he operates in highlights the need to adapt in order to survive difficult circumstances Many other references are possible.

Text 5 — Poetry — *Hallaig* by Sorley MacLean

Question	Expected response	Max Mark	Additional Guidance
49.	Award **2 marks** for detailed/insightful comment plus quotation/reference. Award **1 mark** for more basic comment plus quotation/reference. Award **0 marks** for quotation/reference alone. Award marks 2+2, 2+1+1 **or** 1+1+1+1	4	Possible answers include: • 'The window is nailed and boarded' suggests that MacLean's vision of 'the West' is obscured/time has placed a barrier between MacLean and his home and his past. • 'nailed and boarded' suggests dereliction (introducing the idea of the forced abandonment of the Clearances) • 'through which I saw' suggests that MacLean overcame the difficulty and is able to see the past and his home in his mind, which links to the way that the former inhabitants still seem to walk in Hallaig. • 'my love' is ambiguous but makes clear the strength of MacLean's affection for the place of his origin. • 'a birch tree' introduces the extended metaphor of the trees which come to represent the former inhabitants of Hallaig. • 'the Burn of Hallaig'/'Inver'/'Milk Hollow'/'Baile-chuirn' places the poem clearly in the setting of Hallaig (the cleared village on the island of Raasay).

Question	Expected response	Max Mark	Additional Guidance
50.	Award **2 marks** awarded for detailed/insightful comment plus quotation/reference. Award **1 mark** for more basic comment plus quotation/reference. Award **0 marks** for quotation/reference alone. Award marks 2+2, 2+1+1 **or** 1+1+1+1	4	Possible answers include: • 'birch, a hazel' are trees native to the island of Raasay, representing the native inhabitants of the island. • word choice of 'pine cocks crowing' refers to trees recently brought to the island, supplanting the native trees. • 'They are not the wood I love' is a simple statement, rejecting the pines and the Clearances which they embody. • 'I will wait for the birches to move' reinforces MacLean's determination to re-establish a link with the pre-Clearance past. • more general comment which makes the link between the population and the native forests of Raasay.
51.	Award **2 marks** for detailed/insightful comment plus quotation/reference. Award **1 mark** for more basic comment plus quotation/reference. Award **0 marks** for quotation/reference alone. Award marks 2 **or** 1+1	2	Possible answers include: • 'the Sabbath of the dead' — suggests MacLean's purpose in worshipping the former residents, remembering them. • 'where the people are frequenting,/every single generation gone' emphasises the connection of a long line of ancestors, stretching far back into the past. • 'still in Hallaig' suggests that they live on in the land itself. • 'MacLeans and MacLeods ... Mac Gillie Chaluim' — names the former inhabitants, populating the village again with its actual residents. • 'The men ... at the end of every house that was' makes the place seem crowded by the ghosts of those who have left. • 'the girls a wood of birches' reinforces the previous connection between the population of Raasay and its native trees.
52.	Candidates can answer in bullet points in this final question, or write a number of linked statements.	10	Candidates can gain up to 2 marks for identifying elements of commonality as identified in the question, i.e. how Maclean develops the theme of humanity's connection to place. Award a further 2 marks for reference to the extract given. Award 6 additional marks for discussion of similar references in at least one other poem by the poet. In practice this means: Identification of commonality (2) for example, the poet identifies closely with aspects of the landscape (1) to develop a more profound consideration of change/mortality/nature/time .... (1) • from the extract: Award **2 marks** for detailed/insightful comment plus quotation/reference Award **1 mark** for more basic comment plus quotation/reference Award **0 marks** for quotation/reference alone

Question	Expected response	Max Mark	Additional Guidance
52.	*(continued)*		for example, MacLean's love for Hallaig is demonstrated through his recollection of the tragedy of the Clearances 'every single generation gone'/'the dead have been seen alive' (1) but hope lives on in the redemptive power of love 'my love ... a birch tree' (1)
			• from at least one other part of the text:
			Award **2 marks** for detailed/insightful comment plus quotation/reference
			Award **1 mark** for more basic comment plus quotation/reference
			Award **0 marks** for quotation/reference alone
			In comments on other poems, possible references include:
			• *I gave you Immortality* the way that MacLean's romantic love is connected to his love of place. • *Shores* power of nature is captured in a variety of settings and is compared to enduring love. • *An Autumn Day* nature can bring comfort despite a war setting. • *Kinloch Ainort* the power of the mountains and surrounding landscape is evoked/described almost entirely in active human terms. • *The Girl of The Red Gold Hair* landscape seems to reflect the gloom/mood of the persona in his separation from the Girl of the Red Gold Hair.
			Many other references are possible.

Text 6 — Poetry — *Waking with Russell* **by Don Paterson**

Question	Expected response	Max Mark	Additional Guidance
53.	Award **2 marks** for detailed/insightful comment plus quotation/reference. Award **1 mark** for more basic comment plus quotation/reference. Award **0 marks** for quotation/reference alone. Award marks 2 + 2, 2+1+1 **or** 1+1+1+1	4	Possible answers include: • 'began' suggests the idea of a new start. • 'woke up' suggests the optimism associated with a new day. • 'face-to-face/lovers' suggests the intimacy within the relationship. • 'four-day-old smile' suggests sense of wonder. • 'dawned' reinforces the hopes and energy associated with new beginnings. • 'possessed him' suggests all-encompassing/innocent nature of the happiness. • 'not fall or waver' suggests an indefatigable spirit, determination to carry on.

Question	Expected response	Max Mark	Additional Guidance
54.	Award **2 marks** for detailed/insightful comment plus quotation/reference. Award **1 mark** for more basic comment plus quotation/reference. Award **0 marks** for quotation/reference alone. Award marks 2+2, 2+1+1 **or** 1+1+1+1	4	Possible answers include: • 'not my old' conveys his recognition that he has now moved on to a different stage of his life. • 'hard-pressed grin' suggests a lack of true fulfilment previously. • 'rediscovered' suggests a return to a state of almost childlike innocence. • *mezzo del cammin* appropriate allusions to Dante/a turning point in his life. • 'true path … ever' suggests a sense of meaninglessness which previously characterised his life. • 'lit it as you ran' suggests illumination/dispels the darkness of his previous life.
55.	Award **2 marks** awarded for detailed/insightful comment plus quotation/reference. Award **1 mark** for more basic comment plus quotation/reference. Award **0 marks** for quotation/reference alone. Award marks 2 **or** 1+1	2	Possible answers include: • use of 'true' links back to 'true path' conveying the authentic nature of his love for his son. • 'returned/redelivered/rolled' the sound/repetition conveys the unstoppable, unrelenting progress of his love. • imagery of 'poured … river' suggests the overwhelming effect of his son's love on him. • 'this waking amongst men!' suggests common bond/sense of the future. • 'pledged' suggests the unwavering commitment he will have to his son in the future. • 'forever' positioned as the final word reinforces his commitment to his son.
56.	Candidates can answer in bullet points in this final question, or write a number of linked statements.	10	Candidates can gain up to 2 marks for identifying elements of commonality as identified in the question, i.e. how imagery is used to explore central concerns. Award a further 2 marks for reference to the extract given. Award 6 additional marks for discussion of similar references in at least one other poem by the poet. <u>In practice this means:</u> Identification of commonality (2) for example, Paterson uses imagery to convey ideas/feelings/attitudes concerning individual experiences (1) to explore central concerns such as loss/mortality/change/familial love (1) • from this poem: Award **2 marks** for detailed/insightful comment plus quotation/reference Award **1 mark** for more basic comment plus quotation/reference Award **0 marks** for quotation/reference alone for example, 'the smile poured through us like a river' suggests the powerful love between the speaker and his son highlighting the unbreakable bond between parent and child (2) • from at least one other text: Award **2 marks** for detailed/insightful comment plus quotation/reference Award **1 mark** for more basic comment plus quotation/reference Award **0 marks** for quotation/reference alone

Question	Expected response	Max Mark	Additional Guidance
56.	*(continued)*		In comments on other poems, possible references include:
			• *The Ferryman's Arms* 'the boat … without breaking the skin of water' — the silent, unworldly nature of the ferry's approach suggests the inevitability of death, highlighting human mortality
			• *The Ferryman's Arms* — 'a pool table hummed to itself in the corner' — the personification suggests a menacing presence stalking the persona, highlighting human vulnerability and frailty
			• *Nil Nil* 'the black shell' — the total ruin of the shop suggests the decline/desolation of the community, highlighting transience and change
			• *Rain* 'their fatal watercourse' suggests an inescapable flow of events and consequences highlighting fate and destiny
			• *The Circle* 'we are its living word' suggests that humanity is the physical embodiment of natural evolution and purpose highlighting our place in the universe
			Many other references are possible.

SECTION 2 — Critical Essay

Please see the assessment criteria for the Critical Essay on page 171.

Acknowledgements

Permission has been sought from all relevant copyright holders and Hodder Gibson is grateful for the use of the following:

An extract from the article 'Want to exercise your mind? Try playstation' by Steven Johnson © The Times/News Licensing, 13 May 2005 (2017 Reading for Understanding, Analysis and Evaluation pages 2 & 3);
An extract from the article 'The Writing Is On The Wall' by Boris Johnson, taken from 'The Telegraph', 28 December 2006 © Boris Johnson/Telegraph Media Group Limited 2006 (2017 Reading for Understanding, Analysis and Evaluation pages 3 & 4);
An extract from 'The Slab Boys' © 1982 John Byrne. 'The Slab Boys' was first performed at the Traverse Theatre, Edinburgh, on 6 April 1978. All rights whatsoever in this play are strictly reserved and application for performance etc. should be made to the Author's agent: Casarotto Ramsay & Associates Limited, Waverley House, 7–12 Noel Street, London W1F 8G (rights@casarotto.co.uk). No performance may be given unless a licence has been obtained (2017 Critical Reading pages 2 & 3);
An extract from 'The Cheviot, the Stag and the Black, Black Oil,' by John McGrath. © John McGrath, 1981. Published by Bloomsbury Methuen Drama, an imprint of Bloomsbury Publishing Plc. (2017 Critical Reading pages 6 & 7);
An extract from 'Men Should Weep' © Ena Lamont Stewart, 1947. Reproduced by permission of Alan Brodie Representation Ltd (www.alanbrodie.com) (2017 Critical Reading pages 10 & 11);
An extract from 'The Red Door' by Iain Crichton Smith, taken from 'The Red Door: The Complete English Stories 1949–76', published by Birlinn. Reproduced with permission of Birlinn Limited via PLSclear (2017 Critical Reading pages 14 & 15);
An extract from 'Tartan' by George Mackay Brown, taken from the book 'A Time To Keep', published by Polygon. Reproduced with permission of The Literary Estate of George Mackay Brown (2017 Critical Reading pages 16 & 17);
An extract from 'The Trick is to Keep Breathing' by Janice Galloway, published by Vintage, reprinted by permission of The Random House Group Limited. © Janice Galloway 1989 (2017 Critical Reading pages 18 & 19);
An extract from 'The Cone-Gatherers' by Robin Jenkins, published by Canongate Books Ltd. (2017 Critical Reading pages 22 & 23);
The poem 'Valentine' from 'Mean Time' by Carol Ann Duffy. Published by Anvil Press Poetry, 1993. Copyright © Carol Ann Duffy. Reproduced by permission of the author c/o Rogers, Coleridge & White Ltd., 20 Powis Mews, London W11 1JN (2017 Critical Reading page 26);
The poem 'For my Grandmother Knitting' by Liz Lochhead, taken from 'A Choosing: Selected Poems', published by Polygon. Reproduced with permission of Birlinn Limited via PLSclear (2017 Critical Reading pages 28 & 29);
The poem 'Basking Shark' by Norman MacCaig, taken from 'The Many Days: Selected Poems of Norman MacCaig', published by Polygon. Reproduced with permission of Birlinn Limited via PLSclear (2017 Critical Reading page 30);
The poem 'Heroes' by Sorley MacLean, taken from 'Caoir Gheal Leumraich/White Leaping Flame: collected poems in Gaelic with English translations', edited by Christopher Whyte and Emma Dymock 2011. Copyrighted by Sorley MacLean. Reprinted with permission of Carcanet Press, Manchester, UK (2017 Critical Reading page 32);
The poem 'Nil Nil' from 'Nil Nil' by Don Paterson. Published by Faber, 1993. Copyright © Don Paterson. Reproduced by permission of the author c/o Rogers, Coleridge & White Ltd., 20 Powis Mews, London W11 1JN (2017 Critical Reading pages 34 & 35);
The article 'Cutting down a tree is worse than fox hunting' by Janice Turner © The Times/News Licensing, 12 January 2013 (2018 Reading for Understanding, Analysis and Evaluation pages 2 & 3);
Article is adapted from 'Trees, me, and all of us' by Colin Tudge. Reproduced by kind permission of Colin Tudge (2018 Reading for Understanding, Analysis and Evaluation pages 3 & 4);
An extract from 'The Slab Boys' © 1982 John Byrne. 'The Slab Boys' was first performed at the Traverse Theatre, Edinburgh, on 6 April 1978. All rights whatsoever in this play are strictly reserved and application for performance etc. should be made to the Author's agent: Casarotto Ramsay & Associates Limited, Waverley House, 7–12 Noel Street, London W1F 8G (rights@casarotto.co.uk). No performance may be given unless a licence has been obtained (2018 Critical Reading pages 2 & 3);
An extract from 'The Cheviot, the Stag and the Black, Black Oil,' by John McGrath. © John McGrath, 1981. Published by Bloomsbury Methuen Drama, an imprint of Bloomsbury Publishing Plc. (2018 Critical Reading pages 4 & 5);
An extract from 'Men Should Weep' © Ena Lamont Stewart, 1947. Reproduced by permission of Alan Brodie Representation Ltd (www.alanbrodie.com) (2018 Critical Reading pages 6 & 7);
An extract from 'The Painter' by Iain Crichton Smith, taken from 'The Red Door: The Complete English Stories 1949–76', published by Birlinn. Reproduced with permission of Birlinn Limited via PLSclear (2018 Critical Reading pages 8 & 9);
An extract from 'The Bright Spade' by George Mackay Brown, taken from 'A Time To Keep', published by Polygon. Reproduced with permission of The Literary Estate of George Mackay Brown (2018 Critical Reading page 10);
An extract from 'The Trick is to Keep Breathing' by Janice Galloway, published by Vintage, reprinted by permission of The Random House Group Limited. © Janice Galloway 1989 (2018 Critical Reading pages 12 & 13);